Close Relationships

REVIEW OF PERSONALITY
AND SOCIAL PSYCHOLOGY

Editor

Margaret S. Clark, *Carnegie Mellon University*

Close
Relationships

Editor
CLYDE HENDRICK

10
REVIEW of PERSONALITY and SOCIAL PSYCHOLOGY

Published in cooperation with the Society for Personality and Social Psychology, Inc.

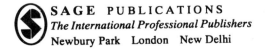

SAGE PUBLICATIONS
The International Professional Publishers
Newbury Park London New Delhi

10-16-95

For information address:

SAGE Publications, Inc.
2455 Teller Road
Newbury Park, California 91320

SAGE Publications Ltd.
6 Bonhill Street
London EC2A 4PU
United Kingdom

SAGE Publications India Pvt. Ltd.
M-32 Market
Greater Kailash I
New Delhi 110 048 India

Printed in the United States of America

International Standard Book Number 0-8039-3377-0
0-8039-3378-9 (pbk.)

International Standard Series Number 0270-1987

92 93 94 15 14 13 12 11 10 9 8 7 6 5 4

CONTENTS

Editor's Introduction
CLOSE RELATIONSHIPS

CLYDE HENDRICK

Clyde Hendrick is Professor of Psychology and Dean of the Graduate School at Texas Tech University. He was previously Chairperson of Psychology, University of Miami. His scholarly interests include close relationships, sex roles, and philosophy of science. He has served as Editor for *Personality and Social Psychology Bulletin* and as Acting Editor for *Journal of Personality and Social Psychology*.

Social psychology and personality, until the recent past, paid almost no attention to the wellsprings that drive much of human life: love, intimacy, closeness, sharing, and the like. Sociology has long studied marriage and the family, but from the perspective of social institutions, rather than as a vital part of ongoing human relations. Psychology generally has had little to say about such warm, fuzzy topics, except for the study of "attachment" in developmental psychology. Even this topic began with Harlow's monkeys, and then cautiously moved to the study of human infants, objects which could safely be studied at a distance. Within social psychology, the fad for many years was the study of "interpersonal attraction," which was presumed to emerge from various types of similarity matching. Personality theory was even more remote in its approach, except that love and affection possibly entered into the structures of traits such as needs for affiliation and succorance.

The history of quietness of our discipline on such topics is very puzzling. It took the genius of Freud many years ago to draw the common sense observation that the two most important things in life are work and love. Despite Freud, love, at least, was little studied by psychology. Why? The answer, if there is one, is not apparent. It may be that the development of rational organization of the modern world created a split between public and private spheres of life, with "public" identified as rational, instrumental, and important, and "private"

EDITOR'S NOTE: In addition to members of the Editorial Board who reviewed chapters, I am indebted to the following individuals for their reviews of one or more chapters: Thomas N. Bradbury, Barry Burkhart, John G. Holmes, Gerrod Parrott, David C. Rowe, Peter Salovey, and Mark Snyder.

identified as nonrational, emotive, and not as important. This theme is suggested by Brown:

> I argue that personal identity is shaped through a "language of self" that is embedded in contemporary political economy. Though this modern Western self is an ideal type and is incarnated differently in different classes, genders, and other groups, its constant characteristic is the loss of positive linkage between person and polity, a bifurcation between a public self defined as a functionary guided by positive, instrumental reason, and a private, affective self that is the locus of arational feelings, values, and emotions. By limiting moral action to the purely private sphere, and by restricting the public sphere to purely instrumental behavior, this bifurcation has engendered a crisis of citizenship, legitimation, and political obligation. (1987, p. 1)

If such a bifurcation between public and private life occurred, psychology may have relatively emphasized those abilities, traits, and processes most relevant to the public facets of life. In this way, the topics of concern were relegated to a secondary status and received little scientific attention.

A change occurred about a decade ago. At the same time that the highly visible cognitive revolution was in full stride, a quiet revolution of research and writing on the affective matrix of social life occurred. Books and articles appeared with "love" in their titles. The study of close or personal relationships has become, in a short decade, a burgeoning field of research activity in several disciplines. Journal outlets now exist. Indeed, the *Journal of Social and Personal Relationships* is devoted solely to the general area. A handbook, edited by Steve Duck, appeared recently. Many other relevant volumes, including textbooks, have appeared in recent years.

The current volume of the *Review* was planned in recognition of this explosion of interest in the topic. The call for proposals for chapters was advertised widely. A total of 58 proposals was received. The selection process resulted in the ten chapters included in Volume 10. Not all possible topics could be included; indeed, many fine proposals had to be declined.

It seems clear that a new discipline has emerged. It is not a discipline in the usual sense because research interest spans several traditional disciplines, including psychology, sociology, communications, areas of home economics, anthropology, and philosophy. The study of personal relationships appears to be similar to the study of language: It is relevant to the interests of many academic disciplines, but no single discipline can encompass all of the relevant facets. Thus, the study of personal relationships must truly become a multidisciplinary enterprise. Toward that end, the present volume is dedicated.

OVERVIEW OF THE CHAPTERS

Chapter 1, by Duck and Pond, sketches a new approach to the study of personal relationships. Many researchers in close relationships come from a background in social psychology with the underlying assumptions of experimental methodology as the way to gain knowledge and the ontological assumption that the world, if not a vast machine, at least is a well-ordered organism. There are other philosophic approaches to knowledge, and Duck and Pond develop one such approach through the study of rhetoric, which basically takes reality to be the symbol world of communication. Most psychologists probably assume that language *represents* reality and is therefore not quite as "real" as the object world. However, Duck and Pond make the assumption that language is a type of *presentation* of reality. In fact, language creates and changes realities in the process of presenting them.

Within this framework, the chapter is an excellent juxtaposition of social psychological approaches to close relationships versus rhetorical approaches to close relationships. The authors do not choose between the two; indeed, they point out the potentially significant contribution of each approach. However, their emphasis suggests that rhetoric has something serious to offer to the study of close relationships. The authors suggest that the study of talk will be very helpful in the understanding of relationships. They note that much research on talk, in the form of narrative accounts of persons' lives, has focused primarily on the breaking up of relationships. The construals, reconstruals, and discrepant construals of the relationship's ending create fascinating material for analysis. In this sense, the study of accounts is also a study of the theater of tragedy. However, Duck and Pond make the telling point that studies of accounts and their language are instructive not only in respect of endings, but for beginning and middle stages of relationships, from the perspective of people who live the relationships from the inside as well as those who observe them from the outside. The authors go on to imply that the study of language is so intermeshed with social actions that social relations per se have a rhetorical quality. The chapter develops this concept in some detail and it is a valuable contribution. On balance, the chapter widens our perspective on the study of personal relationships, in terms of both substantive considerations and methodological possibilities.

Chapter 2, by Harvey, Agostinelli, and Weber, extends the thesis of the first chapter by developing an explicit theoretical framework for the nature of accounts. The focus is on how people explain their relationships, particularly endings of relationships. Accounts are stories. The authors are primarily interested in the cognitive or attributional aspects of the relationship story, but they recognize that giving accounts may serve other functions, such as self-presentation and catharsis. Creation of an account helps generate a cognitive state of expectancy which uses construals of past relationships as templates for the operation of current and future relationships. Creation of an account may be viewed as the joining together of a set of personal constructs (in the sense of George Kelly) in a flowing storyline. Stories help make sense of puzzling events. Personal stories are fabricated from a set of constructs about self and relationship, and the process of creating the story is equivalent to creating the meaning of the relationship or an aspect of it. Lessons are drawn from such self-constructed stories, leading to expectations about future relationships. The authors present preliminary data supporting such a linkage between personal accounts and expectations for relationships. This sensitive, interesting chapter suggests that much useful research can be done on first-person accounts.

The profusion of research on intimate and close relationships in recent years has necessarily drawn attention to issues of measuring various aspects of intimate and close relationships. Chapter 3, by Berscheid, Snyder, and Omoto, is directed to the heart of the problem, that is, to the definition of closeness and the various ways we might measure it. The authors present a fine introduction to the difficulties of defining the construct of closeness and review various ways in which closeness may be measured. They note such approaches as relationship type, comparison of insider versus outsider, phenomenal ratings by participants, and the like.

The main thrust of the chapter is a discussion of a research program on possible measures of closeness. The authors compare and contrast closeness from the point of view of participants in a relationship, from a measure of the hedonic tone of the relationship, and from their own measure, the Relationship Closeness Inventory. These three approaches, using college students as their subjects, yielded somewhat different results as well as some similarities in outcome. Somewhat surprisingly, perhaps, students tended to list romantic relationships as their closest relationships, even though family relationships were of much longer duration. Follow-up data nine months later also showed that these "closest" relationships ended with high frequency. The authors present a masterful comparison of these three general approaches to measurement, and provide very helpful conclusions for future research in this area. This chapter should stimulate substantial progress in the measurement of close relationships in the years ahead.

Social psychologists are biased toward environmental explanations for social behavior, based upon a long tradition of learning theory and environmentalism in psychology generally. During the last decade, heritable aspects of social behavior have become a visible area of research. Indeed, the whole movement of sociobiology, although politically volatile, offers substantial concepts for the study of social behavior. Chapter 4, by Kenrick and Trost, offers a meld of social psychological approaches and evolutionary approaches to the study of heterosexual relationships. The authors note that most social psychologists have ignored the probable importance of reproduction in people's complex courtship rituals, which is partially alleviated by a fine overview of the social psychological economics in courtship, including concepts of selfishness in human relations (usually presented within an equity framework), longitudinal variation in social relations, the content of exchange, the sex differences that seem to exist in courtship exchange, and the contrast of the rational approach of exchange models with the clear irrationalities in much heterosexual exchange. This material is then contrasted with heterosexual relations based on evolutionary economics, using the Darwinian principle of natural selection. Evolutionary theorists use two basic concepts that are quite powerful in explanatory potential, differential parental investment of males and females, and sexual selectivity. The authors do a good job of explicating the explanatory power of the evolutionary framework. At the same time, they point out some of its shortcomings and provide a beginning attempt at integration of the social psychological and evolutionary perspectives. This chapter is a substantial contribution to knowledge and should stimulate further efforts at integration and research, based on a biosocial model of human courtship and close relationships.

Chapter 5, by Bradbury and Fincham, deals with the relation between marital behavior and spousal satisfaction with the marriage. The perspective taken is that of a contextual model in which behavior and satisfaction are linked through possible mediating processes. The authors view their model as broadly integrative, combining previous sociological and behavioral traditions of research on marriage. Basic elements of the model include behavior of each marriage partner over time, as well as a proximal context, a distal context, and a processing stage for each person. Distal context includes personality and long-term relationship variables. Proximal context includes immediate ongoing cognition. These elements affect the processing stage, which in turn feeds back to influence ongoing behavior. Thus, the model assumes multiple feedback loops.

The authors compare their model with other models. In particular, the relevance of the model for existing research on mediational processes is discussed in detail. Several possible directions for future research are noted; the chapter should stimulate new research on marital interaction.

Chapter 6, by Buck, deals with emotion in relationships. The chapter attempts to integrate the cognitive approach of social psychology with the notion of spontaneous emotional communication. This integration assumes the body to be a source of structured information that is processed and used in the general process of making cognitive attributions. The author views his theory as developmental/interactionist in nature. It builds on Schachter and Singer's theory of emotion. However, the concepts of "physiological" and "cognitive" are recast as special and general purpose processing systems. Special-purpose processing systems are structured by evolution to deal with certain important events both within the body and external to the body. These systems provide perceptual information which constitutes genuine knowledge, but it is knowledge by direct acquaintance. In contrast, general-purpose processing systems are structured by the individual's life experience, presumably based on the higher cortical centers involving symbolic learning and language. These systems process the directly known internal and external information, resulting in cognitive attributions.

People learn to understand and label their internal information through a process of emotional education, which proceeds within the context of personal relations in a literal social biofeedback process. Several concepts are introduced. Education of attention is one that applies Gibson's perceptual theory to the notion of internal bodily information. Learning to discriminate internal bodily states is mediated partially by language. Thus, the process of coming to a linguistically-structured understanding of one's emotional states *is* emotional education. Because emotional education always occurs within a social context, relationships may be viewed as emotional regulators. In this way, emotional communication and its regulation underlie social organization.

This chapter is conceptually rich. It is a distinct contribution to knowledge about the role of emotion in personal relationships that, by viewing biologically structured feelings and desires as information that we must learn to *talk* about, suggests a basis for integrating the sociobiological view of relationships presented by Kenrick and Trost with the rhetorical approach discussed by Duck and Pond.

Chapter 7, by Sherrod, explores the extent to which same-sex friendships differ between men and women. Alternatively, the focus is also on gender similarities. Sherrod does an admirable job in reviewing the literature on friendship with respect to gender, and engages in a piece of scientific detective work in trying to pin down the nature of friendship for the two genders. He explores differences in possible definitions of friendship for men and women, sex differences in self-disclosure in friendship, possible differences in affective and non-verbal expressions of intimacy, and the relation of social support to stress reduction as it bears on friendship.

The author considers in detail the possibility that there are substantial gender differences in the ways friendships develop. In reviewing the evidence, he concludes that males prefer less intimacy than females in same-sex friendships, but that males achieve high levels of intimacy nevertheless. However, males follow pathways that emphasize companionship and activities over self-disclosure and emotional expressiveness. The author notes many methodological problems with this area of research, but concludes that gender differences in same-sex friendships are clear and consistent enough to make reasonable the search for causes. Four possible theoretical perspectives are considered: an economic/historical perspective, a psychoanalytic perspective, a biological perspective, and a socialization perspective. The socialization perspective appears to have the strongest support, although there are arguments in favor of the other three perspectives as well. The chapter concludes with a number of questions that could well guide future research. On balance, this chapter is most stimulating and interesting; one that should promote substantial research on the nature of friendship.

Chapter 8, by Holmes and Rempel, deals with trust, an important concept in the study of close relationships. The authors define trust as a sense of interpersonal security that emerges during periods of tranquility in a relationship. They note that trust has its origins in the general approach- avoidance conflicts that people have about relationships. On the one hand, there is a desire for closeness, which seems to be a natural human tendency. That desire is pitted against the need for the safety of distance from others, which also seems to be a natural human tendency. Trust is possible only because of the prospective nature of our cognitive-affective orientations toward relationships. Only in terms of anticipations of future states and the hope and fear that go with such anticipations, does the notion of an emergence of something called "trust" make sense. It follows that trust is based on reduction of uncertainty over time as a relationship develops. However, reduction of uncertainty is a very circuitous process. The authors explore the development of trust through the stages of a relationship. A brief section on the erosion of trust in relationships, a painful but real part of everyday life, is also included. Trust emerges as an anchor concept that involves a large number of cognitive and affective processes over the temporal span of a relationship. The authors do a masterful job in detailed analyses of these processes, relating them to one another, and developing them in ways that make the concept of trust an obviously important concept in the study of relationships. This chapter is excellent, and it is a substantial conceptual contribution to the study of close relationships.

Close relationships involve not only positive emotions, but also negative ones such as envy and jealousy. Chapter 9, by Salovey and Rodin, deals with these two negative emotions. The authors eschew a biological approach and focus on situational and person variables shared by envy and jealousy, as well as characteristics that differentiate between the two states. It is assumed that threats to one's self-evaluation in important interpersonal areas is crucial in provoking these emotional states. Envy and jealousy appear in close relationships whenever self-worth is threatened in a particular self-defining characteristic for the individual involved. Based in part on Tesser's work, the authors argue that envy and jealousy serve the maintenance of positive self-evaluations. Assuming that most people are motivated to maintain positive self-evaluation, they tend to bask in the reflected glory of friends' and loved ones' successes, but only so long as those successes do not affect their self-definitions. When the excellence or competitiveness of another person's behavior threatens one's self-definitions, then, instead of positive regard for the other, envy, jealousy, and related emotions may be aroused. This approach applies well to romantic jealousy, the paradigm case for jealous behavior.

The chapter includes sections on managing envy and jealousy in relationships, and provides a brief overview of the relation of these two emotions to crimes of passion. Cross-cultural considerations suggest that envy and jealousy prosper in competitive cultures with strong individualistic concerns for material possessions, status, affection, and the like. Competition can easily become jealousy when the competition is for the sole affections of a lover. Because envy and jealousy do not seem to be part of the "emotional ideology" of all cultures, their origins may reside in socialization rather than in the genes. The authors conclude that although envy and jealousy tend to make relationships more unpleasant, they also make life more meaningful. To envy or be jealous of another person means that the other matters, and matters enough so that turbulent emotions are created. In summary, the chapter is a fine addition to a growing literature on negative emotions in close relationships.

Chapter 10, by Shotland, explores the dark side of intimate heterosexual relationships. Rape seems endemic to human society. During the last two decades, the pervasiveness of this phenomenon has become well known. Shotland attempts to define one type of rape—date rape, more precisely. He develops a model of three types of date rape, based on the length of the relationship. These include beginning date rape, early date rape, and relationship date rape (the couple has a long-standing relationship). Attention is focused on early date rape, defined in terms of couples who have gone together several times, but for whom the rules for interaction, particularly with regard to sexual matters, are not yet fully defined. Males and females may differ in their perception of sexual intent based on interactional cues. In general, males seem to have lower thresholds for labeling behavior as sexually interested than do females. In addition, males are expected to be initiators of courtship and sexual interactions. Such differences set the stage for miscommunication and misunderstanding of sexual intentions. Shotland presumes that in a courtship situation the discovery of different sexual intentions at critical times may lead to anger on the part of the male, which may enhance sexual excitation through the mechanism of excitation transfer. In addition, many males hold rape-supportive belief systems that, in combination with the other precursors mentioned, may set up a situation that leads to coercive sexual behavior, or rape.

The mechanism for long-term relationship rape appears to depend on other factors, as do the causes for beginning date rape. In beginning date rape it is likely that a selective device is working in which a predatory male simply uses the date as a pretext for rape with less danger of legal action against him. Shotland concludes with several hypotheses that should be open to empirical tests. It may be that the delineation of three types of date rape will not hold up under intense empirical scrutiny, but the hypotheses will nevertheless prove fruitful if they enlarge our understanding of the mechanisms behind this plague on human relationships.

CONCLUSIONS

The chapters constituting Volume 10 of the *Review* indicate clearly that the study of personal relationships is now a vast industry. Very soon it will be impossible to keep up with the relevant literature. Because of the multidisciplinary nature of this enterprise, it is important that tolerance for diverse perspectives and methodologies be cultivated. Otherwise, the scholarship on personal relationships will fragment into many small, noninteracting specialties.

It would be useful at this point in the history of the field to have a diversity of basic conceptual analyses of the nature of relationships. Two people in relationship form a concrete entity. They physically exist in proximity in space and their togetherness and apartness can be tracked over time. They can be videotaped and their utterances to each other can be recorded for later exhaustive analyses. Over the short term, rigorous experimental methods can be applied to many aspects of relational behavior. In this sense, a relationship is as real and concrete as the desk on which these words are being written.

However, there is another sense in which a relationship is as evanescent and fleeting as the wind. Relating is communicating, and without communication there is no relationship. But communication partakes of the world of symbols, and that is another kind of reality. Even the concrete institution of marriage begins in ceremonial ritual that includes the words "I do." These symbolic expressions then lead to a multitudinous host of behaviors, artifacts, and other symbolic expressions that may endure for a lifetime, or they may end in another ceremonial ritual called divorce. Looked at in this way, a relationship is constructed, maintained, and ended in a rhetorical interchange of symbols. Thus, human relating is primarily symbolic relating, and concrete behavior and the material artifacts of a relationship are only shadows in the sunlight of a higher symbolic reality.

These two philosophical images of the nature of relationship may be approached in either of two ways. Both may be taken as interesting, possible worlds of discourse and pursued to see where they might lead. Or, one can choose up sides from the outset, claiming truth, beauty and honor for one view and damnation for the other view. Clearly, I am urging an aesthetic principle that says "choose both." The consequences of a broad net are likely to lead to a richer development of the field of personal relationships, hopefully for the ultimate benefit of all humankind. The study of relationships is a very serious business.

REFERENCE

Brown, R. H. (1987). *Society as text: Essays on rhetoric, reason, and reality.* Chicago: University of Chicago Press.

1

Friends, Romans, Countrymen, Lend Me Your Retrospections

RHETORIC AND REALITY IN PERSONAL RELATIONSHIPS

STEVE DUCK
KRIS POND

Steve Duck is Daniel and Amy Starch Research Professor in Interpersonal Communication at the University of Iowa. He is Founding Editor of the *Journal of Social and Personal Relationships*, Editor of the *Handbook of Personal Relationships*, and author or editor of 15 other books on personal relationships. He was cofounder of the International Society for the Study of Personal Relationships and of the Iowa/International Network on Personal Relationships. He has also organized two series of international conferences on personal relationships and initiated the Iowa/International Network Dissertation Prize and two Distinguished Research Awards, both for work in personal relationships.

Kris Pond is a graduate student in communication research at the University of Iowa. She received her M.A. in interpersonal communication at Purdue University and subsequently taught in the Department of Speech Communication and Theatre Arts at Concordia College, Moorhead, Minnesota. She is interested in the role of talk, including the role of account-making in interpersonal communication.

Some 10 years ago a book summarizing the advances in research on long-term, close personal relationships (excluding marriage) would have been very short, and a simple listing of research on initial attraction would have extended well beyond that. There were only a handful of academic books with "personal relationships" or "close relationships" in the title published between 1969 and 1978, whereas between 1979 and 1988 there have been around 30. During the past decade, research on close personal relationships has grown not only in quantity but also in conceptual sophistication, and consequently differentiated itself from work on initial attraction. There are three elements to this development:

AUTHORS' NOTE: We are grateful to Bob Sanders for his illuminating comments on an earlier draft and to Clyde Hendrick, Richard P. McGlynn, and Susan S. Hendrick for their help in, as Clyde put it, "clearing Duck and Pond of frogs."

(1) a renewed vigor in describing real-life relationships (e.g., Baxter & Wilmot, 1986; Miell, 1987; Sants, 1984) without completely abandoning the laboratory work that is such a necessary adjunct to this activity (e.g., Gottman & Parker, 1987); (2) an emphasis on process, such as the subtleties of social negotiation and interpersonal management that develop a relationship's life (e.g., Surra, Arizzi, & Asmussen, 1988) or the social processes through which cognitive and emotional forces are actualized in the real world of interacting pressures, forces, and social networks (e.g., Milardo, 1982; Milardo, Johnson, & Huston, 1983); and (3) a greater awareness of the contributions of other disciplines than one's own, facilitated by the medium of journals, conferences, and networks.

Partly as a result of these changes, "new" phenomena are studied. For example, researchers now look at personal needs and personal relationships (McAdams, 1988), functions of nonverbal behavior in close relationships (Patterson, 1988), ontogeny, phylogeny, and relationships (Nash, 1988), relations among relationships (Dunn, 1988), persuasion in personal relationships (Miller & Boster, 1988), personal relationships and patterns of interaction (Cappella, 1988), quality communication in personal relationships (Montgomery, 1988), intimacy as an interpersonal process (Reis & Shaver, 1988), roles and gender in relationships (Hendrick, 1988), intimate relationships in task environments (Dillard & Miller, 1988), the organizational life-style of relationships (McCall, 1988), processes and mechanisms of social support (Hobfoll & Stokes, 1988), and advanced work on loneliness (Rook, 1988). Such a list of topics was almost inconceivable 20 years ago and is promoted by the fact that researchers now adopt a processual approach to relationships and treat relaters as (inter)active processors of stimuli.

The present chapter outlines some "process" elements in this momentous growth and advocates their continued investigation—with one important change. It points researchers toward the influences and roles of talk on relationship growth, management, and definition, and encourages study of real-life, everyday talk as a necessary part of the larger enterprise. We see talk as having three closely connected roles in personal relationships: (1) it is *indexical*; that is, it indicates or reveals the emotional status of a relationship; (2) it is *instrumental*; that is, it effects certain purposes in relational development, maintenance, management, repair and dissolution, and it is the vehicle for social negotiation about respective roles and relational climate; (3) it is *essential*; that is, it embodies the relationship and, in a sense we shall explore, *is* the relationship for the participants. From such a perspective we will draw out some constructive overlaps and some tensions between social psychology and communication studies of rhetoric. Also, we will indicate some useful parallels between talk in relationships and talk about relationships in the social scientific research community.

PROCESS AS A FRAMEWORK FOR RELATIONSHIP RESEARCH

It seems inevitable that researchers and subjects alike should adopt a terminology best suited to their goals, one rich in metaphors that may have implications for the framework in which they treat their various enterprises. In the field of interpersonal attraction, the dominant metaphor was clearly magnetic: A was attracted to B. Implicit in such language is a style of thinking that credits and directs attention to certain issues: a terminology of magnetism sets researchers and subjects alike to think in terms of characteristics that draw persons together or repulse one another. In such a framework, the attraction itself is essentially passive and mysterious: It is taken for granted as the result of the juxtaposition of characteristics of the two attracted persons. The process, we say again, is taken for granted and not really explored: It is "what happens when" two correctly correspondent characteristics are aligned and "what does not happen when" two opposites are aligned. Such a view essentially treats relationships as structures that are created as a result of some alignment of necessary components.

In contrast, the emphasis of the current research on close personal relationships is clearly on *process*; as urged by Duck and Sants (1983). Research on process pays closer attention to the "what happens when" and the "what does not happen when" parts of the sentence above, but also has a terminology that sets us to think in particular ways. Thus, some researchers talk of trajectories toward marriage (Huston, Surra, Fitzgerald, & Cate, 1981), a metaphor that invites us to chart the predictable course of relationships through fixed landmarks. Sure enough, the subsequent papers of that team have titles including "turning points," "progress through courtship," and "alternative pathways toward marriage" without mixing a single metaphor. What remains to be examined is the *process* of movement rather than the fact of movement, and we believe its engine is talk.

Our purpose here, however, is not so much to dwell on the terminology of researchers (but see Duck, 1987a); rather, we wish to dwell on the rhetorical framework in which close personal relationships are conducted and to explore ways in which this can help us to clarify the psychological nature of relationships. We intend to expand such points to argue (1) that the study of rhetoric offers some natural links (and some natural tensions) with social psychology and (2) that how subjects use language in relationships is at least as interesting and forceful in the definition of relationships as how researchers use language in defining their focus of attention. We accept Kelly's (1955) view that if you seek to understand people's behavior you must find out how they represent their circumstances to themselves (and, we add in this context, to other people, through talk).

A Process Orientation

In considering some difficulties with the paradigm of initial attraction research and proposing a process orientation to personal relationships, Duck and Sants (1983) emphasized the influences of time on relationship processes. Had they known about the passage then, doubtless they would have quoted Proust, who remarked: "It does us no good to know that the years go by, that youth gives way to old age, that most stable thrones and fortunes crumble, that fame is ephemeral; our way of forming a conception—and so to speak, taking a photograph—of this moving universe, hurried along by time, seeks on the contrary to make it stand still." Thus it does us little good to know that relationships are in flux, developing, declining, or staying at a stable level (whatever that actually means) because as both human beings and investigators we find it easier and more satisfying psychologically to represent them as essentially static or state-like. It is important, therefore, to note that such states are essentially arbitrary impositions for descriptive purposes and that the purposes of investigators and subjects may not always coincide. Thus researchers have traditionally represented relationship growth as a movement, usually a progressive incrementation, from one *state* to another *state*, from one sort of relationship to another or one level of intimacy to another. We have done this by paying little attention to the fact that our subjects actually find it quite hard to make clear relationship-related distinctions about such movements. They can do it if we force them, but they experience lots of fuzzy edges. These very difficulties contain some psychological meaning, if we choose to think about it in a different way, since the representation of relationships perhaps depends on the person who is doing the representing.

We argue that in everyday life much of the process of relational definition, development, and change results not from the direct influence of disembodied cues upon a passive recipient, but from the evaluation and active representation (to self and to other people) of "events" that are deemed important by the person. Thus, people typically "editorialize" their relationship, in the sense of describing it differently as a function of instant needs and circumstances. Such descriptions are part of the process of creating a sense of "being in a relationship" and are one influence that brings it into existence, changes its form, and accounts for partners' feelings about it. In this view, relationships are created as psychological entities for people by their attempts to discern system and meaning in the otherwise unstructured flow of time and to represent that perceived system through language.

Duck and Sants (1983) challenged the four unwanted heirlooms of research on initial attraction that were seen to hinder adoption of a process orientation to relationships.

Relationships as the chemistry of partner attributes. The erroneous view that partners' attributes (e.g., similarity on key dimensions) create relationships, predict ralational growth and affect partners' satisfaction. This is consistent with common sense and the view espoused by dating agencies that psychological matching makes for successful relationships. We take the contrasting view that active social processes such as talking, acting together, disclosing, making joint decisions, arguing, and the like are in fact the key social processes here. Huston et al. (1981) implicitly support this challenge in their work on courtship as an interpersonal process. Even if matching is an important influence on courtship, we need to know how matching is negotiated, displayed, detected, and translated into behavior through the real-life communication between the partners. Duck (1987b) answered that matching is displayed and discovered through talk, which consequently creates the environment for satisfaction and progress in relationships. If this is the case, then some interesting questions arise: How does talk in the early stages of the relationship differ from that at later stages? What tasks does it accomplish that are different from those accomplished later? How does the structure and content of the talk change as particular intimacy goals are reached? How does the talk create a symbolic presentation of "a relationship" or help the partners to see themselves as belonging to it? Hopper, Knapp, and Scott (1981) began work on the personal idioms or private languages that are developed by partners as relationships grow, but a full understanding of such issues has not been reached.

Relationships as undigested interactions. The erroneous view that the raw fact of interaction defines relationships. It involves believing that people do not ponder their interactions, do not plan or reminisce, and do not reformulate their understandings of "what really happened" (Duck, 1980). In contrast, we argue that *people* define relationships, both inside and outside interactions, by means of cognitions ("self-talk") and social interaction involving talk.

Social psychology has so far paid less attention than it might to such "out-of-interaction" personal thoughtwork as, for instance, anxiety, regret, strategies, intentions, plans, and reminiscences or retrospections as psychological entities in their own right. Each is, in its own way, a discrepancy between a present state of affairs and a past or future one. Thoughtwork is manifest in talk, whether talk to oneself or to others, and we might expect both talk and description of relationships to be reformulated in parallel with the developing reformulation of a relationship. What are the influences on relational thoughtwork? How does social relating affect it? In many cases, talk and accounts to friends serve to assess and create or modify the "digestive juices" for prior or subsequent interaction. Questions such as "Was I right?" "Do you think I was silly?" "What should I do to change this state of affairs?" can lead to talk that changes one's views of a relationship. Such discussions also modify one's view of appropriate future behaviors in that relationship.

Other forms of friendship expectations (La Gaipa, 1987) are of interest here also, as is the role of planning and strategy in some aspects of relationships (Berger, 1988). These two also represent discrepancy between present and future. If (a) a strategy or expectation is a plan for the shaping of things to come, and (b) its successful accomplishment requires the influencing of others to share the vision (e.g., to go on a date, get serious, or break off a relationship), and (c) an account is a version of events that is intended to do the same, then (d) the language of expectations, daydreams, reminiscences, strategies and accounts requires social psychological analysis.

As relationships unfold, we would expect differences not only in the patterns of talk content between partners and by partners to outsiders, but also in the "orders" of discussion within the social network. It is likely that the orders of talk change as relationships unfold: for example, people consult or inform others, form alliances, seek support, bitch, give comfort, disclose, and so on, as relational needs presently dictate. Further, the objectively assessable orderings of talk within the network also change (Duck, 1985): As trouble is discovered in a relationship, so are people more likely to spend proportionately more time with confidants and proportionately less with partners; when things go from bad to worse they spend more time arguing or trying to become reconciled with partners and less with friends, and so on. The orderings or proportions of time spent communicating with particular others from the available pool are thus perhaps an index of the internal "state" of a relationship with a particular partner.

Relationships as crocks of gold at the end of the rainbow. The erroneous assumption that a "relationship" is a clear and clearly observable fixed object that researchers should be able, if only we knew how, to study objectively. Our position, in contrast, is that there are many perspectives on a relationship. These differ not only between perceivers but also across time in the same perceiver, resulting in and being detected through the perceiver's different accounts of the relationship, which embody the essence of the relationship from the perceiver's current perspective. In other words, the two persons "in" a relationship are not in a static rhetorical environment as the relationship unfolds from time to time, nor are they in the same rhetorical environment as the outsiders. We speculate that there would be a gradual convergence of these environments as time passes, but see no reason why they should be identical (compare Olson, 1977, and Duck & Sants, 1983, on the differences between insider and outsider perspectives on relationships).

For these reasons, we urge that attention be paid to the ways in which retrospections about a relationship alter over time, to the ways in which the rhetoric of self-reports of relationships coincides with the rhetoric of outsiders, and to the influences on subjects' rhetoric about relationships in different circumstances (e.g., describing the relationship to a scientist, to a friend, to outsiders). Miell (1984) reports some interesting work on the changes in content that occur when couples talk on their own, individually to an interviewer, and together to an interviewer, for instance, and it seems a reasonable, though untested, speculation that "being overheard" provokes some changes to the style of discourse between partners.

Relaters as air traffic controllers. The erroneous belief that human beings are in perfect control of their actions. It assumes that people invariably do everything thinkingly, that when they process information they do so entirely rationally, that they can hold enormous amounts of relevant detail at their fingertips, and that they are constantly self-aware and competent. This point is different from the second one above, which argues that people occasionally make plans and have forethought, however misleading or erroneous or mistaken it might turn out to be. We suspect that, perhaps more at the start of the relationship than later, subjects may show considerable incoherence in their talk about a relationship and that one feature of the development of relationships is a greater coherence both between and within subjects. For example, subjects begin to converge in their stories of where a relationship started, even if at first they were innocently discrepant on the matter (Duck & Miell, 1986). We also suspect that retrospections of contemporaneously recorded events will show a tendency to impute a rationality and control over the course of events that reflect cultural expectations about the course of relationships (see Duck & Miell, 1986). We certainly feel strongly that the vagaries of retrospective data are worth investigation and that any "biases" in them can be studied for systematic rhetorical change, over and above those changes that could be attributed to "pure" memory loss. Changes are psychologically informative both about the ways in which memories for relationships are forged and about the nature of human social activity. We posit an instrumental function for talk here: talk about relationships will "create" those relationships and will affect how participants perceive them. This assertion is true not only during or after the ending of the relationship but also at the start and during the middle. Accounts are not just a reformulation of incoherent material, but are a *symbolic* effort that mediates the formulation of the relationship as a psychological entity in flux.

Such formulations are negotiated through talk with partners and others. Relationship creation, we believe, involves the making of joint accounts of relationships and joint "memory" of relational history that presupposes negotiated agreement on episodes, and which implies a system of communication. We postulate that change and growth are not merely emotional increments but reflect psychological reorganization requiring communicative action (see Wegner, Giuliano, & Hertel, 1985). Talk is thus both instrumental in bringing the relationship about and also essential in constituting a large element of the relationship's character.

This discussion has emphasized the role of talk in constructing and reifying relationships. We do not conclude that talk makes relationships all by itself, but we do claim that it has three very significant roles in framing the social processes that make relationships. It is more than just an indexical medium for other social psychological processes in relationships. In proposing this we explore a present tension between social psychology's approach to talk and that of rhetorical studies.

TALK AS A FRAMEWORK FOR SOCIAL PROCESSES

Whatever else people do in social life (the subject matter of social psychology), a very high percentage of their behavior seems to consist of talking to others. Talk is the crucible wherein relationships are conducted: Almost every day we need to communicate effectively, to influence or inform others, to ask advice, to deliver comfort, to offer help, to chat informally, and to discourse with friends, enemies, colleagues, patrons, subordinates, and kin.

Strikingly, however, this aspect of everyday social experience receives little direct attention in social psychological assessments of social participation (for example, it is not explicitly included for direct assessment in the otherwise excellent and innovative Rochester Interaction Record; see Wheeler & Nezlek, 1977). Talk is typically relegated to the status of a simple medium in much social psychological work on relating. It is represented as the channel through which social psychological processes are conveyed or expressed, or by means of which investigators are directly informed about the affective working of their subjects (e.g., Harvey, Hendrick & Tucker, 1988). Our own work on the Iowa Communication Record (Cook, 1988; Cortez, Duck & Strejc, 1988; Duck & Rutt, 1988) indicates, however, that talk is framed in many ways to effect particular relational purposes, but that in so doing, subjects affect the nature of the relationship. As Watzlawick, Beavin, and Jackson (1967) noted, talk contains literal content and a relational dimension.

Rhetorical studies amplify the latter approach to the nature of talk. Utterances can be framed in many ways, are not affectively neutral, create impressions by means of speech style, and influence people, including self. Such influence ranges from obvious persuasive outcomes to such "minor" persuasive effects as making someone like us, trust us, or form a general impression of us. To paraphrase Weaver's (1983, pp. 284-285) discussion of language, expression cannot be purged of all *tendency* (that is, of all attitudes, preferences, and inclinations to act). Such a claim would rest upon a misconception of the nature of language, both as a symbol system and as it is *used* in the social discourse of everyday life. Language is a social tool by which values and percepts are first framed in the mind and are then imputed to things, including relationships. It is also a symbolic means of indicating relational strength. For some rhetoricians, language is, therefore, "sermonic": It adopts views, offers a perspective, and preaches an outlook. When we utter words, we give impulse to other people to look at the world in our way: We speak as rhetoricians, affecting one another for good or ill.

Social psychological research on social relationships has paid less attention to the structure and content of utterances during relationship formation, growth, and decline. For example, self-disclosure research has focused on the "objectively rated" level of intimacy presumed to be inherent in statements classified as more or less intimate. In such a view, the paramount conveyor of developing emotional attachment is merely the graduated intimacy of the topics chosen for disclosure (e.g., Davis & Sloan, 1974). Communication researchers such as Montgomery (1981) reacted to the narrowness of this view some time ago, and showed that intimate material can be conveyed in nonintimate language forms, and intimacy often comes from context, mode of presentation, manner of communication, and various other stylistic variables rather than content itself.

There are, of course, some social psychological studies of talk, but they tend to be "second-order" studies of the quantity or rate of speech, such as effects of amount of talk on group perceptions of leadership roles (Stang, 1973). There is, of course, also a tradition in social psychology where talk is prominent in the analysis (e.g., Fraser & Scherer, 1982) or where its role is contrasted with that of nonverbal behavior (e.g., Mehrabian & Wiener, 1967), but its role in creating relationships is only indirectly implied in such work.

Phenomena relatively disregarded by social psychologists but not by communication researchers include language style or structure changes as relationships develop and are defined (e.g., Hopper, Knapp, & Scott, 1981), the cohesive functions of language in friendly social chats, the relational role of gossip, and the role of language in testing affinity, escalating intimacy, handling conflict and dissolving relationships (e.g., Daly, Vangelisti, & Daughton, 1987; Douglas, 1987; Planalp, Graham, & Paulson, 1987). These issues are truly interpersonal, and emerge clearly through talk. In like manner, talk is obviously central in nearly all the negotiative processes of relationship development identified in recent social psychological research on courtship progress, but that talk remains relatively uninvestigated (e.g., Huston et al., 1981; Lloyd & Cate, 1985).

Talk and relationship characteristics are nondetachable. That is to say, not only do relationship definitions and transitions affect or influence talk, but also talk defines relationships, both directly through relational negotiation and indirectly through conveying to "the world" subtle signs of intimacy or distance (Watzlawick, et al., 1967). Thus relationships are to be found partly in the discourse and communicational styles that partners adopt over and above the feelings that partners express about one another (e.g., the degrees of control or frequency of attempts at relational definition that characterize their talk; see Rogers & Millar, 1988). It follows that when two people develop (or dissolve) their relationship, their language usage and communication patterns will change in parallel with any changes in conversation topics (for example, they will use more/less intimate or immediate forms of address). Such changes reflect, or possibly even help to create, changes in the "emotional tone" of the relationship for partners themselves as well as "outsiders." In social discourse emotions are represented as much by speech style as by red faces, long stares, or other bodily expressiveness.

Our claim is that current processual emphases justify attention to activities in personal relationships that are mirrored in other disciplines, particularly in communication studies, and that they are exactly those concerns for which attention to talk would be most fruitful. The perspective provided by rhetorical theory would, we believe, be a useful adjunct to, rather than a replacement for, other perspectives.

We suggest that even everyday talk is rhetorically persuasive. It would follow that relational accounts, all sorts of such accounts and not just those focused on the ending of relationships, are persuasive or "invitational." That is to say, relational accounts segment reality in various ways, take a perspective and then invite the listener to share it. This process, of course, involves three related phenomena: (a) ignoring many of the stimuli that might be perceived, (b) focusing on a limited number of those stimuli, and (c) often combining or rearranging initial stimuli in order to make them fit into some meaningful pattern (Condon, 1985). This process helps to retain control, manage impressions or sustain identity, all of which are functions also performed by rhetoric.

Watzlawick et al. (1967) introduced the important notion of "punctuation" of discourse and experience and, as does Gottman (1979), they thereby acknowledge that people differ in the way they segment reality. Before we account for anything, it must first be noticed as a disjunction in the experiential flow and must be seen to require explanation (see Berscheid, 1983). Only then must it be explained. Our choices about the key events and where they are to be delimited are of interest in the relational sphere because the boundaries of social "events" are largely a matter of personal choice or joint negotiation. Our reasons for selecting certain chunks of reality as "events" are of at least as much interest as are the explanations offered for the chunks, once chunked. This, we believe, is especially important when there is the previously noted tendency for humans (including social scientists) to want to perceive life and relationships in segments that do not necessarily reflect its dynamic continuities.

To extend beyond the specific causal attributions that such language structures contain, we advocate attention also to their overarching narrative composition (e.g., whether they attempt to explain, accuse, define, or excuse) and also to the metaphors that they use, their implicit persuasive contents—in short, the rhetoric from which they are composed.

Accounts have often been regarded in social psychology as largely *representational* of reality, and investigators accordingly voice concern over the accuracy of such reports (McGhee, 1987) or mention the risks of (usually unspecified) "biases" in retrospective data or accounts or subjective self-reports. Nevertheless, the exact nature of these biases has never been determined and indeed would, we believe, make an interesting focus of study in their own right as a indication of subjects' psychological processes. In this framework, though, social psychological explanations would be sought for deviations from the "true account".

An alternative view is adopted by rhetoricians: accounts, like other rhetorical acts, are *pre*sentational, not representational. That is to say, accounts offer a view of reality rather than a description of it; they present the perspective of the speaker/writer, who may have the hope of persuading others to adopt the presented view. In this framework, accounts could be analyzed for system and coherence without any assumption that one view is the objective truth. Psychologists such as Kelly (1955) argued similarly that subjects' statements should be treated as presentational or hypothetical, or, in Kelly's terms, invitational. However, that opinion has not been widely adopted by social psychologists.

On the other hand, within some different traditions, such as symbolic interactionism or more general interpretive sociological approaches, such views of the presentational nature of accounts have been widely discussed. Not only are they seen to "explain" what goes on in a relationship, they serve various important social functions for the participants. La Gaipa (1982) and McCall (1982) have both supported a presentational perspective by pointing out that accounts preserve a person's "face" for future relationships. McCall also draws attention to the metaphors that are used in such accounts, because they can reveal the attitudes and emotions of the person toward the relationship, and thus may be of use to therapists. For instance, talk of being smothered in a relationship is one metaphor, whereas talk of being chained, stuck, or united to a partner uses different metaphors with different implications for partner satisfaction with the relationship (and also for relational repair; see Duck, 1984).

(RE)PRESENTING RELATIONAL REALITY THROUGH TALK

Rhetoric regards communication as a *presentation* of reality. Such presentation involves coordinating social actions through use of symbols that create meaning in and for other people. Communication presents reality through the organizing and projecting power of the symbols in language. The presentational character of communication stems also from the situational context in which communication occurs, for actions follow from our understanding of situations, just as scientists' use of particular metaphors constrains them to "see" particular phenomena, as we indicated above. People present scenes, facts, and relationships in ways that constrain the appropriate responses and the subsequent nature of their interactions with others.

Communication and Relationships

The rhetorical approach to social reality suggests that communication about relationships very often *is* the reality of the relationship. This assertion holds for phases of relationships, including initiation, development, and maintenance, as well as dissolution. For instance, the supposed bias, idealization, self-interest, and so on reflected in postdissolution accounts for relationships are "probably not mere accidents or psychological epiphenomena; they are probably psychologically crucial to the persons coming to terms with the relationship dissolution" (Duck, 1982, p. 28). Research on such presentations has often focused on dissolutions as a major crisis that needs explanation; however, we would urge researchers to attend to explanations of growth or stability in relationships as much as to their decline (see Surra et al., 1988).

For both rhetoricians and social psychologists an important fact is that accounts often differ markedly from one telling to the next (Weber, Harvey, & Stanley, 1987). Some accounts may be repeatedly offered in an almost ritualized manner. More often, however, accounts vary across auditors and across time in ways that reflect both listeners' and tellers' (perceived) contemporary needs for presenting a view of themselves or for explaining the present nature of a relationship. Thus, our general proposal is that the principles uncovered by existing work on accounts of the breakup of relationships are extendible to other forms of talk in social relating. All that is necessary for such extension is that (a) we acknowledge the role of the rhetoric of everyday talk in structuring and interpreting aspects of our experience, and (b) beyond this general rhetorical, functional approach, we attend to the persuasive intent of such talk in everyday social activity.

Burke, Rhetoric and Relationships

One of the most influential rhetorical theorists, Burke (1945, 1950), regards language as an arbitrary system of symbols used to ascribe meaning to reality by agents capable of symbolic action and able to reflect upon their actions. Rhetoric is discourse by design and researchers should study the personal and social psychological designs, needs, and strategies that influence talk. Language as used in social settings is inherently persuasive, inherently reflects stances and perspectives, inherently communicates via symbols accepted in a given cultural community, inherently invites us to view reality from a particular vantage point. Rhetoric is a mode of strategic action using language, and it is used to mold and to maintain community and community values.

When a social psychologist looks more closely at Burke's work, a remarkable coincidence is evident between his terminology and Goffman's (e.g., both see life as a drama). Burke's outlook is also similar to that in current use by social psychologists and sociologists, particularly as they write about relationships (which Burke does not do specifically). Yet while social psychologists are interested in attribution and the factors related to the location of causality in social acts, Burke is interested in the whole language by which people describe motives or make attributions. Burke (1945) proposed a "dramatistic pentad" to account for the language of motives: "In a rounded statement about motives, you must have some words that name the *act* (names what took place, in thought or deed), and another that names the *scene* (the background of the act, the situation in which it occurred); also you must indicate what person or kind of person (*agent*) performed the act, what means or instruments he [or she] used (*agency*) and the *purpose*" (p. xv).

For Burke there are so-called grammatical "ratios" among these five terms of his pentad. These ratios have implications for understanding talk. In all there are ten possible ratios, but we supply only one example, using the scene-act ratio. Once the scene has been cast in a particular metaphorical style, certain analogous qualities can readily be imputed to an act: for instance, if the scene is "unusual" then it calls for an "unusual response." Such a ratio was used by F. D. Roosevelt in seeking to invoke the war powers act: he requested the granting of "unusual powers" because the country was "in an unusual international situation." The "because" seems natural in the argument, given the scene as set for the act. Burke (1945) indicates that the scene-act ratio can be applied deterministically in two ways: that an action *had to be* taken in light of the situation as described by the speaker; or that it *should be* taken in that same light.

To extend this analysis to the talk of friends, we can see that the manner of presenting the situation/scene of the relationship's current state or partner's recent behavior renders certain actions by the speaker as *determined*, and so as logical, predictable, normative, reasonable, understandable, or absolved of blame. It also provides a context for evaluating partners' behavior, a context that depends on the speaker and listeners sharing a common symbol system for understanding relationships.

Rhetorical Nature of Sociality

Burke (1950, p. 36) asserts that "the basic function of rhetoric" is "the use of words by human agents to form attitudes or to induce actions in other human agents." It is "rooted in an essential function of language itself, a function that is wholly realistic and is continually born anew; the use of language as a symbolic means of inducing cooperation in beings that by nature respond to symbols" (1950, p. 43). It is the communal understanding of these symbols that makes communication possible, and it is clear that as we learn language so we also learn the rhetorical strategies inherent in language itself. The implication is that as the individual acquires language, he or she also acquires a set of values, rules, and strategies for gaining and maintaining social acceptability (Ambrester & Holm Strause, 1984, p. xii). Thus talk or the formulation of language strategies in a community of friends is a cohesive force as much as it is a simple explanation of a relational event. Talk is not purposeless or capricious, but serves a number of ends, including the definition of self, supplying of the other with expectations of us, and publication to outsiders of several aspects of a relationship. People adapt messages to audiences via the intentional use of the "perspectival vehicle" of language in such ways that "the story-telling process" serves one or more of a variety of such functions. For instance, the need to present self as a well-judging entrant to relationships can perhaps account for the frequency of postdissolution accounts that claim the finally fatal problem was always inherent from the start (Weber, 1983). Yet it is not only the dissolution of relationships that requires the presentation of that image in talk and people rarely present themselves as "easy-to-get" in relationships (e.g., Wright & Contrada, 1986).

Another obvious requisite function of relational talk, for example, is to help one "make sense of" a relationship. Weick writes of establishing meaning retrospectively by attending to what has already occurred. "Since the attention is directed backward from a specific point in time. . . whatever is occurring at the moment will influence what the person discovers when he [or she] glances backward" (Weick, 1969, p. 65). Miell (1987) indicates that subjects very often predict the future of their relationship not on the basis of its long-term stabilities or well established past, but rather on the most recent three days of experience of it! Also, in keeping with Weick (1969), Harvey, Agostinelli, and Weber (this volume) speak of the need to find meaning in the past as well as hope and direction for the present and future, agreeing that the accounts we construe accomplish these functions, even to explain why or how a relationship exists and perhaps express surprise at its growth.

Another pervasive use of talk is to facilitate self-knowledge and self-acceptance. This function assumes added significance during relationship change, when we face questions such as, "Who am I now?" or "Where am I headed?" Nonetheless, language structures also serve to impose continuity on otherwise discontinous events as manifested in the dispositional language used to describe relationships ("we *are* [dispositionally] in love", for instance, as noted by Duck & Sants, 1983). Continuity can also be dramatized as we retell the history of a relationship, reminisce with partners (Edwards & Middleton, 1988) or employ relational symbols in talk (Baxter, 1987). As a form of self-disclosure, such historical recountings have the potential to increase intimacy and trust or to "arrange" expectations in terms of the scenes created when we rehearse our perceptions of relational "events."

Talk can thus serve to constrain behavior or define a relationship's future because of the terms in which the past or present are discussed. Talk also serves to increase identification, another essential function of rhetoric. Burke (1950) writes of identification and consubstantiality and their counterpart, division, noting that only because of the fact of our individuality and uniqueness (a form of division) do we need rhetoric to facilitate identification. He notes that earlier conceptualizations of rhetoric reflected a persuasive paradigm based on separateness: persuasion involved a source attempting to convince a receiver according to an adversarial or agonistic model. Burke's reconceptualization of rhetoric centers on incorporation instead, the idea of evoking meanings in one's auditors by the joining of interests and focusing on common principles, as well as acting together to accomplish some goal. "You persuade a man *[sic]* only insofar as you can talk his *[sic]* language by speech, gesture, tonality, order, image, attitude, idea, identifying your ways with his *[sic]*" (1950, p. 55).

CONCLUSION: ACCOUNTS AND BEYOND ACCOUNTS

The foregoing discussion represents an initial attempt to explicate the rhetorical underpinnings for the functions performed by talk, particularly as it changes over time. As needs and goals change, so we engage in rhetorical symbolization to meet new needs and achieve new goals. People interpret reality rhetorically, as Vatz (1973, pp. 156-157) explains:

> Meaning is not intrinsic in events, facts, people, or "situations" nor are facts "publicly observable"... There is a choice of events to communicate ... The very choice of what facts or events are relevant is a matter of pure arbitration.... The translation of the chosen information into meaning... is an act of creativity. It is an interpretative act. It is a rhetorical act ... Thus rhetoric is a cause not an effect of meaning.

We have argued that such talk as occurs in relationships itself contributes to the definition of the relationship and hence to its psychological creation. By means of accounts presented in public, whether as justification or as gossip with friends, humans structure for themselves the parts that they see as most significant and salient in their relationships and this in turn constrains expectations.

Accounts help people to create life narratives through which they can "market" their relationships to other people and explain what they think is going on in their lives. As has been noted by other social psychologists, people develop accounts of the origin of their relationships just as much as they do for their demise (see Belove's 1980 work on FECKs, stories about First Encounters of the Close Kind). We are convinced that talk about current relationship events is equally important, though we are at present still gathering the data to test this speculation. Discrepancies between partners' stories of quarrels or of other persons' behavior are as significant in the conduct of relationships as are accounts of relationship dissolution, and so too are any forms of talk that "describe" a relationship.

The presentational view inherent in a rhetorical perspective of both accounts and attributions indicates some interesting avenues for research on relationships. All such attributions and accounts not only are, but have to be, *used* by people in a communal context that constrains liberty to describe relationships in just any way we choose: They must be reported in a terminology that is socially acceptable and which reflects normative beliefs about the nature of relationships; they must be presented in terms that people understand as appropriately applicable to relationships; they sometimes serve a symbolic function; they are often edited to serve social and personal requirements at the time of their utterance, such as ingratiation or self-presentational needs; they refer to an agent who does something; their purpose may be persuasive, not just in the obvious sense, but in creating opportunities and constraints for subsequent interactions, e.g., forming a climate of opinion about a person's action or behavior so that certain other influence attempts can be built upon that base.

In sum, we postulate several different, simultaneous, and powerful influences of talk on the creation, existence, and representation of relationships that cry out for further study by personality and social psychologists. In providing an anvil on which to hammer out some of the alloys of qualitative and quantitative methods and some of the blends of mechanistic with symbolic approaches to science, the study of talk offers many opportunities in the multidisciplinary study of close personal relationships. Talk is influenced by psychological, developmental, sociological, and rhetorical forces that make it a natural object, in its own right, for study in this field. As we have tried to show, some lines of research require very little lengthening in order to reach the direct study of talk in relationships. We are hopeful for social psychological research on "relationship editorializing" (Duck & Sants, 1983), the editing of stories, talk, and accounts about relationships in which people constantly engage. Such editorializing emphasizes the relational function of talk; relationships have a communal function and are conducted in a community with its own systems and symbols.

Indeed, relationships are to a considerable extent symbol systems in the minds of participants and observers of those relationships, and relational behavior reflects the development and change of those symbols. Indeed, when people romance in one sense (fall in love), they also romance in another sense (create stories). We are tempted to ask, "which is the noblest romance of them all?"

REFERENCES

Ambrester, M. L., & Strause, G. H. (1984). *A rhetoric of interpersonal communication.* Prospect Heights, IL: Waveland.

Baxter, L. A. (1987). Symbols of relationship identity in relationship cultures. *Journal of Social and Personal Relationships, 4*, 261-280.

Baxter, L. A., & Wilmot, W. W. (1986). Interaction characteristics of disengaging, stable, and growing relationships. In R. Gilmour & S. W. Duck (Eds.), *The emerging field of personal relationships* (pp. 145-159). Hillsdale, NJ: Lawrence Erlbaum.

Belove, L. (1980). First encounters of the close kind (FECKS): The use of the story of the first interaction as an early recollection of a marriage. *Journal of Individual Psychology, 36*, 191-208.

Berger, C. R. (1988). Uncertainty and information exchange in developing relationships. In S. W. Duck (Ed.), *Handbook of personal relationships* (pp. 239-255). Chichester: John Wiley.

Berscheid, E. (1983). Emotion. In H. H. Kelley et al. (Ed.), *Close relationships.* San Francisco: Freeman.

Burke, K. (1945). *A grammar of motives.* New York: Prentice-Hall.

Burke, K. (1950). *A rhetoric of motives.* New York: Prentice-Hall.

Cappella, J. N. (1988). Personal relationships, social relationships and patterns of interaction. In S. W. Duck (Ed.), *Handbook of personal relationships* (pp. 325-342). Chichester: John Wiley.

Condon, J. C., Jr. (1985). *Semantics and communication* (3rd ed.). New York: Macmillan.

Cook, J. (1988, November). *Testing the Iowa Communication Record in families with an alcoholic member.* Paper presented to the Speech Communication Association.

Cortez, C., Duck, S. W., & Strejc, H. (1988, November). *The heart is a lonely communicator: The ICR (Iowa Communication Record) and dating communication in the lonely.* Paper presented to the Speech Communication Association.

Daly, J. A., Vangelisti, A. L., & Daughton, S. M. (1987). The nature and correlates of conversational sensitivity. *Human Communication Research, 14* , 167-202.

Davis, J. D., & Sloan, M. (1974). The basis of interviewee matching of interviewer self-disclosure. *British Journal of Social and Clinical Psychology, 13*, 359-367.

Dillard, J. P., & Miller, K. I. (1988). Intimate relationships in task environments. In S. W. Duck (Ed.), *Handbook of personal relationships* (pp. 449-465). Chichester: John Wiley.

Douglas, W. (1987). Affinity-testing in initial interaction. *Journal of Social and Personal Relationships, 4*, 3-15.

Duck, S. W. (1980). Personal relationships in the 1980s: Toward an understanding of complex human sociality. *Western Journal of Speech Communication, 44,* 114-119.

Duck, S. W. (1982). A topography of relationship disengagement and dissolution. In S. W. Duck (Ed.), *Personal relationships 4: Dissolving personal relationships* (pp. 1-30). London: Academic Press.

Duck, S. W. (1984). A perspective on the repair of personal relationships. In S. W. Duck (Ed.), *Personal relationships 5: Repairing personal relationships* (pp. 163-184). New York: Academic Press.

Duck, S. W. (1985). Social and personal relationships. In M. L. Knapp & G. R. Miller (Eds.), *Handbook of interpersonal communication* (pp. 655-686). Beverly Hills, CA: Sage.

Duck, S. W. (1987a). Adding apples and oranges: Investigators' implicit theories about personal relationships. In R. Burnett, P. McGhee, & D. Clarke (Eds.), *Accounting for relationships* (pp. 215-224). London: Methuen.

Duck, S. W. (1987b). How to lose friends without influencing people. In M. Roloff & G. R. Miller (Eds.), *Interpersonal processes: New directions in communication research* (pp. 278-298). Newbury Park, CA: Sage.

Duck, S. W., & Miell, D. E. (1986). Charting the development of personal relationships. In R. Gilmour & S. W. Duck (Eds.), *The emerging field of personal relationships* (pp. 133-143). Hillsdale, NJ: Lawrence Erlbaum.

Duck, S. W., & Rutt, D. J. (1988, November). *Developing the Iowa Communication Record.* Paper presented to the Speech Communication Association.

Duck, S. W., & Sants, H. (1983). On the origin of the specious: Are personal relationships really interpersonal states? *Journal of Social and Clinical Psychology, 1,* 27-41.

Dunn, J. (1988). Relations among relationships. In S. W. Duck (Ed.), *Handbook of personal relationships* (pp. 193-209). Chichester: John Wiley.

Edwards, D., & Middleton, D. (1988). Conversational remembering and family relationships: How children learn to remember. *Journal of Social and Personal Relationships, 5,* 3-26.

Fraser, C., & Scherer, K. (Eds.). (1982). *Advances in the social psychology of language.* Harmondsworth: Penguin.

Gottman, J. (1979). *Marital interaction: Experimental investigations.* New York: Academic Press.

Gottman, J. M., & Parker, J. (1987). *Conversations of friends.* Cambridge: Cambridge University Press.

Harvey, J. H., Hendrick, S. S., & Tucker, K. (1988). Self-report methods in studying personal relationships. In S. W. Duck (Ed.), *Handbook of personal relationships* (pp. 99-113). Chichester: John Wiley.

Hendrick, C. (1988). Roles and gender in relationships. In S. W. Duck (Ed.), *Handbook of personal relationships* (pp. 429-448). Chichester: John Wiley.

Hobfoll, S. E., & Stokes, J. P. (1988). The process and mechanics of social support. In S. W. Duck (Ed.), *Handbook of personal relationships* (pp. 497-517). Chichester: John Wiley.

Hopper, R., Knapp, M. L., & Scott, L. (1981). Couples' personal idioms: Exploring intimate talk. *Journal of Communication, 31,* 23-33.

Huston, T. L., Surra, C. A., Fitzgerald, N. M., & Cate, R. M. (1981). From courtship to marriage: Mate selection as an interpersonal process. In S. W. Duck & R. Gilmour (Eds.), *Personal relationships 2: Developing personal relationships* (pp. 53-88). New York: Academic Press.

Kelly, G. A. (1955). *A psychology of personal constructs*. New York: Norton.

La Gaipa, J. J. (1982). Rules and rituals in disengaging from relationships. In S. W. Duck (Ed.), *Personal relationships 4: Dissolving personal relationships* (pp. 189-210). London: Academic Press.

La Gaipa, J. J. (1987). Friendship expectations. In R. Burnett, P. McGhee, & D. Clarke (Eds.), *Accounting for relationships* (pp. 134-157). London: Methuen.

Lloyd, S. A., & Cate, R. M. (1985). The developmental course of conflict in premarital relationship dissolution. *Journal of Social and Personal Relationships, 2*, 179-194.

McAdams, D. P. (1988). Personal needs and personal relationships. In S. W. Duck (Ed.), *Handbook of personal relationships* (pp. 7-22). Chichester: John Wiley.

McCall, G. J. (1982). Becoming unrelated: The management of bond dissolution. In S. W. Duck (Ed.), *Personal relationships 4: Dissolving personal relationships* (pp. 211-232). New York: Academic Press.

McCall, G. J. (1988). The organisational life cycle of relationships. In S. W. Duck (Ed.), *Handbook of personal relationships* (pp. 467-484). Chichester: John Wiley.

McGhee, P. (1987). From self-reports to narrative discourse: Reconstructing the voice of experience in personal relationship research. In R. Burnett, P. McGhee, & D. Clarke (Eds.), *Accounting for relationships* (pp. 289-315). London: Methuen.

Mehrabian, A., & Wiener, M. (1967). Decoding of inconsistent communications. *Journal of Personality and Social Psychology, 6*, 109-114.

Miell, D. E. (1984). *Strategies of self disclosure*. Unpublished doctoral dissertation, University of Lancaster, UK.

Miell, D. E. (1987). Remembering relationship development: Constructing a context for interactions. In R. Burnett, P. McGhee, & D. Clarke (Eds.), *Accounting for relationships* (pp. 60-73). London: Methuen.

Milardo, R. M. (1982). Friendship networks in developing relationships: Converging and diverging social environments. *Social Psychology Quarterly, 45*, 162-172.

Milardo, R. M., Johnson, M. P., & Huston, T. L. (1983). Developing close relationships: Changing patterns of interaction between pair members and social networks. *Journal of Personality and Social Psychology, 44*, 964-976.

Miller, G. R., & Boster, F. (1988). Persuasion in personal relationships. In S. W. Duck (Ed.), *Handbook of personal relationships* (pp. 275-288). Chichester: John Wiley.

Montgomery, B. M. (1981). Verbal immediacy as a behavioral indicator of open communication content. *Communication Quarterly, 30*, 28-34.

Montgomery, B. M. (1988). Quality communication in personal relationships. In S. W. Duck (Ed.), *Handbook of personal relationships* (pp. 343-359). Chichester: John Wiley.

Nash, A. (1988). Ontogeny, phylogeny and relationships. In S. W. Duck (Ed.), *Handbook of personal relationships* (pp. 121-141). Chichester: John Wiley.

Olson, D. H. (1977). Insiders' and outsiders' views of relationships: Research studies. In G. Levinger & H. L. Raush (Eds.), *Close relationships: Perspectives on the meaning of intimacy* (pp. 115-135). Amherst: University of Massachusetts Press.

Patterson, M. L. (1988). Functions of nonverbal behavior in close relationships. In S. W. Duck (Ed.), *Handbook of personal relationships* (pp. 41-56). Chichester: John Wiley.

Planalp, S., Graham, M., & Paulson, L. (1987). Cohesive devices in conversation. *Communication Monographs, 54*, 325-343.

Reis, H. T., & Shaver, P. (1988). Intimacy as an interpersonal process. In S. W. Duck (Ed.), *Handbook of personal relationships* (pp. 367-389). Chichester: John Wiley.

Rogers, L. E., & Millar, F. F. (1988). Relational communication. In S. W. Duck (Ed.), *Handbook of personal relationships* (pp. 289-305). Chichester: John Wiley.

Rook, K. S. (1988). Toward a more differentiated view of loneliness. In S. W. Duck (Ed.), *Handbook of personal relationships* (pp. 571-589). Chichester: John Wiley.

Sants, H. K. A. (1984). Conceptions of friendship, social behaviour and school achievements in six-year-old children. *Journal of Social and Personal Relationships, 1,* 293-309.

Stang, D. (1973). Effects of interaction rate on ratings of leadership and liking. *Journal of Personality and Social Psychology, 27,* 405-408.

Surra, C. A., Arizzi, P., & Asmussen, L. A. (1988). The association between reasons for commitment and the development and outcome of marital relationships. *Journal of Social and Personal Relationships, 5,* 47-63.

Vatz, R. E. (1973). The myth of the rhetorical situation. *Philosophy and Rhetoric, 6,* 154-161.

Watzlawick, P., Beavin, J., & Jackson, D. D. (1967). *Pragmatics of human communication.* New York: Norton.

Weaver, R. M. (1983). Language is sermonic. In J. L. Golden, G. F. Berquist, & W. E. Coleman (Eds.), *The rhetoric of Western thought* (pp. 275-285). Dubuque, IA: Kendall-Hunt.

Weber, A. (1983, May). *Breaking up.* Paper presented to the Nags Head Conference, North Carolina.

Weber, A. L., Harvey, J. H., & Stanley, M. A. (1987). The nature and motivations of accounts in failed relationships. In R. Burnett, P. McGhee, & D. Clarke (Eds.), *Accounting for relationships* (pp. 114-133). London: Methuen.

Wegner, D., Giuliano, T., & Hertel, P. T. (1985). Cognitive interdependence in close relationships. In W. Ickes (Ed.), *Compatible and incompatible relationships* (pp. 253-276). New York: Springer Verlag.

Weick, K. R. (1969). *The social psychology of organizing.* Reading, MA: Addison-Wesley.

Wheeler, L., & Nezlek, J. (1977). Sex differences in social participation. *Journal of Personality and Social Psychology, 35,* 742-754.

Wright, R., & Contrada, R. J. (1986). Dating selectivity and interpersonal attraction: Toward a better understanding of the "Elusive Phenomenon." *Journal of Social and Personal Relationships, 3,* 131-148.

2

Account-Making and the Formation of Expectations About Close Relationships

JOHN H. HARVEY
GINA AGOSTINELLI
ANN L. WEBER

John H. Harvey is Professor and Chair of the Department of Psychology at the University of Iowa. His interests and writings have been in the area of attribution (e.g., editor with William Ickes and Robert Kidd of a three-volume series, *New Directions in Attribution Research*, 1976, 1978, 1981) and close relationships (e.g., author with Kelley et al., *Close Relationships*, 1983).

Gina Agostinelli is Assistant Professor of Psychology at the University of New Mexico. Her past research has been on biases in social perception (i.e., the false consensus effect) and people's abilities to detect and identify change. More recently she has been developing a theory for studying confusion (i.e., mental perplexity). She is also coauthor of a chapter in *Analysing Lay Explanation: A Casebook of Methods* (Antaki, Ed.).

Ann L. Weber is Associate Professor of Psychology at the University of North Carolina at Asheville. Her research and teaching interests have focused on close relationships and the role of cognitive processes in relationship maintenance and breakdown. She is coauthor of chapters in *Personal Relationships 4: Dissolving Personal Relationships* (Steve Duck, Ed., 1982) and *The Emerging Field of Personal Relationships* (Robin Gilmour and Steve Duck, Eds., 1986). She is currently working as coauthor on two books in preparation, also in the field of close relationships psychology, and is active as a consultant, conducting workshops and seminars on topics including stress management, communication and conflict resolution, and how to fall out of love.

BACKGROUND AND THEORETICAL
CONSIDERATIONS FOR ACCOUNTS WORK

This chapter has two main concerns. First, we will discuss the nature of the accounts people form to explain major problems in or at the end of their close relationships. Second, we will consider how people form

AUTHORS' NOTE: We thank Clyde Hendrick, three anonymous reviewers, and Steve Duck for excellent advice and commentaries on earlier drafts of this chapter. We also appreciate Becky Huber's outstanding help in preparing the manuscript.

expectations for current and future close relationships and the possible relation of such expectations with their explanations of endings of their past loves.

In our previous work (e.g., Harvey, Weber, Galvin, Huszti, & Garnick, 1986; Harvey, Wells, & Alvarez, 1978; Weber, Harvey, & Stanley, 1987), we have approached the concept of accounts from the framework of attribution theory in social psychology. We define accounts as people's story-like explanations for past actions and events which include characterizations of self and significant others. Essentially, they are meanings organized into a "story" and thus represent more than collections of disparate attributions.

Whether or not accounts are accurate in their depiction of causal factors, we argue that accounts play an important role in enabling individuals to make sense of and arrive at acceptable explanations for an often complex network of causal forces (see also Duck & Sants, 1983). We have previously theorized that accounts develop over a period of time, are rehearsed and periodically elaborated in front of audiences varying in size (from oneself to a set of close others), are triggered by a variety of stimuli including many emotionally relevant sights and sounds, and endure in varied forms until our deaths (Harvey, Flanary, & Morgan, 1986; Harvey, Turnquist, & Agostinelli, 1988).

Following other writers who have emphasized the social psychological dynamics of accounts (e.g., Fletcher, 1983; Newman, 1981; Orvis, Kelley, & Butler, 1976; Weiss, 1975), our own work has emphasized a broad attribution-cognitive approach. That is, we focus on how people arrive at explanations for major events in their lives and the cognitive properties of those accounts or explanations.

In this article we are concerned mainly with account-making as a response to provocative or troubling experience. Account-making, whether reported to others or privately carried out, is as basic to the human mind as are the most mundane queries of our daily lives. In a time of fast-paced lives filled with many moments of unarticulated emotional pain, accounts may serve as the poetry of the masses; we all have our poignant lines. For many, until some of this pain is turned into an explanatory story, it has not really happened in the sense of taking a definite form and reality. Over the years, writers, including those who keep journals and diaries, often use such stories in the hope of giving shape to their grief and inchoate lives (Rosenblatt, 1983). Accounts may serve to help people establish the value of their different life passages and provide such perspective for younger persons. In this regard, accounts may serve as the sliver of immortality each person leaves behind in influencing how others make sense out of their lives.

Scholars focusing on the cognitive properties of accounts for past close relationships have defined accounts as involving underlying knowledge structures, or more specifically, schemata about close relationships (Burnett, McGhee, & Clarke, 1987). As schematic knowledge structures, accounts may lead to certain expectations for future close relationships. The cognitive aspects of accounts will be further developed in our later section on the accounts-expectation link.

Although our focus is on the attributional and cognitive aspects of accounts, in our analyses of account-making we have also recognized other dynamics, including cathartic-emotional, or psychodynamic, and self-presentational, or social, processes (see Harvey et al., 1986). We believe that these processes may also be relevant to the study of accounts. This eclecticism may be vital to the breadth of the phenomenon and our understanding of accounts at this time. Accounts appear to serve a variety of functions as people use them in their attempts to deal with different types of dilemmas. Specifically, in his work with recently separated persons, Weiss (1975) argues that accounts are valuable because they help people make better sense of the loss of a close relationship and thus achieve a greater sense of psychological control. He notes that accounts may serve as a cathartic pathway for emotional release. The reader is also referred to Harvey et al. (1986) for a discussion of different self-presentation strategies that appear to unfold in account-making as people attempt to present themselves via their stories in different ways to different audiences (e.g., an ex-husband's emphasis on communicating to his new lover his innocent-victim role in his previous marriage).

Accounts have become a frequent vehicle for exploring sensitive human problems in much recent writing and scholarship. The following is a list of relevant works: Glick, Weiss, and Parkes's (1974) *The First Year of Bereavement,* regarding the coping and grieving reactions and memories reported by widows during the first year after their husbands' death; Abramson's (1984) *Sarah: A Sexual Biography,* regarding the sexual development of a young woman from college student to prostitute to middle class wife and mother; Schuchter's (1986) *Dimensions of Grief,* regarding people's attempts to cope with the loss of loved ones; Rubin's (1983) *Intimate Strangers,* regarding men and women in their attempts to forge closeness in the midst of imposing dilemmas of changing times, values, and identities; Vaughan's (1986) *Uncoupling,* regarding people's perceptions of the crucial turning points in the failing of their close relationships; Matthews's (1986) *Friendships through the Life Course,* regarding people's life-long quest for and transition in personal friendships; Rosenblatt's (1983) *Bitter, Bitter Tears,* a study of nineteenth-century diarists' grieving responses for lost loved ones; Weissberg's (1985) *Children of the Night,* about the circumstances leading to and impact of adolescent prostitution; Brende and Parson's (1985) *Vietnam Veterans,* about the attempts of Vietnam veterans to cope both with the effects of the war and adjustment to personal life and work; Bernikow's (1987) *Alone in America,* regarding the plight of millions of Americans who experience major periods of loneliness in their lives; Lichtman and Taylor's (1986) treatment of the close relationships of female cancer patients; and Allen and Pickett's (1987) analysis of streams of action in the family life courses of women. These works are only illustrative of the writing and research that uses accounts to explore humans' grappling with emotional pain and loss. Such works delve deeply into issues and have wide popular appeal because they emphasize the ordinary, common-sense reports of individuals experiencing problems. They also take advantage of people's common need/quest to impart their stories to interested others. We believe that such works provide examples of the richness of personality and social psychological dynamics that may be probed via accounts.

Comparisons with Other Conceptions of Accounts and Account-Making

We agree with Cochran (1986) that people use stories often to make sense of puzzling events. While Cochran seems to emphasize the story as deciphered by the scientist or scholar, our emphasis is on the story as told by the actor. Over time, we contend that people develop "master accounts" of their life stories containing the various bits and pieces of their ongoing accounts. A similar point may be made about how the accounts topic is treated in ethogenic psychology. Harré, Clark, and DeCarlo (1985) assert that in producing their accounts, actors are displaying knowledge of the ideal ways of acting and ideal reasons for doing what they have done or omitted doing. They say: "When we collect the accounts from a subculture, like football fans, or a family, or a hospital ward, etc., we search through the accounts for descriptions of what *should* happen. And we *represent* this material as a system of rules *representing a system of knowledge and belief"* (p. 88). Harré et al. go on to say that the rules so cited can be checked against the ethnographic hypotheses about the meanings of the actions and that these accounts are not introspective descriptions of cognitive processes such as plans and intentions.

We have no qualms with this rule-oriented conception in depicting the underlying structure of account-making. We do, however, accord significance to the original contents of the reported knowledge displayed by actors, whether or not this knowledge always reflects ideal ways of acting and reasons for action. The original content (including reports of plans and intentions), style, and context of the report are of primary importance to our analysis, whereas such factors have not been treated prominently in ethogenic psychology.

In other related work, Scott and Lyman (1968) advanced the idea of accounts as either justifications or excuses about socially undesirable actions; such statements presumably are given in order to protect the ego or status of the account-maker. They emphasized verbal statements as the form of accounts. An example of an account according to Scott and Lyman is the following: "I was going to night school to get an M.A. degree, and holding down a job in addition, and the load got too much for me" (p. 52, given by a mental patient). Their analysis did not address various aspects of account-making nor the specific contents of accounts. A more recent analysis of excuses and justifications offered by people in various social settings is provided by Semin and Manstead (1984).

Another work that focuses on the ego preservation/restoration nature of accounts (although the term account is not explicitly used) is Jellison's (1977) *I'm Sorry I Didn't Mean To and Other Lies We Love to Tell*. Similar to Scott and Lyman, Jellison emphasizes social justification as the key motivation for the presentation of accounts. He also does not present an analysis of account-making or the contents of accounts. He did argue that such presentations are designed to win approval from others and that their content is influenced by this motivation. If the individual achieves such liking from others, he or she is more likely to gain material resources from them. The focus on social justification also is related to the social-resource exchange literature of factors involved in viewing others accountable (or negotiating with others about account-ability) in exchange situations (Couch & Weiland, 1986). Again, the emphasis is not so much on the content of the "holding of other accountable" and the impact thereof, as it is on the conditions under which one may be held accountable (a concern found also in Scott and Lyman and in Jellison's writings).

Our own position on accounts differs from that of Scott and Lyman and Jellison mainly in its breadth and focus. In addition to social justification, we include as bases for account-making the enhancement of a personal sense of control and closure, catharsis and emotional release, with an emphasis on a sheer desire to understand. In contrast to what Jellison would seem to argue, we do not believe that people always are seeking approval or material gain from others in their presentations of accounts. They may be so motivated. But we recognize that the other motivations as noted above do not pertain to seeking personal material reward. Finally, unlike Scott and Lyman, we emphasize that accounts are often written, not just verbal statements.

There is an emerging strand of conceptions of accounts quite similar to the conception we are advancing. Antaki (1987) describes various types of accounts within close relationships and also emphasizes their breadth of function. In addition, he makes the useful distinction between performable accounts (that a person could choose to broadcast to others) and unperformable accounts that exist quietly but that are impactful in indirect ways on a person's actions, thoughts, and feelings. As discussed in an earlier paper (Harvey, Turnquist, & Agostinelli, 1988), we, too, believe that people have accounts that they display to others and accounts that they more or less keep private (though there may be overlap with the displayed version). The private version may be a "master account" that requires many years of sorting in order to begin to fulfill. This private version may also more generally be an overview account into which an individual places not only the story of a lost love but also related stories regarding other losses and triumphs that as a whole forms the mosaic of his or her life story.

In addition to Antaki's analysis, there are other views similar to our conception of accounts. In his writing, Shotter (e.g., 1984) also has focused on how people talk about themselves and their behavior and, in general, make their conduct accountable in a moral world. One difference, though, Shotter follows the rule-oriented view of ethogenic psychology in also emphasizing how people *must* talk about themselves in terms of the social order and socially constructed morality in which they exist. People, thus, must account for their experiences in ways that are intelligible and legitimate in their current social context. Our analysis, while less formal in this regard, also involves the view that account-making occurs in a social context and may be affected in substantial ways by this context.

In other writing similar to our position, Birren (1987) has suggested that when the young and old alike make their autobiographical statements, this gives new meaning to their present lives by helping them understand their pasts more fully. This view is consonant with our depiction of the merits of account-making. Coles (1986) also stressed the importance of arriving at meanings for events when he urged teachers to use story-telling (personal as well as literary masterpieces) to make education more meaningful. Various theorists in the psychodynamic tradition (e.g., see Horowitz, 1986) deal with people's inclination to use a variety of defenses that may include account-making-like processes in their attempts to cope with stressful events. Similar types of quests to find meaning are posited by Frankl (1963) and Klinger (1977) in their analyses of how people try to deal with difficulties that involve despair and feelings of meaninglessness and void in their lives.

In the more mainstream literature of attribution work, Read's (1987) knowledge structure approach to causal reasoning stressed people's roles as story understanders and storytellers. In these roles, Read argued that people take sequences of actions and integrate them into a coherent, plausible scenario. They presumably do so via the making of numerous inferences based on detailed knowledge about people and the world. Also, in several valuable studies, Huston, Cate, Surra, and their colleagues have used account-like probes to examine how couples explain the decisional processes involved in their movement toward or away from marriage (e.g., Huston, Surra, Fitzgerald, & Cate, 1981; Surra, 1985). Other scholars as well have emphasized a "narrative mode of knowing" without explicitly discussing accounts or account-making (e.g., Cochran & Claspell, 1987, Gergen & Gergen 1983; Mancuso & Sarbin, 1983).

As Read has suggested, this storyteller-narrative knower type of approach is consistent with Heider's (1958) pioneering statement on the dynamics of social perception, which emphasized the merit of studying people's naive causal theories. Similarly, in the area of social perception, cognitive psychologists concerned with story schemas and scripts (e.g., Mandler, 1984) often work on problems quite distant from the nature of people's accounts; nevertheless, there likely is a fertile interface awaiting the scholar who can readily make connections between these disparate literatures on account-making in relationships and schema activity in recall and recognition phenomena. We believe that accounts, like schemata, presumably affect future encoding of information, anticipation and reconstruction of events, and actual interaction patterns. Later, we will elaborate on how accounts for personal relationships as schemata may lead to expectations for future relationships. Finally, memory work on vivid recollections of past relationships that form a centerpiece in most accounts (Harvey, Flanary, & Morgan, 1986) might be of value to cognitive psychology investigators of autobiographical or personal memory.

Examples of Accounts and Methodological Issues

At this point, we will introduce more concrete examples to be clear on what we mean by an account and to speak to some of the issues involved in examining interpretive material found in accounts. The first example below is from Rubin's (1983) book that involved a host of accounts taken from her patients engaged in psychotherapy and others whom she has interviewed. A woman speaks of the conflict in her mind regarding her ongoing relationship:

> I can't figure out what's happening to me. I'm so anxious and churning inside I can't stand it. I try to read a book, and I find myself thinking of him. But it's not loving thoughts; it's critical, picky thoughts—anything negative, just to get me out of the relationship. Then, once I've convinced myself, I wonder: Why did I love him yesterday? And, if I did, how can it feel so miserable today? I get so confused I want to run and hide just to get away. But now I understand better what I'm scared of; I know it's my problem. I can't tolerate the intimacy, but I can't just break off the relationship like I used to and justify my escape by talking about his faults and inadequacies. But, at times, I actually feel myself being torn apart by this conflict going on inside me. [Tears streaming down her cheeks] How could it be such a burden to be loved? (p. 847)

The next illustrative account is taken from Brende and Parson's (1985) work on the difficulties experienced by Vietnam veterans when they come back home to the United States. This veteran is speaking about the agony he experienced in discovering that his girlfriend could no longer maintain her relationship with him:

> My girlfriend told me she didn't know how to relate to me . . . I had expected things to be the way they were; but they weren't. She said she thought I had been killed in the war, because I stopped writing to her. Honestly, I didn't know how to relate to her now either. I dreaded going to bed with her . . . She also said that I wasn't the loving guy she used to know and love, that something horrible must have happened to me over there to change me so completely. I told her I didn't know what she was talking about. She said the look in my eyes was the look of a deeply terrorized person, with a long-distance stare . . . She also mentioned that my

> frightened look and pallid complexion, my uptight way of sitting, talking, walking, you name it, my aloofness, and all that, made her too uncomfortable for us to continue our relationship. She said that besides, she had found somebody else anyway. That really hurt me. (p. 46)

Methodologically, the study of accounts can be a relatively non-reactive process, and can be undertaken by examining both written and oral reports (Harvey, Turnquist, & Agostinelli, 1988). More generally, this area of work involves the combined use of qualitative and quantitative approaches. The qualitative approaches have evolved from several schools of thought, including dramatism, ethnomethodology, ethogeny, and social constructivism (see Cochran, 1986; Gergen & Davis, 1985). In our work on accounts, we have treated accounts as an example of material containing relatively naturalistic, free-response attributions (e.g., Harvey, Yarkin, Lightner, & Town, 1980). As a set of reported thoughts and feelings, accounts often contain many attributions of causality and responsibility, besides trait ascriptions. These attributions may be identified through the coding of free-response interview, diary, and other archival sources of information. They are likely to be especially sensitive indicators of thought and feeling because they are not influenced by the format of research questions. Further, such methods allow the study of attribution in instances when traditional measures are not easily administered (e.g., resistant populations, sensitive topics).

A general issue, then, is how to define and code attributions and, as importantly, other theoretically meaningful material. In the work by Harvey et al. (1980) on free-response attributions, one approach was suggested. Attributions were defined as "phrases or clauses denoting or connoting causality or responsibility or ascribing traits." Thus, in the material illustrated above, further reduction of the content would be necessary to identify causal, responsibility, or trait phrases. For example, in the first account, the woman's statement indicates a critical view of her lover, but it also is one of ambivalence and her own fears of intimacy. Hence, the attributions of ambivalence about the relationship and of various kinds of psychological states to self would be identified. In the second example, the veteran makes a number of attributions including an inability to communicate with his lover, a major change in the feeling of intimacy especially on the part of his lover, and an ascription of various types of discomfort to her about him.

The investigator of accounts may also wish to identify more specific interpretive dimensions in such material. Such dimensions may be coded on a continuous or dichotomous scale. They may include positive-negative valence of interpretation, stability, globality, and locus of control. For instance, in the veteran's account, his comments may be coded as representing negative valence, some globality in judgment/imputation to other, and an external locus of control for events occurring in his love life. As emphasized by Harvey, Turnquist, and Agostinelli (1988), it is imperative in this type of methodology to obtain multiple coding carried out by well-trained coders who are unaware of the hypotheses and to demonstrate reliability of coding. This reasoning is advanced especially for attributional material but also has applicability for other theoretically interesting material that may be found in accounts.

We would emphasize the further need to evaluate the overall structure of accounts in order to grasp the meaning of the story beyond the individual elements (i.e., to understand its "Gestalt"). One-word and short-phrase responses to probing survey questions are clearly qualitatively different from free-form stories people tell, whether spontaneously or in response to a solicitation. However, the affect and attribution reported in those short answers appear to represent a shorthand version of the longer, richer narratives, as can be seen from the few examples quoted in this chapter. One of the methodological challenges of conducting research on accounts must be identifying some of the least common denominators of the account-making process. In constructing narratives, words and phrases may prove to be such basic components. We prefer to begin with the assumption that people's account-making may become manifest in a variety of forms, and that we can identify the connections between these manifestations as all part of the same process. This is also the parsimonious approach: Phrases are short stories, and stories are verbalized or written accounts.

With the accounts concept now defined and elaborated, we will turn to a discussion of how people's accounts of close interpersonal relationships may be linked to their expectations for future relationships.

ACCOUNTS AND EXPECTATIONS

How are people's expectations about their present and future close relationships affected by their accounts for past loves? Theory and evidence on this question are scant. We will present some theorizing and illustrative results from a survey of young adults and case studies. It seems clear to us that people's future behavior often has some basis in past experience; such a position indeed has a long history of advocacy in psychology (e.g., Miller, Galanter, & Pribram, 1960). If past experience is crucial to the formation of expectations for present and future behaviors, then accounts and account-making may represent the means toward linking experience with expectations. We will agree with the view that accounts and expectations usually are embedded within matrices of interpersonal understanding. Further, they may represent socially negotiated understandings that are then integrally connected with many other activities in which people engage (see Gergen, 1985).

To some extent the assertion of a relationship between accounts and expectations may be similar to the question regarding whether cognitive sets about people in general influence later perceptions. The literature of social psychology suggests the potency of such sets (e.g., Brehm & Aderman, 1977; Regan & Totten, 1975). There also has been explicit work aimed at examining how sets and attributions may affect subsequent perception and behavior (Town & Harvey, 1981; Yarkin, Harvey, & Bloxom, 1981). It is not clear, though, what meaning this evidence has for our concern with expectations. Moreover, the literature of close relationships only indirectly speaks to the accounts-expectation association.

In a related analysis, Cochran (1985) argued that meaning arises through the capacity of memory and anticipation to make events seem coherent over time. He theorized that prior experiences are seen as steps to the present, and the present is seen as a step toward one's future. Along this line, Cochran and Claspell (1987) conceived part of the value of stories (which are like accounts in our analysis) as that of providing an integrative, contextualized explanation combining diverse explanatory terms regarding an event. They suggested that if such an event causes grief, the story in effect provides an antidote to the grief and may even provide a stimulus for plans and hope for the future.

These suggestive leads do not provide much clarity in defining expectations regarding future close relationships. Just as accounts were suggested to be represented as schematic knowledge, expectations can also be represented schematically. Consider the cognitive psychologist's concept of story schema. Mandler (1984) defines a story schema as a "mental structure consisting of sets of expectations about the way in which stories proceed" (p. 18). For our purposes, we would first add that the sets of expectations may pertain to self's own involvement in the unfolding of various real-life stories. Thus, expectations may be specific plans of action for obtaining specific goals. Second, expectations may also include more general expectancies about the outcome of one's close relationships. Thus, the principal question asked by most of us at least on occasion in our lives is, "What can I expect to have/find in the future with my close, intimate others?" It may be an optimistic expectation of a happy marriage, or a pessimistic expectation of loneliness. Or, expectations may be about finding "new others" or about different experiences or plateaus of closeness with "old others."

For our present purposes, noting the potential link between accounts and expectations, the latter posed question can be elaborated as follows: "Based on my previous life experiences, what can I expect to have/find in the future with my close, intimate others?" We turn now to a discussion of George Kelly's (1955) theory of personal constructs. Kelly's work provides one of the most promising theories for providing perspective about accounts-expectations linkages.

Accounts and Constructs

George Kelly's concept of a personal construct bears some similarity to the notion of an account that we have developed (see Harvey, in press). For example, each essentially refers to a set of cognitions or verbal expressions, and each is concerned with explanation. Further, each presumably affords some predictive capacity regarding one's own or others' future actions. Kelly discusses and defines a personal construct in the following way:

> as a template which a person . . . creates and then attempts to fit over the realities of which the world is composed. The fit is not always very good. Yet without such patterns the world appears to be such an undifferentiated homogeneity that man is unable to make any sense out of it. . . . Let us give the name "constructs" to these patterns that are tentatively tried on for size. They are ways of construing the world. They are what enables man . . . to chart a course of behavior, explicitly formulated or implicitly acted out, verbally expressed or utterly inarticulate, consistent with other courses of behavior or inconsistent with them, intellectually reasoned or vegetatively sensed. (Kelly, 1955, p. 9)

Kelly goes on to discuss his view that people regularly increase their repertory of constructs, alter them to provide better fits, and combine them and reorganize them into larger systems of constructs. Unlike accounts, constructs are treated as having rather clearcut, dichotomous qualities (e.g., "light versus dark") and presumably people exhibit idiographic systems of constructs. Nonetheless, both accounts and personal constructs can be linked to specific expectations.

This line of reasoning is congenial to the types of broad accounts-expectations linkages implied by the writers described at the beginning of this section. A wife, for example, may develop a set of personal constructs about her husband that focuses on his gentleness and warmth, perhaps also with illustrative stories, or accounts, containing such themes. Such a construct system then permits her to anticipate her husband's future critical acts toward her and the relationship. Under certain conditions, she expects her husband to exhibit gentleness—that is the way she construes him. Presumably, representative accounts form the evidence for the development of her constructs about her husband.

A Survey of Explanations for Breaking Up and Expectations in Young Adults

To provide some evidence about the relationship between explanatory accounts and expectations in young adults, we asked 440 (male and female) University of Iowa undergraduates to "give as many explanations as you can" for why their most recent significant close relationship had ended and then to list their "most important expectations" about how their current or future relationships would develop. Subjects simply listed their explanations and expectations on a questionnaire.

To provide information about the nature and frequency of respondents' explanations and expectations, a content analysis was conducted on subjects' written responses. An initial screening of all explanations and expectations listed was carried out. There was a consensus (interrater reliability = .98) in identifying the various explanations and expectations in this initial screening procedure which later formed the basis for deriving categories. These categories are presented along with the percentage with which each category was endorsed in Table 2.1.

Table 2.1 shows that "differences" (as in interests, lifestyles, etc.) was mentioned by the greatest number of respondents (42%) as an explanation for their break-ups. For the expectation categories, "seek good relationship" (e.g., trust, honesty, respect) was mentioned most frequently (48.2%).

Beyond this descriptive information, these data provide evidence about degree of association between the different categories of explanations and expectations. Chi-square analyses were conducted on the frequency with which each explanation and expectation co-occurred. The most statistically reliable association obtained was between the "communication problems" explanation category and both the "work at

TABLE 2.1
Type and Content of Explanation and Expectation Categories

Categories	Percent of Respondents Mentioning
Explanation Categories	
1. Differences	42.0
e.g., different interests, lifestyles, views, ideas, religion, race, background, age; found differences, nothing in common	
2. Communication problems	21.8
e.g., lack of communication, not open with each other, couldn't agree, argued	
3. Too much seriousness	22.9
e.g., too serious, too close, better as friends, felt pressured, too fast, went on too long, pregnancy, needed time and space	
4. Different definitions of relationship	16.7
e.g., only physical relationship, different expectations, unreasonable expectations, conflicts about having sex, different degrees of liking	
5. "CLAlt" (third person involved)	37.2
e.g., other man/woman, wanted to date others, cheated on, ex-lover returns, jealousy	
6. Negative/no affect	25.3
e.g., lost attraction, lost feeling, dead end, just didn't work, not satisfied, bored, depressed	
7. Negative qualities of "ex"	31.3
e.g., stubborn, not understanding, immature, insecure, jerk, bitch, insensitive, irresponsible, no personality, dishonest, domineering, drug/alcohol problem, mean	
8. Bad circumstances	39.9
e.g., distance, moved, went away to college, wrong place, wrong time, not enough time to spend with each other, too busy	

(*continued*)

relationship" and "achieve happiness" expectation categories. Specifically, respondents who had identified a communication problem as the reason for a recent breakup more frequently listed expectations from the "work at relationship" expectation category (60.5%) than respondents who had not listed a communication-related explanation for their breakups (38.3%) (χ^2 = 12.7, p < .001). Further, the frequency with

TABLE 2.1 continued

Categories	Percent of Respondents Mentioning
Expectation Categories	
1. Seek happiness e.g., be happy, enjoy it, have fun, have a companion/friend	41.2
2. Work at relationship e.g., change personal problems, work at relationship, spend more time together, commitment, don't domineer, value other's opinion, expect mutual concern, understanding, trust	43.1
2a. Seek slow development e.g., wait for sex, start as friends, be careful, take it slow and naturally	16.4
2b. Seek open communication e.g., open communication, openness, get to know each other better	25.3
3. Develop a stimulating relationship e.g., want sex, attractive partner, variety, romance, stimulating relationship	14.8
4. Develop future closeness e.g., marriage, back with ex, live together, have children, make future plans, vacations, long-term relationship, security, commitment, serious, solid	26.9
5. Seek good relationship e.g., trust, honesty, sincerity, monogamy, fidelity, acceptance, fairness, compromise, understanding, respect, equality, really care, love	48.2
6. Seek compatibility e.g., similar goals, religion, values, interests, getting along with each other's friends and family	24.0
7. Seek freedom e.g., not permanent, independence, freedom, space	11.3
8. None e.g., no expectation	4.6

which expectations from the "open communication" subcategory were listed was greater for respondents who had listed a "communication problems" explanation (38.3%) than for respondents who had not listed a "communication problems" explanation (21.7%) ($\chi^2 = 9.16, p < .01$).

Finally, those who had listed explanations from the "communication problems" explanation category had more expectations from the "happy" expectations category (54.3%) than subjects not listing a "communication problems" explanation (37.6%) ($\chi^2 = 7.32$, $p < .01$).

The above results suggest that, if one can develop an explanation that identifies a solvable problem within a past failed relationship (e.g., communication problems), then one's expectations for future relationships may be influenced by these accounts. Both expected plans of action (e.g., working at relationship) and expected relationship outcomes (e.g., expecting happiness) were influenced by the accounts subjects held. Accounts are useful. People can learn from their accounts in understanding past failures and losses in their lives. This may lead to more optimistic expectations (e.g., overcoming more communication problems and expecting happiness). Indeed, one male respondent initially listed the following communication problems to explain a past failed relationship: "Me not listening. Her not listening. Communication not good on either side. Me seeing more than there was. I was so excited about the relationship, I couldn't see she wasn't. Me not letting her breathe. Communication." His explanation for the relationship breakup apparently influenced his reported expectations for future relationships as well: "We will be more open. More truthful. Actually talking to each other. Not always pointing out what I do is special."

We also found that in assessing the association between accounts and expectations, it was sometimes important to consider which person in a past relationship was reported as initiating the breakup. For example, when the association between explanations and expectations is analyzed as a function of which person in a past relationship was reported as initiating the breakup (excluding respondents who reported that the breakup was "mutual"), an interesting explanation-expectation link emerged. Of respondents who reported explanations from the "too much seriousness" account for a relationship breakup, those who had been "left behind" (partner had initiated breakup) went on more frequently to report expectations from the "seek slow development" subcategory of the "work at relationship" category (54.5%) than when the respondents themselves had initiated the breakup (17.8%) ($\chi^2 = 4.56$, $p < .03$). For example, one woman's explanation listed that her partner had initiated the breakup, and that they had broken up because it "started to get too serious." She then went on to list the following expectations for future relationships: "First become friends. Begin to date, give each other freedom, become committed when ready, continue to grow on own, get married when ready, not rushed or pushed." These results suggest that those who feel that their significant other left them will develop an expectation for future relationships that emphasizes caution.

A major issue that limits the merit of these illustrative data for the present concerns is that the respondents were not explicitly asked to indicate what specific expectations derived from what particular past experiences and previous accounts for such experiences. Essentially, these results refer to highly generalized expectations that may or may not be linked clearly to the specific explanations for the ending of a particular relationship.

Nonetheless, these survey data are suggestive of specific accounts-explanations linkages that are logical and follow from people's attempts to make sense of past meaningful events and to prepare carefully for the future. The data derived from these college students contain a host of implied messages and agendas for action (e.g., consider the various implications of the reported expectation, "wait for sex"). The suggested links between explanations and expectations may represent the seeds of personal constructs that respondents are developing regarding their lovers (e.g., "open vs. closed"; "honest vs. dishonest").

We now turn to some case history evidence that also speaks to these bridges of the past with the present and the future. The explanations given by the college students in our survey for the endings of past relationships contained a variety of themes. But such explanations were obtained using a simple listing procedure which limited the amount of detail respondents could include in presenting their explanations and expectations. Accounts themselves are much more convoluted, richer and more complex. Would an examination of full narrative accounts yield any inkling of an account-expectation link as we have pinpointed in our college student survey?

Case History Accounts

Two years ago we requested written accounts of past relationships from participants in a Summer Elderhostel class. All volunteers who completed and mailed in free-response survey forms were over 60 years of age. Most apparently saw themselves more at the end than at the beginning of their relationship "lives," in probable contrast with our college student respondents above. The Elderhostelers' survey probed for memories of past relationships, descriptions of how they began, significant events, and endings (if the relationship had ended). General open-ended queries were used by the interviewer to solicit accounts (e.g., "Would you tell me about some of the most memorable experiences you have of your marriage?"). The goal of this type of probing was to elicit in a nonintrusive way the respondent's recall of key events in her own words.

There is a clear autobiographical quality to these accounts, subsuming other personal and world events as well as the course of the remembered relationship. We include three excerpts here from the Elderhostel stories to illustrate more forcefully what they have to offer in richness and complexity, as well as relevance to the quest for meaning, control, and expectations of the future.

This first account, that of a 68-year-old woman, is included in its entirety. Note the respondent's efforts to interpret as well as report her recollections, to conclude and learn lessons.

> I was not particularly attracted to him in the beginning. However, as I sat in the car with him, along with other students, my palms were sweaty, my heart was pounding. I was confused and didn't understand my reaction since he had not even touched me or held my hand. I remember our first kiss—an immediate sexual desire. The emotional response seemed to consume me. I had not experienced anything like this with other relationships. I remember it like it was yesterday. Years later [came his] proposal of marriage at family summer cottage—a full moon by a mountain stream, passionately in love. My whole being was engulfed in this man who became my husband. I have memories of a happy and satisfying life. Our wedding night: Two persons very much in love, ardent desire, exhausted from all the wedding "hoopla." Sexual union a complete failure. Inexperience grew into perfection! The birth of our first child seemed to bring us closer together. The realization that this union had created a new life. These children to me now are loving memories of my life with him. My husband's work involved international travel, which resulted in separations of a year or more. Reunion when we joined him in Japan and a second honeymoon in Hawaii—an oasis—an unforgettable reunion. Sustaining memories that are written on my mind. . . . I remember our last interaction. I kissed him goodbye as I dashed off to take our grandchildren who were visiting to the Air and Space Museum. Upon our return, I was called to Holy Cross Hospital, where I was informed my husband had died. My whole life revolved around this man. I still think of him every day. I feel his presence at times—the many happy memories of good times we shared keep me going. We were a very close family and my children have been very supportive since my husband's death. Death of a mate is an experience that is difficult to explain—it is so final. It's like part of you is gone. The loneliness is difficult to adjust to. . . .

It is a major emotional loss—life will never be the same. One has to create a new life style. Older women rarely remarry. I have no desire to. I was married to a very intelligent man. Had a wonderful outlook on life. He respected me and was very proud of his family. It gave me great joy to make him happy. Thinking back on this relationship, perhaps the flame of love and devotion for one another and the intense sexual desire was more intense due to my husband's travel and long periods of separation. We cherished the time we had together.

The next excerpt, from the account of a 62-year-old woman reflecting on her divorce, focuses on the ways in which her marriage and her divorce shaped the rest of her social life, especially her expectations about friendships with others and a sense of social belongingness.

After the divorce my life changed completely, the people I had known left me, the organizations I belonged to no longer welcomed me. Fortunately I could go to church because he didn't go. Occasionally I would meet new people and they would ask me if I knew Dr. So-and-so, and I would reply, "Yes, he is the father of my children." Let them figure it out.... Now, after working until I could retire, I have a few friends I met at work or other places, but don't replace the ones I knew before, the ones I shared my married life with. Of course they probably wouldn't relate to me any more, since I have made my own way. To sum it up, I feel cheated. I put in the hard years of helping a man get ahead, bore his children, raised them, and then find myself alone and unable to enjoy the fruits of my efforts.... I feel society is pretty hard on the divorced woman. Probably nothing can change that. We are a natural threat in the minds of others. It is heartbreaking to try to continue friendships with women met during marriage and being rejected. In my case I went with my husband to a new area of the country and the only people I knew were people connected with his job. I didn't feel like moving and I certainly didn't want to uproot my children any more than the divorce did—school, church, scouts, etc. And so I had to somehow make new friends, brave the stigma of divorce, etc., all by myself, with little or no support system. Things may be better now but it is still tough.

Many of the Elderhostel respondents made reference in their stories to the different cultural values and norms that prevailed when they were young and first seeking partners. A few admitted that some recent changes might be for the better in encouraging better communication, more openness, or greater freedom to pursue one's own self-expression. Most, however, seemed to be presenting their accounts as testimony to the value of their experiences and the lessons they had learned, as if it were especially important to pass on their insights and conclusions to an audience of young relationship-seekers or relationship-researchers. As we noted earlier, this heritage of understanding for others would appear to be one of the driving forces behind account-making as people age and try to tie together their life stories. This last excerpt shows such an instructive motive in a 64-year-old woman's memories of love and loss before World War II and also speaks indirectly to the accounts-expectations relationship. She begins by recalling the circumstances of the first meeting with her long-ago love:

> His boat upset in front of the lake cottage. He was wet and wore braces. I was shy and had pimples on my back. Wow! After 41 years I remember this. Maybe I should have married him to recall such sweet, simple memories. . . . (Then came World War II). He was at basic camp and I went into training to become a nurse. Our "breakup" happened gradually at a busy time in my life. I still think of him now about two or three times a month, when I hear certain Glenn Miller recordings and some classical music. I sometimes dream about his family house—white clapboard with "gingerbread." I always wanted one like it. . . . [In those days] you didn't have to have a sexual relationship to enjoy dating. I think this is best to emphasize activities to faster understand each other—bedding down can come later. The more we understand ourselves and each other, the better equipped we will be to face living. There is such social-cultural revolution going on, from the industrial revolution to high technology. Our parents and we are all living longer. The old adage, "Old too soon and smart too late," is so true from my standpoint. Now that I've learned so much, no one wants to listen and younger people seem bound to make the same mistakes. I think more research could be done regarding life after 60, retirement with your mate, and adjustments, and not meeting expectations.

One of the main conclusions we wish to draw from these accounts given by the Elderhostel respondents is that they are similar to the college-aged respondents in their grappling with loss and their attempts to find meaning in the past that will give them hope and direction for the present and future. At their age, though, the content of the future expectations held by the Elderhostel respondents often is somewhat more directed toward maintaining friendships and being open to human contact than it is toward finding a mate and living happily ever after. It is clear, too, that as they plot the emotional terrain of their final years, they are assembling, dissecting, categorizing, and filing away in sacred memorial quarters their own precious memories and accounts of their significant loves in other times and places. In so doing, these loves continue to exist cognitively, even until the death of the account-maker. Like biographers and the writers of memoirs, account-makers also are validating their versions of events by committing them in some form of story-telling, to an audience consisting of themselves and sometimes others as well. The account makes its subjects memorable in the very matrix of remembering, however accurate or melodramatic.

SUMMARY AND CONCLUSIONS

In this chapter, we have reviewed conceptual work on account-making and some of the forms of evidence illustrating this phenomenon. We have provided a modest amount of original data pertaining to accounts and accounts-expectations linkages. We also have described how personal construct theory as formulated by George Kelly provides a useful "meta-account" for understanding the link between account-making and expectations for future relationships.

Our overall quest in this analysis and empirical work has been to argue that accounts should be accorded a meaningful and valid stature in the array of concepts that social scientists use in understanding close relationship phenomena. In so arguing, we have suggested that in principle, account-making can be subjected to the same rigors of theory and method that apply to the investigation of other, more well-established phenomena in the domain of relationship research. Although the evidence is far from conclusive, we think that a case is emerging for the import of account-making in the cycles of thought, feeling, and action associated with close relationships.

We do not know if account-making or accounts of particular types and/or contents cause more long-term effects. Only longitudinal, prospective work can provide a vigorous test of that possibility.

Finally, we believe that the study of people's accounts yields themes and explanations that can usefully be transformed into resolutions and skills for improving future relationships. The study of one's *own* accounts contributes as well to an accruing and developing framework for one's personal constructions of life events in a more general sense: "I learn from my losses, not only about how I ought to behave in the future, but about who I am, in the context of past and present relationships." At the outset of this chapter, we defined an account as meanings organized into a story. In his epilogue to *Sarah: A Sexual Biography* (1984), Abramson offers the following concluding comments about the value of studying and considering the story of someone like Sarah, whose own life involved painful and frightening struggles with victimization and abuse, and that unexpectedly endured and prevailed:

> Sara is by no means a hero. Her story has the potential to annoy, dismay, disgust, or excite. And it is *these* characteristics which make this an important case study. It is not pretty. It does not flow smoothly. Resolution is slow and questionable. There are no fireworks. But against all odds Sarah made it. Consequently, it offers hope to others. (p. 140)

REFERENCES

Abramson, P. R. (1984). *Sarah: A sexual biography.* Albany: State University of New York Press.

Allen, K. R., & Pickett, R. S. (1987). Forgotten streams in the family life course. *Journal of Marriage and the Family, 49,* 517-526.

Antaki, C. (1987). Types of accounts within relationships. In R. Burnett, P. McGhee, & D. Clarke (Eds.), *Accounting for relationships* (pp. 97-133). London: Methuen.

Bernikow, L. (1987). *Alone in America.* New York: Harper & Row.

Birren, J. E. (1987, May). The best of all stories. *Psychology Today,* pp. 91-92.

Brehm, S. S., & Aderman, D. (1977). On the relationship between empathy and the actor versus observer hypothesis. *Journal of Research in Personality, 11,* 340-346.

Brende, J. S., & Parson, E. R. (1985). *Vietnam veterans: The roads to recovery.* New York: Plenum.

Burnett, R., McGhee, P., & Clarke, D. (Eds.). (1987). Introduction in *Accounting for relationships* (pp. xvii-xviii). London: Methuen.

Cochran, L. (1985). *Position and the nature of personhood.* Westport, CT: Greenwood.

Cochran, L. (1986). *Portrait and story.* Westport, CT: Greenwood.

Cochran, L., & Claspell, E. (1987). *The meaning of grief.* Westport, CT: Greenwood.

Coles, R. (1986). *The moral life of children.* Boston: Atlantic Monthly Press.

Couch, C. J., & Weiland, M. W. (1986). A study of the representative-constituent relationship. In C. Couch (Ed.), *Studies in symbolic interaction* (pp. 375-391). Greenwich, CT: JAI.

Duck, S. W., & Sants, H. (1983). On the origin of the specious: Are personal relationships really interpersonal states? *Journal of Social and Clinical Psychology, 1,* 27-41.

Fletcher, G. J. O. (1983). The analysis of verbal explanations for marital separation: Implications for attribution theory. *Journal of Applied Social Psychology, 13,* 245-258.

Frankl, V. E. (1963). *Man's search for meaning.* New York: Washington Square.

Gergen, K. J. (1985). Social constructionist inquiry: Context and implications. In K. J. Gergen & K. E. Davis (Eds.), *The social construction of the person* (pp. 4-18). New York: Springer-Verlag.

Gergen, K. J., & Davis, K. E. (Eds.). (1985). *The social construction of the person.* New York: Springer-Verlag.

Gergen, K. J., & Gergen, M. M. (1983). Narratives of the self. In T. R. Sarbin & K. E. Scheibe (Eds.), *Studies in social identity* (pp. 254-273). New York: Praeger.

Glick, I. O., Weiss, R. S., & Parkes, C. M. (1974). *The first year of bereavement.* New York: John Wiley.

Harré, R., Clarke, D., & DeCarlo, N. (1985). *Motives and mechanisms.* New York: Methuen.

Harvey, J. H. (in press). People's naive understandings of their close relationships: Attributional and personal construct perspectives. *International Journal of Personal Construct Psychology.*

Harvey, J. H., Flanary, R., & Morgan, M. (1986). Vivid memories of vivid loves gone by. *Journal of Social and Personal Relationships, 3,* 359-373.

Harvey, J. H., Turnquist, D. C., & Agostinelli, G. (1988). Identifying attributions in oral and written explanations. In C. Antaki (Ed.), *Analyzing lay explanation: A casebook of methods* (32-42). London: Sage.

Harvey, J. H., Weber, A. L., Galvin, K. S., Huszti, H. C., & Garnick, N. N. (1986). Attribution and the termination of close relationships: A special focus on the account. In R. Gilmour & S. Duck (Eds.), *The emerging field of personal relationships* (pp. 189-201). Hillsdale, NJ: Lawrence Erlbaum.

Harvey, J. H., Wells, G. L., & Alvarez, M. D. (1978). Attribution in the context of conflict and separation in close relationships. In J. H. Harvey, W. J. Ickes, & R. F. Kidd (Eds.), *New directions in attribution research* (Vol. 2, pp. 235-259). Hillsdale, NJ: Lawrence Erlbaum.

Harvey, J. H., Yarkin, K. L., Lightner, J. M., & Town, J. P. (1980). Unsolicited interpretation and recall of interpersonal events. *Journal of Personality and Social Psychology, 38,* 551-568.

Heider, F. (1958). *The psychology of interpersonal relations.* New York: John Wiley.

Horowitz, M. J. (1986). *Stress response syndromes* (2nd ed.). Northvale, NJ: Jason Aronson.

Huston, T. L., Surra, C. A., Fitzgerald, N. M., & Cate, R. M. (1981). From courtship to marriage: Mate selection as an interpersonal process. In S. Duck & R. Gilmour (Eds.), *Personal relationshhips 2: Developing personal relationships* (pp. 53-88). London: Academic Press.

Jellison, J. M. (1977). *I'm sorry I didn't mean to and other lies we love to tell.* New York: Chatham Square.

Kelly, G. A. (1955). *The psychology of personal constructs.* New York: Norton.

Klinger, E. (1977). *Meaning and void.* Minneapolis: University of Minnesota Press.

Lichtman, R. R., & Taylor, S. E. (1986). Close relationships of female cancer patients. In B. L. Andersen (Ed.), *Women with cancer* (pp. 233-256). New York: Springer-Verlag.

Mancuso, J. C., & Sarbin, T. R. (1983). The self-narrative in the enactment of roles. In T. R. Sarbin & K. E. Scheibe (Eds.), *Studies in social identity* (pp. 233-253). New York: Praeger.

Mandler, J. M. (1984). *Stories, scripts, and scenes: Aspects of schema theory.* Hillsdale, NJ: Lawrence Erlbaum.

Matthews, S. H. (1986). *Friendships through the life course: Oral biographies in old age.* Beverly Hills, CA: Sage.

Miller, G. A., Galanter, E., & Pribram, K. H. (1960). *Plans and the structure of behavior.* New York: Holt, Rinehart & Winston.

Newman, H. (1981). Communication within ongoing intimate relationships: An attribution perspective. *Personality and Social Psychology Bulletin, 7,* 59-70.

Orvis, B. R., Kelly, H. H., & Butler, D. (1976). Attributional conflict in young couples. In J. H. Harvey, W. Ickes, & R. F. Kidd (Eds.), *New directions in attribution research* (Vol. 1, pp. 353-386). Hillsdale, NJ: Lawrence Erlbaum.

Read, S. J. (1987). Constructing casual scenarios: A knowledge structure approach to casual reasoning. *Journal of Personality and Social Psychology, 52,* 288-302.

Regan, D. R., & Totten, J. (1975). Empathy and attribution: Turning observers into actors. *Journal of Personality and Social Psychology, 32,* 850-856.

Rosenblatt, P. C. (1983). *Bitter, bitter tears.* Minneapolis: University of Minnesota Press.

Rubin, L. (1983). *Intimate strangers: Men and women together.* New York: Harper & Row.

Schuchter, S. R. (1986). *Dimensions of grief.* San Francisco: Jossey-Bass.

Scott, M. B., & Lyman, S. (1968). Accounts. *American Sociological Review, 33,* 46-62.

Semin, G., & Manstead, A.S.R. (1984). *The accountability of conduct.* London: Academic Press.

Shotter, J. (1984). *Social accountability and selfhood.* Oxford: Blackwell.

Surra, C. A. (1985). Courtship types: Variations in interdependence between partners and social networks. *Journal of Personality and Social Psychology, 49,* 357-375.

Town, J. P., & Harvey, J. H. (1981). Self-disclosure, attribution, and social interaction. *Social Psychology Quarterly, 44,* 291-300.

Vaughan, B. D. (1986). *Uncoupling.* New York: Oxford University Press.

Weber, A. L., Harvey. J. H., & Stanley, M. A. (1987). The nature and motivations of accounts for failed relations. In R. Burnett, P. McGhee, & D. Clarke (Eds.), *Accounting for relationships* (114-133). London: Methuen.

Weiss, R. S. (1975). *Marital separation.* New York: Basic Books.

Weissberg, D. K. (1985). *Children of the night.* Lexington, MA: Heath.

Yarkin, K. L., Harvey, J. H., & Bloxom, B. M. (1981). Cognitive sets, attribution, and social interaction. *Journal of Personality and Social Psychology, 41,* 243-252.

3

Issues in Studying Close Relationships
CONCEPTUALIZING AND MEASURING CLOSENESS

ELLEN BERSCHEID
MARK SNYDER
ALLEN M. OMOTO

Ellen Berscheid is a Professor in the Department of Psychology at the University of Minnesota, where she received her doctorate. She is a coauthor of *Close Relationships*, past president of the Society of Personality and Social Psychology (APA, Division 8), and recipient of the Donald T. Campbell Award for Distinguished Research in Social Psychology. Her current interests include the experience of emotion in close relationships, as well as interpersonal attraction and social perception.

Mark Snyder is a Professor of Psychology at the University of Minnesota, where he has been a member of the faculty since 1972. He received his B.A. from McGill University in 1968 and his Ph.D. from Stanford University in 1972. His research interests include theoretical and empirical issues associated with the motivational foundations of individual and social behavior. He is the author of the book, *Public Appearance/Private Realities: The Psychology of Self-Monitoring.*

Allen M. Omoto received his B.A. from Kalamazoo College in 1982 and is currently completing his doctorate at the University of Minnesota with a specialization in social psychology. His primary research interests include interpersonal relationships and stereotyping and prejudice.

THE EMERGING IMPORTANCE OF THE CONSTRUCT "CLOSE"

The development of a systematic body of knowledge about close human relationships depends importantly upon general agreement about the proper basis for classifying any given relationship as "close" as opposed to "less close" (see Berscheid & Peplau, 1983, for a discussion of this point). Without such agreement, investigators in the relationships domain run the risk of developing a confusing and inconsistent body of

AUTHORS' NOTE: The authors wish to acknowledge the support of two grants-in-aid of research from the Graduate School of the University of Minnesota.

findings simply because the object of investigation, the close relationship, surreptitiously changes its identity from one study to the next.

Agreement about the most useful manner of discriminating a close relationship from those that are less close does not now exist despite the great interest that investigators in a variety of disciplines have taken in close relationship phenomena in recent years. Not only is there as yet no agreement about the merits or demerits of different close relationship classification schemes, but the matter is seldom discussed. Only recently, of course, has the need for such discussion become apparent.

The necessity of explicating the construct of closeness and tying it to the base of observable behavior has become obvious as the concept of closeness has moved from the periphery of the relationship domain to front and center in the minds of both investigators and laypersons. There are a number of reasons for the emergence of closeness as a critical concept in understanding relationship phenomena. Perhaps the most important of these have their source in the rapid changes family relationships have undergone in this time.

Until relatively recently, close relationships seemed to be, and probably were, well encapsulated within only a few forms, or types, of relationships. Apart from same-sex friendships (and even these were not regarded as necessarily close), most close relationships were assumed to be family relationships. Of these, marital relationships and parent-child relationships were regarded as exemplars of the close relationship and received, as they do now, special scrutiny. These forms of relationships received special attention not necessarily because they were exemplars of the close relationship, but rather because these types of relationships were simply assumed, and correctly so, to occupy a special place in human affairs—to have, for whatever reason, important consequences for the individual and for society.

That certain relationship forms, especially the marital relationship, did not automatically possess the quality of closeness became apparent as divorce and serial marriage became more and more frequent, and as the shape of the family itself began to undergo dramatic change. As divorce increased, for example, more and more parents were physically separated from their children, with a step-parent often being in closer daily proximity to the child than one of the biological parents. Today, it is projected that by 1990 in North America there will be more "binuclear" families (a family configuration made up of two or more remnants of former families) than there are "nuclear," or original, families (Ahrons & Rodgers, 1987). This new form of social organization has profound implications for society that are, as yet, unknown.

At the same time that more and more variations in family patterns appeared, so too did other alternative relationship forms (e.g., cohabitation). And just as it became obvious that marital and other family relationship types could no longer be as safely assumed as before to be close, it also became clear that some of these new relationship forms encompassed very close, even the individual's closest, relationships. Perhaps society's awareness of the new lack of union between relationship closeness and relationship type was most clearly revealed in the change in medical forms that now ask people to name their "significant other" or, simply, the person they want notified in case of emergency.

Relationship investigators also have increasingly recognized that while the outward form of the relationship will account for a great deal of the variance in the behavior of the principals of the relationship (due to social norms and expectations associated with that relationship type if nothing else), the closeness of the relationship is also an important causal determinant of relationship phenomena. Thus, for example, Clark and Reis (1988), in their status report on relationship research in the *Annual Review of Psychology*, state that closeness is a process that underlies many relationship phenomena that long have been of interest in their own right. As opposed to the outward form of the relationship, the locus of the construct closeness has been loosely placed in the internal infrastructure of the relationship, which is now recognized to be conceptually independent of external form.

Because the concept of relationship closeness has only recently been considered to be of paramount importance, it is understandable that, usually, only impressionistic and anecdotal definitions of the descriptor "close" have been given. As Berscheid and Peplau (1983) state,

> Such words as *love, trust, commitment, caring, stability, attachment, one-ness, meaningful,* and *significant*, along with a host of others, flicker in and out of the numerous conceptions of what a "close relationship" is. The words used to explain the phrase *close relationship* often carry clouds of ambiguity, and so people are not infrequently driven to concrete single-case illustrations or to highly abstract analogies and metaphors to try to communicate what they mean by the term, often with little success. (p. 12)

Each of these elements—such as caring, or love, or commitment—has been the object of theoretical attention and of measurement attempts. For present purposes, however, it is important to state that no one of these has been conceptually equated with the concept of closeness. Moreover, while some people might be willing to argue that one or more of these elements constitute a necessary condition for relationship closeness—or the reverse, that closeness is a necessary condition for, say, commitment—few would want to go as far as to say that they form sufficient conditions for closeness.

The time has come, then, for investigators to more carefully examine the concept of relationship closeness. This chapter represents a beginning attempt to address the problem of identifying useful ways to conceptualize and to measure relationship closeness. With respect to the measurement of closeness, throughout this chapter we will draw, for illustrative purposes and where appropriate, upon portions of an ongoing empirical investigation we are conducting. We will do so in the faith that knowledge about the characteristics and the consequences of using one means of identifying a close relationship rather than another will permit investigators to make informed choices among these methods. Ultimately, of course, we hope that a consensus about the appropriate criteria for identifying close relationships will develop.

CURRENTLY USED MEANS OF
IDENTIFYING CLOSE RELATIONSHIPS

The current lack of discussion and agreement about the consequences of identifying close relationships by one means rather than another cannot be said to be inhibiting research in the relationship area. The rapid growth of such work is attested to by the fact that this volume of the *Review of Personality and Social Psychology* is exclusively devoted to relationship theory and research (and see Berscheid, 1985; Clark & Reis, 1988). How, then, are investigators proceeding? Given that for many investigators the object of study is a close relationship, how does the investigator know that he or she has identified one for study? Several classification methods are commonly used.

As we have already noted, investigators frequently have identified close relationships by using relationship type as an indicator. Thus, for example, it has been typically assumed that marital relationships are close relationships (e.g., Swenson, 1972), and many would still be willing to guess that these relationships are closer than certain other types of relationships. While it is undoubtedly true that most marital relationships are closer than, say, most co-worker relationships, the number of investigators who would want to argue that all marital relationships are equally close has decreased radically, and the number who recognize that some marital relationships are not close at all has undoubtedly increased.

Thus, those who continue to use relationship type as a divining rod for close relationships run the risk that many relationships included in their sample of close relationships are not close. To the extent that this is so, the conclusions about close relationships drawn from that sample are compromised. Moreover, to the extent that different investigators draw samples from the population of that relationship type which differ significantly in their numbers of close and less close relationships, and to the extent that the dependent variables of interest are causally associated with relationship type rather than with relationship closeness, then findings in the close relationship area (as well as research on relationship types) will be marked by confusion and inconsistency.

Perhaps more important, just how close marital, or parent-child, or other types of relationships generally are, is an empirical question. It is also one with some import. For example, the degree of variability in marital closeness in various populations, how closeness may wax and wane with the age of the marriage or the age of the partners, and so on, are important questions whose answers have both theoretical and empirical implications. In fact, one of our aims, not only in our chapter but also in our program of research, is to investigate the variability in closeness between types of relationships (as well as within types) for various populations, for it is now a reasonably safe assumption that even the prototypes of close relationships—marital and parent-child— are not homogeneous with respect to their degrees of closeness.

Apart from using relationship type to identify close relationships, perhaps the most usual way of identifying close relationships and of assessing their degree of closeness, as well as the method on which most current knowledge about close relationships rests, is to ask one of the principals to the relationship to make the assessment—to characterize the closeness of the relationship using the extensive and special knowledge he or she has about the relationship and whatever meanings the word close has for him or her. As previously noted, these meanings often encompass such concepts as "love," "caring," "intimacy," "trust," "commitment," and so forth.

This method, too, is not without problems. It is increasingly recognized, for example, that there is some variability in meaning among laypersons in the concept of closeness. As a consequence, the question of the meaning of closeness as well as of its popular synonyms (e.g., a "loving" relationship; a "meaningful" relationship) is now the subject of study (e.g., Helgeson, Shaver, & Dyer, 1987; Sternberg & Grajek, 1984). While there is not space to discuss these studies here, their importance should be obvious, as should be the relevance of recent studies examining the lay meaning of concepts describing relationship type, such as "friend" (e.g., Berndt, 1986). One matter that has yet to be addressed is the influence of motivational factors upon the classification the relationship participant makes (e.g., the influence of the belief that all marital relationships should be close, or of the desire that this particular relationship be close, upon the classification).

The point to be made about this popular means of identifying close relationships is that the relationship participant makes the classification, not the investigator, and that the yardstick the participant is using to make the discrimination is not yet known. These "insider" classifications of relationships are undoubtedly useful (e.g., see Berscheid & Peplau, 1983; Olson, 1977), but what they predict is not entirely clear. Neither is it clear how they compare with "outsider" classifications, such as those the investigator or other external observers of the relationship might make.

Among the many meanings the concept of close relationship embodies for laypersons, as well as for some investigators, is the notion that close relationships are characterized by positive affective ties—that close relationships are loving and satisfying relationships frequently punctuated with positively toned emotional events of various kinds and infrequently marred by negative events. As a consequence, few people, when asked by an investigator to classify their own relationships, would designate an acrimonious one as close. Using the emotional tone of the relationship to assess its closeness is thus another scheme sometimes used to identify close relationships.

Though often related to insider classifications of closeness in that the relationship participant reports on these emotional events or on the emotional quality of the relationship, this means of identifying close relationships can be independent of participants' subjective closeness estimates in that the emotional tenor of the relationship can be, and is, used by investigators as well. Investigators not infrequently (and particularly in the case of marital relationships) attempt to make their own assessments of the emotional tenor—often the degree of satisfaction or distress—that characterizes the relationship. The extent of emotional harmony or distress in the relationship plays an important role in the frequently used Locke-Wallace Marital Satisfaction Scale (1959), for example. Respondents to the Locke-Wallace are not only asked to tell whether they typically agree or disagree about a number of issues but also to make a global assessment of the extent to which their marriage has been characterized by "joy." Although assessment of the negative emotions that usually accompany disagreements and a global assessment of emotional tone are important in themselves and have been shown to have predictive value, no one argues that "marital satisfaction" need bear strong association with closeness. Marriages in which the partners are highly involved and interdependent as well as marriages in which the partners lead parallel lives, for example, may both be equally satisfying and marked by little disagreement. At the least, it is not known how the method of sorting relationships according to how satisfied the partners are with them compares with other methods of identifying close relationships, although it has been extensively argued theoretically that it is a mistake at worst, and unprofitable at best, to use a relationship's emotional tone as the only, or even a strong, indicant of closeness (see Berscheid, 1983; and Kelley et al., 1983, for a discussion of this point). The matter is, however, an empirical question, and one that we will address in this chapter.

Whether or not relationship affect is usefully considered as an indicant of closeness, it is clear that interest in affective phenomena in relationships has increased in recent years, particularly affect within marital relationships. One of the most innovative and promising avenues of relationship research in the past decade has been the work of Gottman and his associates, who have examined the patterns of positive and negative affect felt by marital partners as they discuss a problem. (See also Bradbury & Fincham, 1987, for a description of this body of research, as well as for a discussion of what is known of the association between affect and marital satisfaction as measured by the Locke-Wallace and other measures.) No doubt the closeness of a relationship and its affective tone and events are related, but it remains to be empirically demonstrated what the associations are.

In contrast to these approaches to identifying close relationships, Kelley et al. (1983) have argued for the importance of an "outsider" classification made on the basis of an examination of the activities of the relationship partners. They have proposed that it is useful to classify a relationship as "close" when it is characterized by high interdependence of these activities, where "A high degree of interdependence between two people is revealed in four properties of their interconnected activities: (1) the individuals have *frequent* impact on each other; (2) the degree of impact per each occurrence is *strong*; (3) the impact involves *diverse* kinds of activities for each person; and (4) all of these properties characterize the interconnected activity series for a relatively long *duration* of time" (p. 13).

The activities of the relationship partners may be assessed in many different ways. As Kelley et al. discuss, the ideal would be for an omniscient investigator to observe both partners continuously over a very long period of time, recording not only their outward behaviors but also their inner thoughts and physiological responses. Such observation is not possible, of course, and various methods of activity assessment, and the resultant classification of closeness, will be flawed to the extent that they depart from this ideal.

We have developed a method of interdependence assessment, the "Relationship Closeness Inventory" or RCI, described elsewhere (Berscheid, Snyder, & Omoto, in preparation), that is far from ideal but may yield a useful approximation of the extent of interdependence of the partners in the relationship. (See Rusbult, 1980; 1983 for another conceptualization and method of assessing interdependence.) Derived from Kelley et al.'s theoretical conception of closeness, the inventory attempts to assess the *frequency* of impact the partners have on each other, the *strength* of influence, as well as its *diversity*, yielding a "closeness" score. The examination of the activities the respondent has engaged in with his or her relationship partner "during the past week" is based on the respondent's self-report. To blunt the well-known deficiencies of the self-report method, the inventory is highly structured and detailed, as well as time-bound, so that the respondent, in most cases, need report only whether a particular event did or did not occur. The investigator performs an aggregation of events to arrive at indices of the three properties of interaction that help define interdependence: frequency, strength, and diversity of the impact of each person's activities on the other. Because the RCI is essentially based on self-reports, or insider reviews of the relationship, while at the same time the investigator, an outsider, decides what it is that is important in these reports and performs the necessary aggregations, we think of the RCI as a kind of hybrid of the two approaches. As we shall later discuss, though the instrument is based on self-report, the role the outsider plays in the selection and aggregation of the events reported makes a very significant difference in the conclusions that are drawn about the closeness of the relationship, at least where RCI closeness scores are contrasted to the insider's subjective estimate of closeness.

It should be explicitly noted that the fourth interaction property proposed by Kelley et al. to be an important factor in closeness, duration of the relationship (to be referred to throughout this chapter as relationship *longevity*), does not contribute to the RCI closeness score, though longevity is always assessed. There are several reasons for this decision to keep relationship longevity separate from the other indices, perhaps the most important being an unwillingness at this point (in the absence of evidence to the contrary) to make the assumption that closeness along the other three dimensions inevitably increases as the relationship moves through time.

COMPARING AND CONTRASTING
CLOSENESS ASSESSMENT METHODS

Which of these relationship classification schemes is most profitable for an investigator to use? Aside from theoretical argument, who can now say? Little, if any, comparative empirical data exist comparing these different methods of identifying close relationships and of assessing the extent of their closeness. It is possible that each method produces unique and useful information about the relationship in question. It is also possible, of course, that the results of all methods of classification we have outlined above converge, so that, for example, a relationship characterized by the participant as close is also a relationship that has a predominantly positive affective tone as well as one that an outside observer, after examining the activities of the relationship participants, would classify as close.

It would be extraordinarily difficult for anyone to compare and contrast these classification schemes by drawing upon the many existing studies in which they have been used. For one thing, samples of respondents in these studies, while usually homogeneous within a study, vary widely across studies in their demographic characteristics, many of which may influence the results obtained from a particular classification mode. No one study has attempted to use several closeness classification schemes with one sample of respondents, thus permitting clear comparisons of their consequences, at least with that sample. The disadvantage of making comparisons within one sample, however, is that the results can be generalized only to the population from which the sample is drawn. The exercise is, however, a worthwhile one, if only to illustrate the convergence and divergence of various schemes.

In the end, however, while it is interesting to know whether the various classification schemes do or do not speak with one voice about a relationship, as well as useful for the interpretation of previous research using any one of these measures, what is far more important is whether any one of them, or all (if there is convergence), can predict something of interest about the relationship and the phenomena that occur within it. For this reason, we will also address the question of what, if anything, these methods of classification predict. We shall focus upon the prediction of two events with which relationship investigators have been particularly concerned: the stability of the relationship and, if it weakens or is dissolved, the emotional distress that results.

Overview

The study from which we draw our empirical illustrations of the central point we wish to make in this chapter—that it is now necessary for researchers to explicitly examine the consequences of using the various methods identifying close relationships—was one in which young men and women were asked to identify their "closest" relationship. Since a full and detailed report of this study is forthcoming (Berscheid, Snyder, & Omoto, in preparation), we will not take space here to fully describe the details of this study, but rather will focus only on those portions that have immediate implications for conceptualizing and measuring closeness.

To set the stage, we begin with the general question of who people in our sample chose as their closest relationships. We then consider subjective estimates of the closeness of these closest relationships, evaluating this approach to measuring closeness in terms of how these estimates of the closeness of that closest relationship vary with the sex of the respondent, the longevity of the relationship, and with the type of relationship.

Next, we examine the emotional tone of these closest relationships, based on the respondents' reports of the frequency with which they experience various emotions within the relationship. Again, we examine the extent to which the relationship's emotional tone appears to co-vary with the sex of the respondent, the longevity of the relationship, and with the type of relationship.

Afterward, we shall present our own assessment of the closeness of the relationship, based upon the closeness scores yielded by the RCI. And, again, we shall consider how relationship closeness assessed in this way does or does not co-vary with the sex of the respondent, the longevity of the relationship, and the relationship type.

To place these empirical matters in a conceptual perspective, we discuss how the different yardsticks of relationship closeness do or do not produce measurements that correspond to one another. In doing so, we focus upon how an investigator who looks at a relationship through the lens of one classification scheme may obtain a view of that relationship somewhat different from that of an investigator who views it through another classification lens.

Finally, we present the proof of the several classification puddings in the form of their respective abilities to predict relationship stability in a sample of unmarried young adults and, if unstable, the emotional distress experienced when the relationship ends. As part of a longitudinal study, we contacted some of our respondents up to nine months after they told us a great deal about their "closest" relationship with another human. Not surprisingly, when recontacted, many of our respondents were still involved in the relationship they had designated. But some of these "closest" relationships had dissolved. What did we know from our first contacts with respondents that would have allowed us to predict the eventual break-up of some close relationships and the endurance of others? And, for those that did break up, what did we know that would have allowed us to predict the degree of emotional distress experienced when these closest relationships came to an end? Did the respondents' own reports of closeness predict these outcomes best? The emotional tone of the relationship? Or, did our laborious attempt to estimate the partners' closeness through a detailed examination of their activities along the lines suggested by Kelley et al. (1983) provide the most useful predictive information?

THE "CLOSEST" RELATIONSHIP

With whom do people share their closest relationships? To obtain one answer to this question, we asked nearly 250 undergraduates at the University of Minnesota to identify their "closest, deepest, most involved, and most intimate relationship." "Deep," "involving," and "intimate" appeared to us to be the most usual synonyms laypersons use for "close" and we included them all so as not to bias relationship selection toward any one (where the individual respondent believed each described a different relationship). These students then anonymously completed an extensive questionnaire about that relationship.

Approximately equal numbers of men and women completed our questionnaire. The "typical" respondent was a 19-20 year old sophomore who was single and a full-time student at the time of his or her initial entry into our study. When we examined the types of relationships that our respondents nominated as their closest, it was evident that three types of relationships accounted for almost all of our respondents' nominations. Specifically, and as depicted in Figure 3.1, the greatest majority of our respondents (47%) nominated a romantic relationship

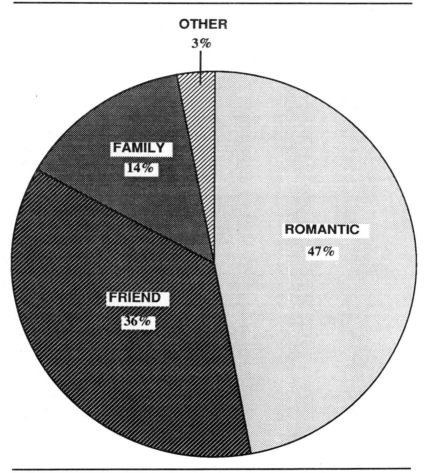

Figure 3.1 Percentage of sample nominating each relationship type.

as their closest relationship. Friendships were the second most frequently nominated type of relationship (36%), and the third major category of relationship nomination was family relationships, although this type of relationship was nominated relatively infrequently (14%). Finally, only a very small percentage of respondents (3%) nominated some other type of relationship as their closest relationship, and these were usually work relationships.

Somewhat surprisingly, there were no differences between men and women in the types of relationships they nominated. (We had guessed that women might be more likely to choose family relationships and that men would be more likely to choose friend relationships, given the popular belief that women retain closer ties to the family of origin than men do, e.g., "When a daughter marries, the family gains a son, but . . . .) The longevities of the relationships designated by males and females as their closest also did not differ. Not unexpectedly, however, we did find that relationship longevity varied as a function of relationship type. The longest relationships, of course, were family relationships; they had lasted an average of over 19 years. The second longest relationships were friend relationships, with a mean longevity of about 5 1/2 years. Finally, the shortest-lived relationships were romantic relationships (mean longevity slightly less than than 3 1/2 years), the relationship type most frequently nominated by this sample.

Thus, there was a great deal of variability in the length of time that the different types of relationships nominated as closest had lasted. There was also considerable variability within relationship categories (e.g., among romantic relationships) as well as between them. Partially, the association between relationship type and relationship longevity in this sample no doubt accurately reflects the close relationship population; that is, family relationships, regardless of sample, will typically be relationships of longer duration. In other part, however, the association may be attributable to this sample of young people; one can hope that in older samples, romantic relationships will not be so short-lived, although some cynics might not care to bet on the matter. In any event, because relationship longevity potentially confounds comparisons between relationship types, we will keep a wary eye on this factor as we examine the view of the relationship that each of these classification schemes of closeness yields.

SUBJECTIVE ESTIMATES OF THE CLOSENESS
OF THE CLOSEST RELATIONSHIP

As previously discussed, the most common manner in which investigators discriminate close relationships from less close relationships is to ask the individual to provide subjective estimates of closeness. Included in our questionnaire were two items which asked respondents to estimate the actual closeness of their closest relationship. The first item read "Relative to *all* your other relationships (both same- and opposite-sex), how would you characterize your relationship with this person?" As we expected, virtually all of our respondents chose the midpoint and above on this scale, demonstrating that they read the instructions accurately. The second item queried "Relative to what you know about *other* peoples' close relationships, how would you characterize your relationship with this person?" In both cases, respondents used 7-point scales to estimate the closeness of their relationship, with higher scores indicating greater closeness. Responses to these two items were highly correlated across respondents, so we summed them to create an *index of subjective closeness.*

Given that our respondents had been given free rein to choose their closest relationship, we expected their subjective closeness scores to be skewed toward the maximum closeness score defined by the subjective closeness index. They were. As shown in Figure 3.2a, however, there was, nonetheless, a surprising degree of variability in these subjective closeness scores. Not all people estimated their closest relationship to be extremely close, and some even went so far as to characterize their relationship as only average *or below* in closeness!

Examining this subjective closeness measure further, we found a significant sex difference: Females claimed greater closeness of their closest relationship than males did. This difference emerged despite the fact that males and females had nominated the same types of relationships. Respondent sex thus appears to be an important moderator of subjective estimates of closeness (see also Rubin, Peplau, & Hill, 1981; Wheeler & Nezlek, 1977; Wheeler, Reis, & Nezlek, 1983). The investigator who utilizes this closeness classification and assessment scheme, then, would be well-advised to keep this sex difference in mind. For example, we can expect investigators who use subjective estimates of closeness to discriminate close from less close relationships will find more women's than men's relationships in the close category. Perhaps this reflects reality, but perhaps it doesn't. We shall return to this point shortly.

With respect to relationship longevity, our data revealed a small and inverse association with subjective closeness; respondents whose closest relationship had lasted longer tended to claim less closeness, whereas shorter-lived relationships were rated as slightly more close. This tendency was not highly reliable, however, and, in any case, it will be recalled that longevity is confounded with relationship type, which itself appears to be significantly associated with subjective closeness. Relevant to the possible influence of the confounding of longevity and relationship type is the fact that within the category of romantic relationships, longevity and subjective closeness were virtually independent of each other.

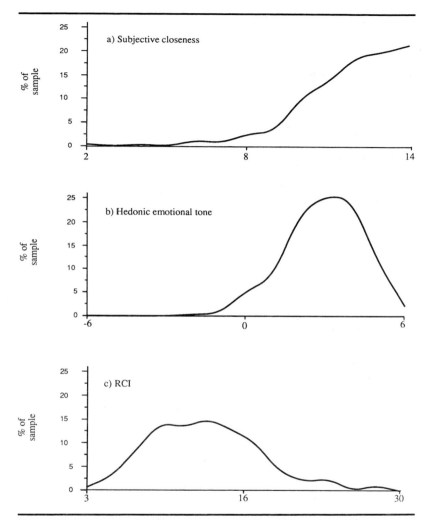

Figure 3.2 Frequency distributions for (a) subjective closeness, (b) hedonic emotional tone, and (c) Relationship Closeness Inventory.

Moreover, while respondents who designated a romantic relationship as their closest believed their relationship to be as close as those of respondents who nominated a friend relationship, both groups claimed significantly greater closeness than those whose closest relationship was a family relationship. Thus, whatever the events or algorithms upon which people base their subjective estimates of closeness, they apparently may differ with relationship type.

Summary. Perhaps the most interesting finding in these data, and a preliminary point in favor of the subjective closeness method of identifying close relationships, is that people do discriminate the degree of closeness of even their closest relationship. People's subjective estimates of closeness of these relationships are not uniformly high: Some "closest" relationships are closer than others in the eyes of the respondents. Additionally, these data indicate that women view their closest relationships as closer than men see theirs and that members of romantic and friend relationships rate their relationships as closer than members of family relationships rate theirs. Finally, subjective estimates of closeness appear to be only slightly (and negatively) related to relationship longevity; in this sample, at least, the sheer endurance of a relationship does not assure that the relationship will be regarded by one of its principals to be extremely close.

EMOTIONAL TENOR OF THE CLOSEST RELATIONSHIP

In our survey we asked respondents to tell us how often they experienced each of several emotions in their relationship with the nominated partner. Specifically, they were asked to rate the frequency with which they had experienced each of 27 emotions in the relationship. Some 12 positive and 15 negative emotions were identified; included were intense emotions, such as "elated" and "angry," and less intense feelings, such as "contented" and "disappointed." Although the Locke-Wallace measure of marital satisfaction differs, no doubt significantly, in its particulars, it should be pointed out that it is similar in concept to what we used here, with respondents indicating the frequency with which they were "satisfied," "joyful," "elated," "delighted," and so forth, as well as emotions generally thought to accompany disagreements.

Not surprisingly, these emotion data revealed that in their closest relationships respondents experienced a significant amount of positive emotion (statistically significant, that is, when the benchmark is taken as "never" responses for the positive emotions). Moreover, it also was not surprising to find that in these closest relationships, positive emotions were experienced significantly more often than negative emotions. What may be regarded by some as surprising, however, is that these closest relationships were also significantly marked by the experience of negative emotions (again, statistically significant in frequency when "never" is taken as the benchmark).

In examining the emotional nature of these close relationships, we split the positive and negative emotion scores into groups that were at or above their respective medians and those below their medians, resulting in a four-fold typology of relationships displayed in Table 3.1: "Happy," or at or above the sample median in the experience of positive emotion and below the median in the experience of negative; "Less Happy," below the positive median and at or above the negative; "Ambivalent," at or above both the positive and negative medians; "Flat," below both the positive and negative medians of frequency of emotion experience. With this typology it is possible to address the issue of the amount of variability in the emotional characterization of even the closest relationship: Are these closest relationships largely characterized as "Happy" or "Less Happy" in the typology, or are all types represented? As Table 3.1 indicates, all types were represented in the sample; a goodly percentage of closest relationships were Ambivalent and Flat, as well as Happy or Less Happy. Evidently, just as even closest relationships are not uniformly close subjectively, neither are they homogeneously positive emotionally.

To further investigate the emotional tenor of people's closest relationships, and directly evaluate the notion that close relationships are positive emotionally, we took the difference between the average of the scores on the experience of positive emotions and the average of the negative emotion scores for each respondent, creating a measure of the relationship's *hedonic emotional tone*, or the relative frequency with which positive and negative emotions are experienced in each relationship. Positive scores on this measure indicate that positive emotions are experienced more frequently in the relationship than negative emotions; negative scores indicate that negative emotion occurs more frequently than positive emotion. The absolute magnitude of these scores, moreover, reflects the degree to which one type of emotion is experienced more frequently than the other type. That is, a score near zero indicates that the experience of positive and negative emotions is nearly balanced, whereas a score that considerably deviates from zero indicates that one emotion type occurs much more frequently than the other.

On this measure of hedonic emotional tone, we found (as expected) that positive emotion occurred more frequently than negative emotion in most closest relationships. There was, however, considerable variability; that is, as shown in Figure 3.2b, there was variation even among relatively positive relationships, with some relationships much more positive than negative and others much closer to being balanced (small difference score).

TABLE 3.1

Distribution of Relationships into Each of the
Four Emotion Characterizations

		Positive Emotion	
		High	Low
		Ambivalent	Less happy
	High	19.6%	30.4%
Negative Emotion		Happy	Flat
	Low	31.7%	18.3%

To date, we have found no differences between males and females in the hedonic emotional tone of their relationships; the closest relationships of men and women both appear to be relatively positive, and the degree of this positivity does not differ between them. (When one *adds* together the amount of positive and negative emotion, however, rather than taking the difference score, there *is* a sex difference: Women claim to experience more *total emotion* than men do in their closest relationships.)

The correlation between hedonic emotional tone and relationship longevity, as expected from recent theoretical statements about emotion in relationships (see Berscheid, 1983), was negative, such that the emotion experienced in longer relationships was relatively less positive in quality than the emotion experienced in shorter relationships, but only marginally so. (Moreover, and also as Berscheid predicts, the sheer amount of emotion experienced in the relationship, positive *plus* negative, was significantly—and negatively—associated with relationship longevity: Long-term relationships are least likely to be marked by a high degree of emotion.)

Finally, we have found no association between the hedonic emotional tone of the relationship and relationship type.

Summary. The quality of emotion experienced in people's closest relationships appears to be generally positive, although there was considerable variability in just how positive, and there was also much negative emotion in evidence. Our data suggest that the relative frequency of the experience of positive emotions as opposed to negative covaries neither with respondent sex nor with relationship type. There seems to be a slight tendency, however, for positive emotion to predominate to a greater extent in shorter relationships (which, in this sample, also tended to be romantic relationships, it should be recalled).

INTERDEPENDENCE IN THE CLOSEST RELATIONSHIP

In the Relationship Closeness Inventory, the *frequency* measure is derived from the amount of time that respondents typically spend alone with each other (not in the presence of others) in each of three time periods: morning, afternoon, and evening. (As previously indicated, frequency is to be distinguished from relationship duration or longevity, which refers to the length of time the relationship has existed.) The *diversity* measure is activity-based; respondents indicate the number of times in the past week they engaged in each of 38 diverse activities, ranging from the mundane (e.g., "did laundry," "ate a meal") to the more unusual (e.g., "went on an outing," "planned a party/social event") in each of four social contexts: alone (by oneself), alone with their partner, with their partner in the presence of other people, and with people other than their partner. The data we utilize in creating a measure of diversity is simply the number of *different types* of activities (of the 38) that respondents have engaged in with their partner alone in the past week (regardless of the number of times each *one* of those activities was performed). Finally, our measure of *strength* is derived from respondent estimates of the current and future impact their partner has on numerous itemized activities, decisions, and plans, including career choice, moods, amount of time spent with friends, and so forth.

For each of these three dimensions, we have devised separate aggregation and scoring procedures that produce a score that ranges from 1 to 10, higher scores indicating higher impact along that dimension. These three scale scores are then summed to form an overall closeness index, with higher scores taken to indicate greater inter-dependence, and thus closeness, between relationship partners.

What do people's closest relationships look like when viewed through the lens of the RCI? First, and again, people's closest relationships are not uniformly close, as is dramatically apparent from looking at Figure 3.2c. In fact, the distribution of closeness scores for these closest relationships is nearly "normal" in appearance, a pattern at odds with the distribution of scores of subjective estimates of closeness (compare Figure 3.2a with Figure 3.2c). The RCI, then, appears to be sensitive to differences between what, on the surface, are all close—in fact, closest—relationships.

Comparisons between males' and females' RCI scores revealed no differences; the degree of interdependence in males' closest relationships was equivalent to that in females' relationships.

Relationship longevity, as with the other classification schemes we have outlined, was negatively related to the RCI index. Again, the absolute magnitude of this association was not large, but it was statistically significant, suggesting that longer relationships tended to be less close relationships, while shorter relationships were characterized by higher levels of interdependence in this sample. (It also should be mentioned in this context that within romantic relationships alone, longevity was not significantly associated with the RCI, nor with emotional tone, nor with subjective closeness.)

Finally, romantic relationships scored higher on our closeness index than either friend or family relationships did. The friend and family relationships, furthermore, did not differ from one another.

Summary. As assessed by the RCI, people's closest relationships were not all close. In fact, the distribution of closeness scores approached a normal distribution within the minimum and maximum range defined by the RCI. While respondent sex was not associated with closeness measured by the inventory, relationship longevity was inversely associated with closeness, although not strongly. Lastly, closeness varied as a function of relationship type, with romantic relationships evidencing higher levels of closeness than either friend or family relationships.

CONVERGENCE AND DIVERGENCE OF THE CLOSENESS MEASURES

A direct comparison of the several closeness assessment schemes we have examined indicates that each draws a somewhat different picture of relationships for the investigator. On one important issue, however, they all sing in unison, though not in harmony: Even among the relationships people regard as their "closest," there is considerable variability in closeness. All of the approaches to quantifying closeness suggest such variability in the closeness of these closest relationships. Whether we apply the yardstick of subjective estimates of closeness, of the hedonic emotional tone of the relationship, or of interdependence as measured by the RCI, we discover a substantial range of degrees of closeness. This range suggests that even when examining *only* the relationships people have identified as their closest, the investigator cannot be entirely confident that he or she has secured a sample of close relationships—certainly not when put up against some absolute Platonic ideal of closeness and probably not even when compared with most garden-variety conceptions of closeness.

While it is clear that some closest relationships are closer than others no matter what yardstick one chooses to measure them, just exactly how many are closer and how many are less close depends on the measuring stick taken in hand. If the investigator were to listen to the subjective estimates of closeness pronounced by the people whose closest relationships they are, he or she would be led to believe that most are pretty close, with only a few less-close stragglers constituting a thin tail to a heavily skewed closeness distribution. If the relative positivity of the emotions experienced in the relationship is the yardstick chosen, the investigator will find that these closest relationships are not quite as close as the principals say they are, with the closeness distribution shifting a bit toward less closeness and the tail somewhat thicker and decidedly shorter. And if the investigator chooses to examine interdependence in the relationship, perhaps through the lens of the RCI, he or she will find even fewer very close relationships, with the distribution of closeness almost bell-shaped in form and situated over the middle of the continuum this closeness measure defines.

Those investigators who select their sample of close relationships on the faith that relationship type will do an adequate classification job for them—that, for example, a sample of family relationships will be a sample of close relationships—will get yet another picture. If our respondents' own subjective estimates of closeness are to be believed, family relationships *are* set apart from other relationships, at least from romantic and friend relationships; but contrary to assumption, they are *less* close. On the other hand, our measure of hedonic emotional tone suggests that *no* one type of relationship is closer than any other and one is as well off selecting family relationships as romantic or friend relationships (if they are designated as "closest," of course). But the RCI would say that if the investigator really wants a sample of very close relationships to examine, he or she would choose romantic relationships, rather than family or friend relationships, at least with this population of respondents. The RCI says that romantic relationships are in a class by themselves, closer than any other type of relationship by virtue of their greater evidence of frequency, diversity, and strength of causal influence on the partners' activities.

The closeness assessment schemes we have examined here quarrel with each other when they answer other questions as well. If you ask each, for example, whether men and women differ in the closeness of their closest relationships, the answer you get depends on which scheme you ask. If you were to trust subjective estimates of closeness, you would conclude that the closest relationships of women are closer than those of men. And you would probably think that the answer makes good sense, for it receives corroboration from other studies (e.g., Wheeler & Nezlek,

1977, as previously noted), as well as all those studies that suggest that women have greater affiliation needs, are especially concerned with relationship intimacy, and so on and so forth (see Huston & Ashmore, 1986, for a review). On the other hand, if you were to listen to the answer provided by the RCI measure of interdependence, you would conclude that there is no difference between the sexes in the closeness of the closest relationship. And if, to break the tie, you were to ask the emotional tenor scheme if there is a sex difference in closeness, you would find that it sides with the RCI: According to the relative positivity of the emotional tone of the relationship, women's and men's closest relationships do not differ in closeness. But, if you were to respond that positivity isn't where it's at, that the closer the relationship, the more emotion should be experienced in it—both positive *and* negative—then the emotion classification scheme would side with subjective estimates, supporting the idea that women experience significantly more emotion in their closest relationships than men do.

On yet another question, however, the various assessment schemes agree, unanimously rejecting the idea that relationships of long duration tend to be closer than shorter-term relationships, as many, including Kelly et al., have assumed. They also agree that, as a matter of fact, at least with this sample of young adults, a short relationship is probably going to be a closer relationship than a long one. Whether one trusts subjective estimates of closeness, relative positivity of emotional experience, or interdependence, relationships of longer standing seem to be less close. Other samples of respondents may yield different answers, but with this population—the one that currently constitutes the backbone of relationship research—long relationships aren't necessarily the closest relationships.

The empirical message, then, with respect to those approaches to closeness we have examined here, is one both of divergence (on questions of differences between the sexes and relationship types), of some convergence (on the question of closeness variability), and good agreement (in the matter of longevity). In at least one respect, this state of affairs is to be expected; the constituent elements of the three approaches to relationship classification (e.g., the individual measures of subjective estimates, the individual reports of positive and negative emotions, the individual measures of frequency, diversity, and strength) are, at best, only modestly inter-correlated, and none are significantly associated with the longevity of the relationship. Although such a pattern may place considerable constraints on the ability of the separate approaches to serve as interchangeable and mutually substitutable measures of closeness, their relative independence does make it possible to compare them—in fact, to pit them against each other—in the critical task of predicting important outcomes of relationships. What each classification scheme _says_ about close relationships is, of course, much less important than what it actually can _do_.

PREDICTION OF BREAK-UP AND DISTRESS

Romantic relationships were the type of relationship most frequently chosen by the men and women in our sample as their closest relationship. We followed these relationships over a nine-month period to explore how well each closeness classification scheme could predict two outcomes of interest: the stability of the relationship (e.g., see Fowers & Olson, 1986) and the amount of emotional distress the respondent felt if and when the relationship ended. In assessing the adequacy of each scheme to predict, we assumed that the relationships identified by that scheme as very close should be _least_ likely to break-up but that if they did, the respondent should have experienced the _most_ distress.

In the beginning we were pessimistic that we would be able to make the competitive outcome comparisons we wished, fearing that the number of break-ups would be so small that reliable analyses could not be performed. After all, these were not just close relationships—they had been identified as the respondents' _closest_. In fact, we had already determined in our follow-up of all relationships that at the 3-month point there were very few break-ups among the _friendship_ closest relationships (of the friend relationships successfully recontacted at 3 months, only 11% had dissolved). We also were able to recontact after 3 months 76 out of those 95 respondents who had designated a romantic relationship as their closest relationship. (No attempt was made to recontact 19 people who chose romantic relationships but who were also married.) The three month follow-up suggested that we might have enough break-ups to examine if we were patient. Thus we tried to contact these people again nine months after they had initially completed our questionnaire, and were successful in finding 86% of these and asking them about the current status of their relationship with the person they had nominated (e.g., "Are you still dating R. K. [or whatever the person's initials were]?"). If that relationship had ended in the intervening months, we proceeded to ask respondents about the intensity and duration of the emotional distress they had experienced at the time the relationship ended. Specifically, respondents answered six items of the type "Immediately after the break-up, how difficult was it for you to make an emotional adjustment?" and "How long were you upset after the break-up?" We then summed these items to create a composite index of emotional distress.

As it happens, we did find enough break-ups within the follow-up period we considered practical (before the academic year ended, residences changed, and students otherwise dropped from our sight) with romantic relationships. In fact, we found a surprising amount of instability in this type of closest relationship: Among respondents who had initially designated a romantic relationship as their closest interpersonal relationship, fully 42% were no longer involved in that relationship nine months later! While romantic relationships are not generally noted for their stability (e.g., Hill, Rubin, & Peplau, 1976), even being chosen as the *closest* relationship did not ensure that a current romantic relationship would survive less than one year later.

We proceeded, then, to examine whether any of the closeness assessment schemes could have forecast which relationships would be terminated and which would endure. In doing so, we elevated relationship longevity from the status of a dependent variable to an independent variable. Despite the fact that all of the closeness measures indicated that the shorter relationships were the closest (and, for this sample, these tended to be the romantic relationships), most predictions of human behavior, like the weather, rest on the relatively safe assumption that what happened yesterday is going to happen today. Thus, in the absence of any other information about a relationship, and even information provided by various fancy closeness measuring devices, it seemed to us that the safest assumption was probably the simple one that the longer this closest relationship had lasted in the past, the more likely we'd see it thriving nine months after we had administered our questionnaires and inventories. In any case, our assessment schemes were required to compete not only against each other but also against the measure of relationship longevity.

And compete they did in a regression analysis in which relationship status was predicted from relationship longevity, subjective closeness, hedonic emotional tone, and interdependence as measured by the RCI. Taken together, this set of measures did significantly predict which relationships would last and which would end. Among this set, however, only the RCI interdependence measure was a significant predictor of break-up, with all other measures unreliable predictors. Relationships characterized by the RCI as being of greater closeness proved to be more likely to endure, whereas relationships it characterized as less close were more likely to have ended. Thus, not only do the assessment schemes examined here offer somewhat divergent views of close relationships, but they are clearly differentially effective in predicting relationship dissolution.

Some may consider it surprising that subjective estimates of closeness did not forecast the status of people's closest relationships nine months later. Others, however, would say that the level of specificity of this predictor was not sufficiently matched to the criterion to allow for adequate prediction (see Ajzen & Fishbein, 1977). That is, they would say that the lessons learned in the attitude and behavior domain suggest that in order to predict a specific behavior, such as relationship dissolution, one must assess a very specific attitude and intention. While we did not directly ask respondents to predict if their relationships would end, we *did* ask them "How long do you anticipate this relationship will last?" Hence, we conducted another regression analysis in which we sought to predict later relationship status from only this measure. The results of this analysis revealed that our respondents were not at all accurate forecasters of the fates of their relationships; the contribution of this single item of projected relationship longevity to the prediction of relationship status was trivial and nonsignificant, even in the absence of competing predictor measures.

Still others may claim that the subjective estimate of closeness could not possibly have predicted relationship dissolution because, as a two-item index, its reliability is relatively limited. However, it should be noted that the hedonic emotional tone index is essentially derived from two items, whereas RCI scores are only three-item aggregates. In fact, the reliabilities of these three approaches to closeness did not appreciably differ from one another. Furthermore, according to the concep-tualization of closeness that relies on people's subjective estimates of their relationships, multiple indicators of subjective closeness are not really required; an investigator can legitimately and easily employ only one subjective estimate to assess closeness. This is indeed the manner of assessment that has typically been employed with subjective estimates of closeness in past research. It would also not appear that sheer number of items is a guarantee of adequate predictive capability. If it were, the hedonic emotional tone index (where the two components are computed from the raw data of ratings of 27 different emotions) should have proved a significant predictor of relationship status; which, of course, it did not. In the end, in fact, many different items may be necessary in order to adequately tap relationship closeness, but this explanation would not seem to be able to account for the failure of the measures of subjective closeness and hedonic emotional tone to predict relationship status.

We should comment here that, frankly, we consider it remarkable that the RCI was able to predict breakup within romantic relationships. From the beginning, we were painfully aware that it takes two people to continue a relationship and only one to terminate it, and that we possessed the RCI score of only one person in the relationship. All of the other predictors were forced to perform under this handicap as well, of course. It is doubtless the case that the predictive accuracy of the RCI, as well as that of the other measures, would be significantly enhanced if the closeness of both partners were to be assessed.

Having found that the RCI measure was the only significant predictor of later relationship status, we moved on to test the relative predictive capabilities of the various closeness measures and of simple relationship longevity for the amount of emotional distress experienced by those respondents whose relationships had broken. Again, relationship longevity, subjective closeness, hedonic emotional tone, and RCI scores were entered as predictors into a regression equation with the composite index of emotional distress serving as our criterion measure. As a set, these four measures only marginally predicted the emotional distress respondents reported at the dissolution of their closest relationship. In terms of individual contributions, only relationship longevity predicted distress, and only at a marginal level: members of longer relationships as compared to shorter relationships tended to be more distressed at the dissolution of their relationships. Thus, prediction of emotional distress at break-up proved to be a difficult task from the relationship measures we obtained, with none of the predictors demonstrating highly reliable contributions. Recent research by Simpson (1987) on romantic relationships (but romantic relationships that are not necessarily the person's closest relationship), however, has shown that the RCI is a significant predictor of emotional distress at relationship dissolution, and that study also replicates our finding that the RCI predicts dissolution of dating relationships.

As with the prediction of break-up in the instance of subjective estimates of closeness, one could take issue with the specificity with which emotional distress was predicted and measured. Again, however, we had asked respondents a direct question nine months earlier about their reactions to the hypothetical dissolution of their closest relationship. Specifically, we solicited respondents' agreement with the statement "If our current relationship was to end suddenly, I could make an almost total emotional adjustment fairly quickly." And, again, responses on this measure did not significantly predict emotional distress at relationship dissolution, even in the absence of our other predictors. Hence, reliable prediction of the emotional distress that people experienced when their closest relationship ended was not possible from any of our classification schemes nor from a simple, specific, and face-valid measure of emotional adjustment obtained earlier.

CONCLUDING COMMENTS

What is a close relationship? How is closeness to be defined? And, how is it to be measured? The answers to these fundamental questions are critically important in the development of the science of close relationships. If our inquiry has taught us anything, it is that it is no simple matter to answer these questions. Starting from different theoretical points of departure, one can devise different approaches to defining and measuring closeness that lead eventually—as the empirical illustrations we have included in this chapter suggest—to differing portraits of close relationships.

As much as our use of a single, limited sample permitted us to draw direct comparisons between various approaches, we now should reemphasize that different subsets of the population of close relationships will quite possibly produce different results. We have tried throughout to keep the reader sensitive to the limitations of this sample. But let us directly point to one such limitation and how another subsample may produce different findings: It will be recalled that for these young men and women, family relationships were less likely to be chosen as closest and, even when chosen, were not as close as other types. T. J. Berndt (personal communication, October 21, 1987) has data suggesting that the association between age and closeness with parents is a U- shaped function, with highest closeness at younger and older ages. Thus, our sample of young adults enter this curve at a time when they are less close to their parents than they were earlier and would be later.

Not only may different views of the relationship be obtained from different subsamples of the close relationships population, views different from those depicted here may be obtained if different dependent measures are used. Moreover, we have seen how one approach to defining and measuring closeness serves particularly well in the prediction of dissolution of dating relationships and attendant emotional distress. However, these are but two phenomena of interest to relationship investigators. Satisfaction, happiness, and love, for example, are of great interest to some. Quite possibly, one or other (or several) of the approaches to defining and measuring closeness may turn out to be effective predictors of these and other relationship phenomena. Whether or not they do, of course, remains to be seen. It is for this reason, then, that we refrain from concluding this chapter with a recommendation about the "true" or most "valid" method for assessing relationship closeness. To do so, we believe, would help close the door prematurely on the discussion and examination of various methods of assessing closeness, only a few of which we have focused upon here, as well as consideration of the fascinating question of whether certain closeness measures, taken in various combinations and weighted in a variety of ways, might allow extremely accurate prediction of a broad number of relationship phenomena.

REFERENCES

Ahrons, C. R., & Rodgers, R. H. (1987). *Divorced families: A multi-disciplinary developmental view.*

Ajzen, I., & Fishbein, M. (1977). Attitude-behavior relations: A theoretical analysis and review of empirical research. *Psychological Bulletin, 84,* 888-918.

Berndt, T. J. (1986). Children's comments about their friendships. In M. Perlmutter (Ed.), *Cognitive perspectives on children's social and behavioral development: The Minnesota symposia on child psychology* (Vol. 18, pp. 189-212). Hillsdale, NJ: Lawrence Erlbaum.

Berscheid, E. (1983). Emotion. In H. H. Kelley, E. Berscheid, A. Christensen, J. H. Harvey, T. L. Huston, G. Levinger, E. McClintock, L. A. Peplau, & D. R. Peterson, *Close relationships* (pp. 110-168). New York: Freeman.

Berscheid, E. (1985). Interpersonal attraction. In G. Lindzey & E. Aronson (Eds.), *The handbook of social psychology* (3rd ed., pp. 413-484). New York: Random House.

Berscheid, E., & Peplau, L. A. (1983). The emerging science of relationships. In H. H. Kelley, E. Berscheid, A. Christensen, J. H. Harvey, T. L. Huston, G. Levinger, E. McClintock, L. A. Peplau, & D. R. Peterson, *Close relationships* (pp. 1-19). New York: Freeman.

Berscheid, E., Snyder, M., & Omoto, A. M. (in preparation). *Assessing interdependence in interpersonal relationships: The Relationship Closeness Inventory.*

Bradbury, T. N., & Fincham, F. D. (1987). Assessment of affect in marriage. In K. D. O'Leary (Ed.), *Assessment of marital discord: An integration for research and clinical practice.* Hillsdale, NJ: Lawrence Erlbaum.

Clark, M. S., & Reis, H. T. (1988). Interpersonal processes in close relationships. *Annual Review of Psychology, 39,* 609-672.

Fowers, B. J., & Olson, D. H. (1986). Predicting marital success with PREPARE: A predictive validity study. *Journal of Marital and Family Therapy, 12,* 403-413.

Helgeson, V. S., Shaver, P., & Dyer, N. (1987). Prototypes of intimacy and distance in same-sex and opposite-sex relationships. *Journal of Social and Personal Relationships, 4.* 195-233.

Hill, C. T., Rubin, Z., & Peplau, L. A. (1976). Breakups before marriage: The end of 103 affairs. *Journal of Social Issues, 32*(1), 147-168.

Huston, T. L., & Ashmore, R. D. (1986). Women and men in personal relationships. In R. D. Ashmore & F. K. DelBoca (Eds.), *The social psychology of female-male relations: A critical analysis of central concepts* (pp. 167-210). Orlando, FL: Academic Press.

Kelley, H. H., Berscheid, E., Christensen, A., Harvey, J. H., Huston, T. L., Levinger, G, McClintock, E., Peplau, L. A., & Peterson, D. R. (1983). *Close relationships.* New York: Freeman.

Locke, H. J. & Wallace, K. M. (1959). Short marital-adjustment and production tests: Their reliability and validity. *Marriage and Family Living, 21,* 251-255.

Olson, D. H. (1977). Insiders' and outsiders' views of relationships: Research studies. In G. Levinger & H. Rausch (Eds.), *Close Relationships: Perspectives on the meaning of intimacy* (pp. 115-135). Amherst: University of Massachusetts Press.

Rubin, Z., Peplau, L. A., & Hill, C. T. (1981). Loving and leaving: Sex differences in romantic attachments. *Sex Roles, 7,* 821-835.

Rusbult, C. E. (1980). Commitment and satisfaction in romantic associations: A test of the investment model. *Journal of Experimental Social Psychology, 16,* 172-181.

Rusbult, C. E. (1983). A longitudinal test of the investment model: The development (and deterioration) of satisfaction and commitment in heterosexual involvements. *Journal of Personality and Social Psychology, 45,* 101-117.

Simpson, J. A. (1987). The dissolution of romantic relationships: Factors involved in relationship stability and emotional distress. *Journal of Personality and Social Psychology, 53,* 683-692.

Sternberg, R. J., & Grajek, S. (1984). The nature of love. *Journal of Personality and Social Psychology, 47,* 312-329.

Swenson, C. H. (1972). The behavior of love. In H. A. Otto (Ed.), *Love today: A new exploration.* New York: Association Press.

Wheeler, L., & Nezlek, J. (1977). Sex differences in social participation. *Journal of Personality and Social Psychology, 35,* 742-754.

Wheeler, L., Reis, H., & Nezlek, J. (1983). Loneliness, social interaction, and sex roles. *Journal of Personality* and *Social Psychology, 45,* 943-953.

4

A Reproductive Exchange Model
of Heterosexual Relationships
PUTTING PROXIMATE ECONOMICS
IN ULTIMATE PERSPECTIVE

DOUGLAS T. KENRICK
MELANIE R. TROST

Douglas T. Kenrick is an Associate Professor in the Social and Environmental Psychology Programs at Arizona State University. His main theoretical interest is the integration of evolutionary models of behavior with psychologically based learning and cognitive models. His recent research has focused on heterosexual attraction and person/environment interactions.

Melanie R. Trost is a doctoral student in social psychology at Arizona State University. Her research interests include attraction, group processes, and business ethics.

When the first author began his graduate training in social psychology in 1974, a professor proudly informed him that there were no grand theories in social psychology. Judging from the fact that the second author heard the same pronouncement when she started graduate school ten years later, times have not changed very much. A glance at any social psychology text still reveals a conglomeration of findings, at best loosely connected to small-range "minitheories" that scarcely overlap from one chapter to the next. Not everyone finds this lack of general theory idyllic. Recently, a colleague lamented that psychology needs "a Charles Darwin," a grand theorist to put our isolated findings into perspective. He was surprised to hear a biologist respond that we already had one. "Who?" he asked. The biologist replied, "Charles Darwin."

Darwin's theory of evolution by natural selection is almost certainly the grandest of theories in the life sciences, and it has particular appeal as a grand perspective for heterosexual relationships. If there is any area in which the fingerprints of Darwinian evolution should be found, it is

AUTHORS' NOTE: We thank Clyde Hendrick, Warren Jones, and three anonymous reviewers for their helpful comments on an earlier draft. This article was written while the first author was a visiting scholar at the University of Tulsa.

mating behavior. Our ancestors might have succeeded in every other aspect of their fight for survival, but had they neglected reproduction, we would not be here to discuss it. For this reason, reproductive arrangements are a central concern, perhaps the central concern, of evolutionary biologists. Since social psychologists share this central interest with evolutionary biologists, it is surprising that evolutionary theory has had so little influence on social psychological research (Cunningham, 1981). The mutual interest in heterosexual relationships raises other important and relatively unexplored links between the two fields: (a) both emphasize resource exchange as a basis for courtship, and (b) both envision a basically selfish individual seeking maximal personal gain from a relationship. The two fields diverge on their underlying assumptions, however. Psychological models generally assume that culture determines the pattern of the exchange, whereas evolutionary models explain the exchange in terms of reproduction opportunities.

Integrating these two perspectives would benefit both research traditions. Social psychologists have gathered extensive data about the proximate exchange mechanisms in human courtship, but rarely consider the central role of reproduction. At a recent meeting of the *Society of Experimental Social Psychology*, prominent relationship researchers met for a day to discuss the central issues in the area. Given that heterosexual relationships are the main focus of their research, it was surprising that no speaker mentioned reproduction as an important issue. Only one speaker referred to it at all, and even then only in passing, mentioning "children" as third on a list of "extrinsic" determinants of "investment size" (after "sharing friends," and "being a tennis partner"). Social psychologists may be missing a principle that could organize a number of isolated psychological findings. A reproductive exchange model can also incorporate other findings, such as: (a) *gender differences* in courtship exchange that are inconsistent with a cultural model; (b) *cross-cultural universalities* suggesting that different human groups mate in ways similar to one another, but different from most mammalian species; and (c) *hormonal influences* on human courtship.

Grounded in a rich history of theory and research on mating behaviors in various species, evolutionary models can place human courtship in a broader perspective. However, evolutionary approaches suffer their own deficiencies. They are often naive regarding psychological and sociological findings, and they generally pay little attention to temporal changes in relationships. These oversights have led to some confusion in evolutionary predictions and findings regarding human courtship.

We will summarize relationship economics from the social psychological and the evolutionary perspectives, and then review a model that integrates both approaches (Kenrick & Trost, 1987). This biosocial model can generate new predictions that do not follow from either approach in isolation. We will review new findings showing that males and females differ in (a) their approach to resource exchange at different phases of the relationship and (b) the resources they demand of a mate at different stages of the life cycle.

SOCIAL PSYCHOLOGICAL ECONOMICS

Three historical influences have shaped psychological exchange models. First is Gouldner's (1960) formulation of a "social norm of reciprocity" that governs giving and taking in diverse cultures around the world. Second is Homans's (1974) application of the Skinnerian model to the exchange of reinforcements in relationships. Third is Thibaut and Kelley's (1959) model of social interactions based on the notion of interdependent outcomes, in which one person's rewards and costs in a relationship are dependent on those of the person's partner (also see LaGaipa, 1977). Later models share an implicit or explicit emphasis on norms, rewards, and joint outcome calculations (e.g., Huesmann & Levinger, 1976; Walster, Walster, & Berscheid, 1978). Exchange-type models typically assume that relationships are based on economic bartering between actors who are motivated to maximize benefits and minimize costs. This emphasis is perhaps best developed in equity theory (Walster, Berscheid, & Walster, 1973; Walster et al., 1978). This theory assumes that individuals are motivated to achieve a fair ratio of rewards and costs in their relationships, and become uncomfortable when overbenefited or underbenefited. The economic emphasis is nicely captured in a study of singles' advertisements that referred to "the heterosexual stock market," noting that "the ads in this paper read a little bit like the ask-bid columns of the New York Stock Exchange. Potential partners seek to strike bargains which maximize their rewards in the exchange of assets" (Cameron, Oskamp, & Sparks, 1977, p. 28).

Theory and research on the exchange perspective have filled many volumes, and there is no need to review it here. We wish to make five points about this area, however: (a) actors seem to be motivated more by *selfishness* than fairness, and achieve fairness only as a side effect of self-interested bargaining; (b) exchange processes are not static, but show *longitudinal* variations; (c) research has focused on the exchange process and paid less attention to the *content* of the exchange; (d) there are a number of poorly explained *sex differences* in the content of commodities desired; and (e) economic models have emphasized conscious, rational cognition and shed little light on *irrationalities* in heterosexual exchange, or on the *powerful motivational processes* underlying romantic relationships.

Selfishness

One line of support for the equity view is the repeated finding that mates tend to be similar to one another in socially desirable characteristics such as physical attractiveness (Berscheid, Dion, Walster, & Walster, 1971; Huston, 1973; Murstein, 1972). When there is a discrepancy in a characteristic such as physical attractiveness, it may be compensated for in other dimensions, such as education or income (Berscheid, Walster, & Bohrnstedt, 1973; Elder, 1969; Holmes & Hatch, 1938). A study by Kiesler and Baral (1970) supports the notion that people are motivated to achieve equity. In that study, men with lowered self-esteem showed more romantic interest in unattractive than in attractive female confederates.

Other research indicates that people are not particularly motivated to end up with someone similar in "value" as much as they are constrained by their own exchange value. For instance, Walster, Aronson, Abrahams, and Rottmann (1966) found that although people's demands in a computer date were limited by their own attractiveness, subjects were most satisfied by good-looking partners, regardless of their own attractiveness. The mismatched pairs were terminated by the attractive partner's unwillingness to continue in an underbenefited situation, not by the unattractive person's unwillingness to date someone more desirable.

"Communal relationships" (Clark & Mills, 1979; Mills & Clark, 1982) present a qualified exception to the rule of selfishness. Clark and Mills found that people who are, or want to be, in an intimate relationship do not keep an explicit tally of what and how much has been exchanged. Instead, intimates exchange resources according to each one's present need. Although this finding sounds like an example of "selflessness," communal relationships do not indicate a true exception to the selfishness rule. People enter communal relationships only with those pretested for trustworthiness, and there is some suggestion that people are especially motivated to enter communal arrangements with unattached, attractive members of the opposite sex. Mills and Clark (1982) noted that "people do not desire communal relationships with unattractive people. They prefer to treat such others in terms of exchange" (p. 130). They also found that even an attractive person is more likely to be treated in exchange terms if that attractive person is attached. Male subjects preferred a communal relationship with an attractive unmarried female, but explicit reciprocation if she was married. As we shall see below, the fact that individuals in relationships are more selfish than they are normatively equitable is quite consistent with a reproductive exchange perspective, as is the suggestion that overt selfishness is reduced in relationships with attractive and available members of the opposite sex.

The Longitudinal Perspective

Several researchers have noted that exchange processes change with the course of a relationship (Altman & Taylor, 1973; Duck, 1978; Levinger & Huesmann, 1980; Levinger & Snoek, 1972; Murstein, 1972). For instance, Murstein presumed that stimulus factors (such as physical attractiveness) are important early in a relationship, and that explicit exchange rules are pertinent at that time. Later, however, similarity of values is emphasized, and exact matching is more important than marketplace exchange. Research has yielded only mild support for discontinuous stage theories of exchange (Murstein, 1981), and more recent theorists favor a modified notion of flexible and overlapping "phases" (Levinger, 1983). In any case, it appears that extended relationships operate according to different exchange rules than brief encounters (Clark & Reis, in press). For instance, Clark and Mills's (1979) research found a more communal orientation in relationships that were expected to continue into the future. This longitudinal perspective can help clarify some findings in the evolutionary literature on relationships, to be discussed below.

The Content of Exchange

Researchers have focused on the process of exchange and paid less attention to what is exchanged. Levinger and Huesmann (1980) simply assumed that reward "is a many splendored thing" and argued that it is unlikely that all of its facets will be captured within a single theory. Some theorists have assumed that the different commodities can all be collapsed into one category, "information" (e.g., Altman & Taylor, 1973; Duck, 1978). However, Foa and Foa (1980) categorized resources into six classes—love, status, information, money, goods, and services. They described love as a "particularistic" resource: It is valued only when it comes from certain intimates, and is mainly exchanged in kind. Money, on the other hand, can be exchanged with anyone for anything (except love). Although Foa and Foa noted that love is restricted to intimate relationships, little research attention has addressed the association between resource content and type of relationship. Hatfield, Utne, and Traupmann (1979) suggested that intimate relationships simply involve the exchange of more types of resources, and that intimates are more likely to substitute resources in one category for those in another. As we shall discuss below, the evolutionary perspective assumes that there are important distinctions between the resources exchanged in heterosexual relationships and in other relationships. Exchange of reproductive value is a qualitatively different game, and it is not the same game for females as it is for males.

Sex Differences

Males and females take different approaches to the "heterosexual stock market." Females are more likely to shop for economic resources and older partners. On the other hand, males seem to be in the market for physically attractive younger partners (Brehm, 1985; Cameron, Oskamp, & Sparks, 1977; Elder, 1969; Harrison & Saeed, 1977; Koestner & Wheeler, in press; Murstein, 1972). A cross-cultural study (Dickemann, 1981) found that high-status men were more likely to demand evidence of virginity in a potential bride.

Social psychologists explain sex differences in partner requirements in terms of social norms. As Brehm said, "Traditionally, in our society, males have been valued for their economic success, and females for their physical attractiveness" (Brehm, 1985; p. 76). Likewise, Cameron et al. (1977) explained their finding that females preferred taller, older, intelligent, high status males as due to "traditional sex-role specifications... frequently valued as sex-appropriate in American society," which specify that women should "look up to" their male partners, both literally and figuratively. The assumption that arbitrary social norms underlie gender differences is an unexamined and "obvious" basic tenet among social psychologists. However, Cameron et al. noted the discrepancy between the advertisements and the liberated norms of California in the late 1970s, and concluded that "traditionally sex-appropriate characteristics were claimed and desired, suggesting that shifting sex role expectations are not evident in this type of mate selection" (p. 27). Inconsistencies between changing norms and gender differences in relationships pose no problem from the biosocial position. Our position assumes that the resources exchanged in relationships pertain to ultimate reproductive capabilities, not variable cultural norms.

Limitations of Conscious Cognitive Calculations

Courtship relationships may have some characteristics of economic exchange, but they are hardly exchanges between "rational man" and "rational woman." For instance, the age requirements in singles advertisements hardly seem adjusted to what the market will bear. Cameron et al. (1977) found that women advertisers were slightly over 41 years of age and looking for men who were an average of 3 years older. Men placing ads were 39, on average, and looking for women 7 years younger. As Cameron et al. (1977, p. 29) noted, "since the average age of the women advertisers was over 9 years older than that desired by male advertisers, a serious problem of matching is evident." Bolig, Stein, and McKenry (1984, p. 592) likewise noted "the men who placed profiles in this magazines were not looking for the women who placed profiles (nor were the women looking for these men)." Though one could argue that people only place advertisements for partners with commodities that are in short supply, scarcity does not explain why the men and women advertisers are discrepant in opposite directions.

After the initial bargains have been struck, established romantic relationships also seem to defy simple rational exchange economics. Berscheid (1987) found that college students chose romantic partners as their "closest" relationship more frequently than friends or relatives, despite the fact that romantic relationships had a shorter history of mutual interaction, and were more likely to involve negative inter-actions. Romantic relationships pose a particular problem for theories of people as cool-headed accountants seeking maximal rewards. Those relationships are powerfully laden with emotion from start to finish, from the ecstasies and agonies of early romantic love to their sometimes painful endings. Divorce and separation are strongly associated with alcoholism, drug abuse, and mental hospital admission (Sarason & Sarason, 1987). If simple exchange of rewards was the rule, people would also seek hospitalization when their butcher of forty years (who has provided delicious rewards, always for a fair price) goes out of business. Likewise, it is easier to bear separation from a same sex friend who has worked by our side for a decade and who is similar enough to be our twin than to leave a battle-torn relationship with a lover who, by every rational standard, is not right for us. If "normative" pressures were the key, why does the anguish of separation persist in the face of unanimous feedback from friends that "you're better off without the jerk"? Normative theorists might argue that heterosexual separations are more unpleasant because of the heavy investment in mating relationships, but that would not explain *why* the discrepancy in investment strategy exists. If one simply considers that successful reproduction is the driving force of evolution, however, the special emotional power of sexual relationships makes immediate sense. We now turn to this issue.

EVOLUTIONARY ECONOMICS

Slightly over a century ago, Darwin outlined the three components of his classical argument for *natural selection*:

(1) Animals reproduce at rates that quickly exhaust their available resources. For instance, a single pair of elephants doubling every 30 years could produce about 4,000,000,000 offspring in 11 centuries. In just a tick of the evolutionary clock the globe would be overrun by pachyderms. Competition for scarce resources, however, limits unbridled population expansion.

(2) There are heritable variations between and within any animal species. For instance, genes influence human individual differences in physical traits such as height and psychological characteristics like shyness. (Loehlin & Nichols, 1976)

(3) Any variation that helps in the competition for scarce resources or more successful reproduction will be selected. To evolutionary biologists, all presently surviving animals are selfish gene-replicating machines, and humans are no exception (Barash, 1977; Dawkins, 1976; Wilson, 1975). Adaptive variations are not limited to "tooth-and-claw" competitive advantages. Even cooperative and helpful acts may be genetically selfish strategies that, in the evolutionary past, assisted relatives with common genes. (Campbell, 1983; Hamilton, 1964)

Successful reproduction is thus the name of the game, according to the evolutionary view. Evolutionary theorists also assume that male and female mammals are selected to play slightly different mating strategies, as a function of *differential parental investment*, and the resulting *sexual selection*.

Differential Parental Investment

As a parable about gender differences in reproductive strategies, evolutionary biologists tell an anecdote about Calvin Coolidge, his wife, and a certain barnyard rooster:

One day the President and Mrs. Coolidge were visiting a government farm. Soon after their arrival they were taken off on separate tours. When Mrs. Coolidge passed the chicken pens she paused to ask the man in charge if the rooster copulates more than once each day. "Dozens of times" was the reply. "Please tell that to the President," Mrs. Coolidge requested. When the President passed the pens and was told about the rooster, he asked "Same hen every time?" "Oh, no, Mr. President, a different one each time." The President nodded slowly, then said "Tell that to Mrs Coolidge." (Bermant, 1976, pp. 76-77)

Many biological theorists would argue that the Coolidge anecdote illustrates a gender difference pervasive enough to span the wide evolutionary distance from humans to barnyard chickens. Across that span, polygyny tends to be more common than polyandry. That is, it is more likely that several females will share one male sexual partner than the reverse. Male and female vertebrates commonly have sexual preferences that parallel these sorts of mating arrangements. For instance, males tend to be more promiscuous. Even after a male rat has had intercourse with one female until he appears satiated to the point of fatigue, his interests will rekindle if a new female is placed into the cage with him. A female rat, on the other hand, prefers a familiar partner over a novel one. Although this gender difference is not as pronounced in some species as in others, it is prevalent enough to have earned a name. In honor of the late president and the famed anecdotal rooster, it has been dubbed the "Coolidge effect" (Dewsbury, 1981).

Evolutionary theorists explain these gender differences in terms of the *differential parental investment model* (Trivers, 1972; Williams, 1966). The model presumes that males and females play different reproductive strategies. Because offspring grow inside the female's body and must later be nursed, mammalian females are constrained to a small number of progeny. Therefore, females invest more resources in any single potential offspring, and must be more selective in their mate choice. Males, conversely, provide less direct resources for any given offspring and have less to lose from an ill-chosen mating.

Sexual Selection

If females' inherently greater parental investment predisposes them to be choosier than males, how do they exercise their greater choosiness? There are two primary possibilities. Charles Darwin (1859/1958) suggested one mechanism called *sexual selection*:

This form of selection depends, not on a struggle for existence in relation to other organic beings or to external conditions, but a struggle between the individuals of one sex, generally the males, for the possession of the other sex. The result is not death to the unsuccessful competitor, but few or no offspring. . . . Generally, the most vigorous males, those which are best fitted for their places in nature, will leave most progeny. But in many cases, victory depends not so much on general vigor, as on having special weapons, confined to the male sex. (p. 94)

This preference for males who overtly display their superiority over their competitors will, over generations of natural selection, lead to a steeply graded dominance hierarchy among males. It will simultaneously select for greater size and weaponry among males. It can also result in ostentatious displays of male success, like the colorful plumage in certain male birds. For instance, Andersson (1982) found that female widowbirds were more likely to mate with males whose tail feather displays were experimentally elongated, and to reject males with experimentally shortened tails. Sexual selection of dramatic physical features has received the most attention, but females may use other selection criteria. They can select males who are willing to directly invest resources in the offspring. Birds, for instance, commonly form *pair bonds* in which the male helps to build the nest, to feed and protect the young, and so on. Compared to species in which females select from a small group of noninvesting males, pair-bonded mates are more similar in physical structure. This particular pattern is not prevalent among mammals, since direct male input is usually less necessary. For instance, herd-dwelling antelopes have calves that can walk shortly after birth, and male input is simply not required.

What About Humans?

Where do we fit in? Humans are not like many other mammalian species in which the female gains little from the male's continual presence. Human offspring are helpless at birth, and continue to be dependent for a long period, two characteristics commonly associated with mating bonds (Barash, 1977). Beyond the theoretical reasons for considering humans atypical among mammals, there are data that make the distinctions obvious. One need only look at our own society to find a well established pattern of male-female parent bonding. According to the 1983 U.S. Census statistics, approximately 95% of all Americans get married. Although one commonly hears claims that cross-cultural data reveal a near infinite variation in mating arrangements, a close examination of the findings does not support that claim. Daly and Wilson (1979) examined data from over 800 societies and found some form of marriage in *every* known society. While there may well be cultural variation in the specifics of mating bonds, the bonds themselves are a universal feature of human society. This is in contrast to most other mammalian species, where parents do not bond.

In many human cultures, the norms have *permitted* the more common mammalian pattern of polygyny, but it is still a very qualified tendency. First of all, no society is purely polygynous. Even in stately India, where several maharajahs had over 100 wives, the most common marital arrangement remained a single man and a woman. Second, even in those polygynous societies, the pattern involved high *direct investment* by the father. The maharajah was not chosen as a mate solely for his dominant genes. He was chosen for his riches. Those resources were sufficient to provide many children and wives with more support than they could have received in a monogamous relationship with a commoner. The human father's direct investment also contrasts with males in highly polygynous nonhuman species, who usually provide little more than genes for their offspring.

Humans are not completely out of line with typical mammalian patterns, however. Sex differences are ubiquitous in the human sexuality literature. In line with the "Coolidge effect," males are generally more sexually eager and less discriminating. For instance, one of us found that males were more likely to volunteer for experiments on erotica than were females (Kenrick, Stringfield, Wagenhals, Dahl, & Ransdell, 1980). This result fits with other evidence that males seek more experience with erotica (e.g., Kinsey, Pomeroy, & Martin, 1948; Kinsey, Pomeroy, Martin, & Gebhard, 1953; Shepher & Reisman, 1985). More generally, males are overrepresented in virtually every category of sexual deviation (Davison & Neale, 1982). Such differences in sexual inclination are found cross-culturally, too. From the Mangaian islanders, famous for their promiscuity, to the Inis Beag islanders off the Irish coast, famous for their prudishness, men are reputedly more sexually eager (Marshall, 1971; Messenger, 1971).

In support of the differential investment hypothesis, Hinde (1984) reviewed findings that men are often willing to sleep with someone they desire sexually, even in the absence of love, whereas women are more likely to see sex and love as inseparable. For instance, Peplau, Rubin, and Hill (1977) found that females tended to lose their virginity in a relationship where both partners reported high love and intimacy, whereas male's loss of virginity was not related to love or other measures of emotional intimacy in the partners. Similarly, Lewis, Casto, Aquilino, and McGuffin (1978) found that men, compared with women, were more likely to view sex and intimacy as separate.

In the animal kingdom, direct investment of resources by the male is generally associated with low *sexual dimorphism* (or physical differences between males and females; Hinde, 1984). In promiscuous species, only a few males mate, and they face fierce competition as a result of differential sexual selection by females. In baboons, for instance, males are twice the size of the females, and have elaborate "special weapons," like those Darwin noted. However, the sexes are more similar in appearance in monogamous species (since the monogamous female is not in the strong position of a comparison shopper, and the monogamous male can lose more from an ill-chosen match). Relatively speaking, humans exhibit some dimorphism, but it is not dramatic. The average man is 25% to 30% heavier than the average woman, and only 8% to 10% taller. At equivalent levels of training, male upper body strength is about 50% more than that of females, but lower body strength is about equal (Doyle, 1985). Compared with peacocks and baboons, our species differs much less on secondary sexual characteristics. Males have additional bodily and facial hair, but females also have special features such as fatty deposits on their breasts and hips. To evolutionary biologists, the lack of extreme differences would suggest that *both* male and female hominids were subject to sexual selection pressures (Daly & Wilson, 1979).

Monogamous males select females for slightly different characteristics than those for which females select males. Since a female mammal carries and nurses the young, her reproductive hardiness is important to the male. On the other hand, females select males for characteristics that indicate their ability to provide direct resources for the offspring (Buss & Barnes, 1986).

In sum, humans are neither a pure case of mammalian polygyny nor of the monogamous patterns common among birds. Our helpless and slow-developing offspring seem to have co-evolved with male parental investment, but our mammalian reproductive physiology maintains some constant differences in parental investment and sexual selection (Daly & Wilson, 1979).

Beyond our "impurity" as a typical polygynous or monogamous species, there may be biologically-based individual differences in mating strategies within our species. There is some evidence of stable and heritable individual differences between people in the extent to which they adopt either what biologists call the *K*-strategy (high investment in a small number of offspring, associated with monogamy) versus the *r*-strategy (lower investment, high fecundity strategy, associated with early mating and promiscuity) (Kenrick & Trost, 1987; Rowe, Rodgers, Meseck-Bushey, & St. John, 1987; Rushton, 1985).

Explanatory Power of the Evolutionary Framework

The evolutionary model places a number of social psychological findings in ultimate perspective. It explains the "selfishness" that predominates in social exchange, despite all the normative pressures towards selflessness (Campbell, 1975). The evolutionary perspective also has no difficulty making sense of the fact that relationships with attractive, available mating partners drift toward "communal exchange." It has obvious implications for explaining the gender differences found in the "heterosexual stock market." Findings that females seek older partners who can provide financial resources and that males seek younger, attractive partners do not leave the evolutionary theorist puzzled about the genesis of the arbitrary norms underlying those differences. They fit with the evolutionary view that women select men for their resource contributions to the offspring, while men select women for their reproductive potential (as signaled by physical signs of health and youth; Buss & Barnes, 1986; Cunningham, 1986). As we noted above, the evolutionary model explains why romantic relationships are often motivated in powerful and irrational ways. Since human courtship involves extensive testing and bonding for the purpose of reproduction (Kenrick & Trost, 1987), a romantic relationship is much more significant than, and less interchangeable than, a relationship with a friend or a butcher.

In addition to placing the social psychological findings in a wider perspective, the evolutionary model easily incorporates some findings that make no sense from the cognitive/normative perspective of social psychology. First, there are a number of *cross-cultural universals* in human courtship. At the most basic level, Eibl-Eibesfeldt (1975) found fascinating evidence of a universal nonverbal language in flirtation. He unobtrusively filmed flirting couples all around the world, and then had observers examine the films in slow motion. To quote him,

> we found agreement in the smallest detail in the flirting behavior of girls from Samoa, Papua, France, Japan, Africa (Turcana and other Niloto-hamite tribes, Himba, Bushmen) and South American Indians (Waika, Orinoko). The flirting girl at first smiles at her partner and lifts her

eyebrows with a quick, jerky movement upward so that the eye slit is briefly enlarged. . . . After this initial, obvious turning toward the person, in the flirt there follows a turning away. The head is turned to the side, sometimes bent toward the ground, the gaze is lowered, and the eyelids are dropped . . . the girl may cover her face with a hand and she may laugh or smile in embarrassment. She continues to look at the partner out of the corners of her eyes and sometimes vacillates between that and an embarrassed looking away. (p. 465)

Eibl-Eibesfeldt thought it unlikely that this universal pattern was *taught* to young women in widely separated cultures. Instead, he viewed the sequence as akin to courtship gestures in other animals. Just as peacocks and peahens can flirt without words, so can humans.

We mentioned another universal in human mating arrangements: All human cultures have some form of marriage. This fact seems unsurprising when we confine our observations only to our species, but it is important to note that it is contrary to the typical mammalian pattern. So despite the wide cultural relativity that anthropologists have touted, no human culture has randomly hit upon the pattern so common among other mammals—polygyny with no emotional bond between parents. Polygyny is *permitted* in the majority of human cultures (708 out of 849 examined) and polyandry is also permitted in 4 of the 708, but even polygamous attachments are bonded, and most individuals in polygamous cultures nevertheless mate monogamously. Social exchange theory would assume that polygyny is much more common than polyandry because males have more resources. If so, then males should demand a better bargain in heterosexual relationships. We will present new data below that directly contradict that assumption.

Psychological models that assume conscious cognitive causes also cannot address the relationship between hormones and courtship behaviors. Elsewhere, we review evidence that testosterone is involved in initiating sexual contacts at several stages of the relationship (Kenrick & Trost, 1987). Testosterone is also associated with sexual interest in both sexes (Bancroft, 1978; Svare & Kinsley, 1987), and while females produce some testosterone in their adrenal glands, males produce much greater quantities in their testes. Testosterone is also associated with dominance behaviors (Mazur & Lamb, 1980; Rose, Holaday, & Bernstein, 1971). In line with the sexual selection literature, dominance behaviors are associated with male attractiveness in a number of vertebrate species, including our own (Sadalla, Kenrick, & Vershure, 1987). The fact that males chronically produce greater quantities of testosterone is therefore consistent with cross-cultural and cross-methodological findings of more sexual advances by males. Hormonal findings fit with the argument that humans have not evolved away from the pattern of differential sexual selection in which females select males for evidence of dominance.

INTEGRATING THE TWO PERSPECTIVES

We have been discussing the advantage of expanding exchange models to include the evolutionary perspective. On the other hand, evolutionary theorists often focus too heavily on nonhuman species (Alexander, 1979), and could profit from attending to research and theory in the psychological tradition. We have previously reviewed findings supporting a biosocial integration that incorporates the two perspectives (Kenrick & Trost, 1987). Consistent with the psychological models, we assume that (a) there are longitudinal changes in relationship exchange, and (b) partners seek information about rewarding characteristics in the partner. Consistent with the evolutionary models, we assume that (c) reproduction is the organizing theme of courtship, the most crucial traits in the partner being those that signal direct or indirect contribution to potential offspring; and (d) male and female courtship strategies differ in accord with the parental investment model. Our general scheme is depicted in Figure 4.1.

Kenrick and Trost (1987) used the biosocial framework to integrate a number of existing findings in the psychological and biological literatures. Here, we wish to address the heuristic potential of the biosocial model to generate new findings. Below we summarize two recent lines of research that combine the insights of the two perspectives.

A Time-Qualified Parental Investment Model:
I. Relationship Course

As noted above, evolutionary theorists view humans as combining the mating characteristics of polygynous and monogamous species. This has led to some confusion in applying the differential parental investment/sexual selection model to humans, as evidenced by two recently published studies. Testing a prediction derived from the parental investment hypothesis, Sadalla, Kenrick, and Vershure (1987) found that college age females were more sexually attracted to male strangers who expressed nonverbal dominance. Male subjects' attraction was not influenced by dominance in female targets (one way or the other). The results were robust, dominance enhanced male attractiveness

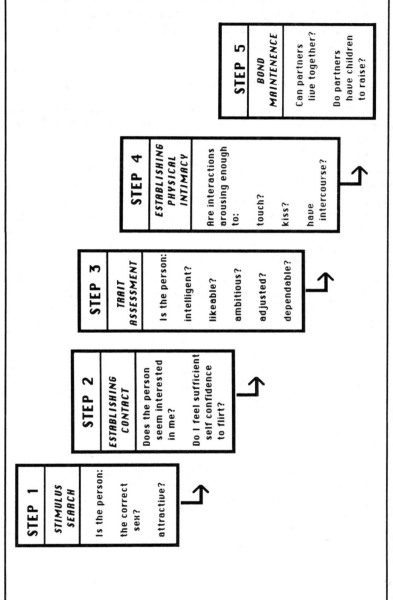

Figure 4.1 Schematic representation of Kenrick and Trost's (1987) Biosocial Model of Relationship Formations.

across four different studies using three very distinct operationalizations, and Sadalla and Fausal (1980) found similar results with middle-aged workers at a large factory.

Buss and Barnes (1986) used a survey design and asked students to rank the characteristics they preferred in a mate. Consistent with findings of earlier surveys, they also found sex differences. Females ranked "good earning capacity" and "college graduate" as more important than males did, while males ranked "physically attractive" higher than did females. Applying the sexual selection hypothesis, Buss and Barnes suggested that earning capacity and education level may provide cues about a male's potential to invest resources in the offspring, whereas physical attractiveness may relate to a female's health and age, and so reflect on fertility. However, the most striking feature of the Buss and Barnes data was the similarity between males' and females' mate preferences. Seven of the ten highest rated preferences did not differ between the sexes. Consistent with our earlier argument, Buss and Barnes mentioned that differential sexual selection is diminished in species like ours (i.e., species that are monogamous and in which most mating-age individuals pair off). This point fits with the suggestion that humans have an inclination toward differential sexual selection that is moderated by strong monogamous tendencies.

When do humans act like polygynous species, with females being more selective (as in the Sadalla et al., 1987 study) and when do we act like monogamous species, with both sexes showing high selectivity (as in the Buss and Barnes, 1986 study)? Our awareness of the social psychological focus on longitudinal changes in relationship exchange suggested a possible answer to this question. An evolutionary perspective offers compelling reasons to expect that the sex difference in selectivity will interact with the amount of time that the partners have invested in one another. In fact, monogamous species typically have a lengthy courtship period that precedes mating. Presumably this lengthy courtship gives *both* members of the pair time to appraise one another's value as a potential parent (Barash, 1977). Polygynous species, on the other hand, have very brief courtships. Here it is common to find a pattern in which multiple females mate with males who are demonstrably superior to their competitors (as indicated by high dominance rankings and/or physical characteristics).

We would therefore expect longer human courtships to be associated with increasing selectivity by the male. When it comes to choosing a marital partner, in whose offspring the male is going to invest resources for what may be a lifetime, males' pickiness should start to approach

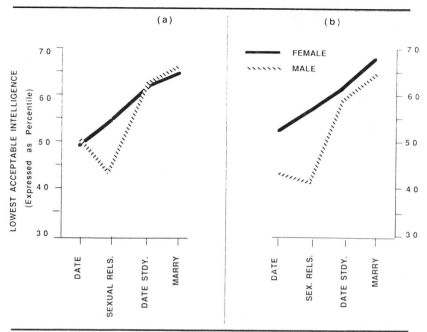

Figure 4.2 Minimum percentile intelligence required by males and females at different levels of relationship involvement: Based on (a) "Gender and trait requirements in a mate: An evolutionary bridge between personality and social psychology," by D. T. Kenrick, E. K. Sadalla, G. Groth, and M. R. Trost (in press), and (b) "Gender differences in mate selection criteria vary with different phases of courtship," by D. T. Kenrick, M. R. Trost, G. Groth, and E. K. Sadalla (1988).

that of females'. On the other hand, males should be less selective when they have a chance for a casual mating opportunity. Under these circumstances, males stand to invest less time and resources in the partner. Casual mating opportunities should most clearly highlight the gender differences, and reflect a pattern closer to that of the polygynous species. That is, males and females should differ most in casual sexual relations. To test this hypothesis, Kenrick, Sadalla, Groth, and Trost (in press) asked college women and men about their minimum standards in a partner at four different levels of relationship involvement: (a) a single date, (b) sexual relations, (c) steady dating, or (d) marriage. Consistent with a time-qualified parental investment hypothesis, we found an interaction between subject gender and level of involvement. In moving from a single date to sexual relations, females increased their minimum criteria; males tended either to decrease or to remain level in their demands. Figure 4.2 depicts the results for the "intelligence" variable, and also includes results from a second study in this series, which replicated the same pattern of findings at a different university (Kenrick, Trost, Groth, & Sadalla, 1988).

As indicated in the figure, men were willing to have sexual relations with someone that did not meet their minimum intelligence criteria for a date.

This research shows the advantage of enlarging the evolutionary models to include the temporal dimension usually considered by social psychologists. Evolutionary models have not adequately considered the distinction between different levels of involvement in human relationships. We replicated the findings of both Buss and Barnes's (1986) study and Sadalla et al.'s (1987) research. Our findings suggest that Buss and Barnes's focus on criteria for a "mate" led them to find fewer strong sex differences than they would have found had they examined other levels of involvement. Conversely, Sadalla et al. (1987) found clear sex differences because they focused on a stranger's "sexual attractiveness."

The approach used here extends the traditional social psychological models, as well. In both studies, we found stronger results than one usually sees in temporal interaction studies. Social psychologists may have missed the point of courtship by focusing too heavily on normative explanations. Normative models would not have led us to expect the sex differences found by Kenrick, Sadalla, Groth, and Trost (in press) and Kenrick, Trost, Groth, and Sadalla (1988). Since males have greater earning potential and higher position in the social status hierarchy (see Tavris & Wade, 1984), a simple equity account that ignored the central role of reproductive potential would be unlikely to predict that females are *more* demanding than males.

A Time-Qualified Parental Investment Model:
II. Life Course

Several psychologists have used "lonely-hearts" advertisements as an unobtrusive measure of economic exchange in the mating process. Advertisements in "singles" newspapers allow for the nonreactive, naturalistic examination of mating preferences, and are particularly well suited for examining what are usually tacit economic exchange considerations (Bolig et al., 1984; Cameron et al., 1977; Harrison & Saeed, 1977; Lynn & Bolig, 1985). One of the clearest findings from these studies is a gender difference in age preferences: Females tend to

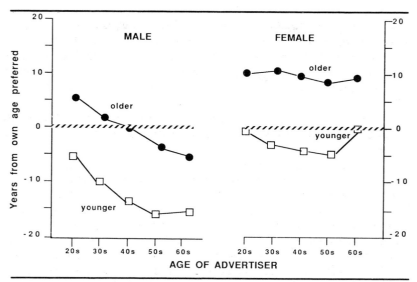

**Figure 4.3 Minimum and maximum age preferences specified by males and
females in singles advertisements, plotted as a function of the solicitor's
age. Based on "Gender and age requirements in a mate fit a reproductive
exchange model," by D. T. Kenrick and R. C. Keefe. Manuscript
submitted for publication.**

seek older males, males to seek younger females. This finding is
compatible with a reproductive exchange model. However, the model
leads to another prediction that would not follow from the normative
exchange models. We would expect that advancing age will change the
shape of the gender difference, mainly by affecting the male pattern of
preferences. It is not youth, in itself, that should be attractive to males.
Youth should only be attractive to the extent that it is associated with
differential reproductive value. Therefore younger males should show
less attraction toward younger females than do older males. However,
the difference should become more pronounced with age, as males and
females diverge in the number of remaining reproductive years.

The previous studies only considered the general "norm" that females
prefer older males, and did not further partition the preference data
once the normative expectation was supported. To test the reproductive
exchange model, Kenrick and Keefe (1988) examined advertisements
from a source similar to those used in the earlier studies. Kenrick and
Keefe used only advertisements that specified a minimum and maximum
desired age for a partner, as well as the age of the advertiser. Breaking
down these data by advertiser's gender and decade of age yields the
pattern shown in Figure 4.3.

As can be seen, there was a significant gender by age interaction for both minimum and maximum age specified. Female specifications remained fairly constant throughout the age range. Females were not particularly averse to partners who were slightly younger than themselves, and were, at all ages, interested in males up to a decade older than themselves. Males, on the other hand, changed substantially as they grew older. Males in their twenties were not very dissimilar to younger females in their preferences, specifying partners ranging, on average, from five years younger to five years older. As males got older, however, their preferences increasingly diverged from those of females. Males in their 50s and 60s specified a maximum acceptable age below their own age and a minimum almost a generation discrepant from their own age.

These data indicate that age preferences are more complex than earlier analyses led us to expect. Previous studies suggested a simple relationship: males seek younger females, and females seek older males. Our results are consistent with half of that generalization; females do seek males who are, on average, slightly older than them (although a bit younger is generally acceptable). For males, however, the preference for younger females is hardly evident during the 20s, but becomes exaggerated in older males.

Previous authors did not detect the developmental variations in the gender discrepancy in age preference. However, they did note that the age discrepancies were somewhat irrational in terms of the usual "marketplace" analogy. Our data also seem to support Bolig et al.'s (1984) observation that the people who place these ads are not looking for one another. The discrepancy becomes even more marked when the data are analyzed developmentally. Older males also violate the strong similarity/attraction principle in their search for women a generation younger. However, the economic rationalities of the male preferences weigh differently from a reproductive viewpoint. The pattern can be explained parsimoniously by assuming that reproductive value weighs heavily, and by noting that older females have increasingly fewer reproductive years left.

CONCLUSION

As social psychologists tuned to proximate environmental variations, we have often been frustrated when our carefully manipulated situations seem to produce effects that can only be detected with the aid of a square root transformation on a special contrast performed under an electron microscope on Windsorized data. In that context, we have been impressed with how differently males and females have acted in our studies of attraction and sexuality, even when we did not expect them to (Kenrick, 1987). If one stays within the bounds of the traditional social psychological explanations, each sex difference is explained as due to another arbitrary norm thrown onto the heap of random historical accidents that need to be drummed into the heads of the next generation by rote. The "collection of arbitrary norms" viewpoint cannot address several troublesome questions: Why do males and females differ on traits related to aggressiveness, dominance, and child care across all human cultures (Daly & Wilson, 1979; Williams & Best, 1982)? Why do other primates share so many of the same "historical accidents" in role assignment with our own species (Hinde, 1974, 1984; Lancaster, 1975)? Why does the hormone testosterone have effects on sex-stereotyped male behaviors such as aggressiveness, dominance, and overworked libido (Rose, Bernstein, & Gordon, 1975; Mazur & Lamb, 1980; Svare & Kinsley, 1987)? An evolutionary perspective not only allows us to connect these findings with one another, but also to organize them into a framework that can clarify numerous disconnected findings in the psychology of relationships (Kenrick & Trost, 1987). That perspective weaves the relationship findings into a nomological network that connects not only personality and social psychology (Kenrick, Montello, & MacFarlane, 1985), but all of the social and biological sciences (Lumsden & Wilson, 1981; McDougall, 1908).

We therefore think that the biologist who said Charles Darwin was the ultimate grand theorist was partly right, but only partly. Evolutionary theory provides a necessary structure for organizing many psychological findings, but a multidisciplinary approach is necessary if we are to answer crucial questions about how ontogenetic learning processes lock into that evolutionary base, and how ongoing processes of cognition are in turn nested in ontogeny and phylogeny. Elsewhere we have reviewed evidence to support our conviction that the study of social cognition must be nested within the framework of social learning, and that both need to be nested within the framework of social biology (Kenrick, 1987; Kenrick, Dantchik, & MacFarlane, 1983; Kenrick, Montello, & MacFarlane, 1985). The self-contained study of social psychological mini-phenomena, with no regard to their ultimate significance, may be fun, but it is like a theory of pyramids based on the study of isolated bricks shipped from Egypt to London and New York without a note of explanation.

REFERENCES

Alexander, R. D. (1979). Natural selection and social exchange. In R. L. Burgess & T. L. Huston (Eds.), *Social exchange in developing relationships* (pp. 197-221). New York: Academic Press.

Altman, I., & Taylor, D.A. (1973). *Social penetration: The development of interpersonal relationships.* New York: Holt, Rinehart & Winston.

Andersson, M. (1982, October 28). Female choice selects for extreme tail length in a widowbird. *Nature*, pp. 818-820.

Bancroft, J. (1978). The relationship between hormones and sexual behavior in humans. In J. B. Hutchison (Ed.), *Biological determinants of sexual behavior* (pp. 493-520). Chichester, England: John Wiley.

Barash, D. P. (1977). *Sociobiology and behavior.* New York: Elsevier.

Bermant, G. (1976). Sexual behavior: Hard times with the Coolidge effect. In M. H. Siegel & H. P. Ziegler (Eds.), *Psychological research: The inside story* (pp. 76-103). New York: Harper & Row.

Berscheid, E. (1987, October). How should we define and measure closeness? In E. Berscheid, K. Davis, I. Sarason, & M. Snyder (Discussion leaders), *Controversies in the conceptualization and measurement of relationship phenomena.* Discussion session conducted at the Pre-conference Meeting of the Society of Experimental Social Psychology, Charlottesville, VA.

Berscheid, E., Dion, K., Walster, E., & Walster, G. W. (1971). Physical attractiveness and dating choice: A test of the matching hypothesis. *Journal of Experimental Social Psychology, 7,* 173-189.

Berscheid, E., Walster, E., & Bohrnstedt, G. (1973, November). The body image report. *Psychology Today,* pp. 119-123, 126, 128-131.

Bolig, R., Stein, P. J., & McKenry, P. C. (1984). The self-advertisement approach to dating: Male-female differences. *Family Relations, 33,* 587-592.

Brehm, S. S. (1985). *Intimate relationships.* New York: Random House.

Buss, D. M., & Barnes, M. (1986). Preferences in human mate selection. *Journal of Personality and Social Psychology, 50,* 559-570.

Cameron, C., Oskamp, S., & Sparks, W. (1977). Courtship American style: Newspaper ads. *Family Coordinator, 26,* 27-30.

Campbell, D. T. (1975). On the conflicts between biological and social evolution and between psychology and moral tradition. *American Psychologist, 30,* 1103-1126.

Campbell, D. T. (1983). The two distinct routes beyond kin selection to ultrasociality: Implications for the humanities and social sciences. In D. Bridgeman (Ed.), *The nature of prosocial development: Interdisciplinary theories and strategies* (pp. 11-41). New York: Academic Press.

Clark, M. S., & Mills, J. (1979). Interpersonal attraction in exchange and communal relationships. *Journal of Personality and Social Psychology, 37,* 12-24.

Clark, M. S., & Reis, H. T. (in press). Interpersonal processes in close relationships. *Annual Review of Psychology.*

Cunningham, M. R. (1981). Sociobiology as a supplementary paradigm for social psychological research. In L. Wheeler (Ed.), *Review of personality and social psychology* (Vol. 2, pp. 69-106). Beverly Hills, CA: Sage.

Cunningham, M. R. (1986). Measuring the physical in physical attractiveness: Quasi-experiments on the sociobiology of female facial beauty. *Journal of Personality and Social Psychology, 50,* 925-935.

Daly, M., & Wilson, M. (1979). *Sex, evolution, and behavior: Adaptations for reproduction.* North Scituate, MA: Duxbury.

Darwin, C. (1958). *The origin of species* (6th ed.). New York: New American Library. (Original work published 1859)

Davison, G. C., & Neale, J. M. (1982). *Abnormal psychology* (3rd ed.). New York: John Wiley.

Dawkins, R. (1976). *The selfish gene.* Oxford: Oxford University Press.

Dewsbury, D. A. (1981). Effects of novelty on copulatory behavior: The Coolidge effect and related phenomena. *Psychological Bulletin, 89,* 464-482.

Dickemann, M. (1981). Paternal confidence and dowry competition: A biocultural analysis of purdah. In R. D. Alexander & D. W. Tinkle (Eds.), *Natural selection and social behavior* (pp. 417-438). New York: Chiron.

Doyle, J. A. (1985). *Sex and gender.* Dubuque, IA: Brown.

Duck, S. (1978). *The study of acquaintance.* Westmead, England: Saxon House.

Eibl-Eibesfeldt, I. (1975). *Ethology: The biology of behavior* (2nd ed.). New York: Holt, Rinehart, & Winston.

Elder, G. H., Jr. (1969). Appearance and education in marriage mobility. *American Sociological Review, 34,* 519-533.

Foa, E. B., & Foa, U. G. (1980). Resource theory: Interpersonal behavior as exchange. In K. J. Gergen, M. S. Greenberg, & R. H. Willis (Eds.), *Social exchange: Advances in theory and research* (pp. 77-94). New York: Plenum.

Gouldner, A. W. (1960). The norm of reciprocity: A preliminary statement. *American Sociological Review, 25,* 161-178.

Hamilton, W. D. (1964). The genetical evolution of social behavior. *Journal of Theoretical Biology, 7,* 1-52.

Harrison, A. A., & Saeed, L. (1977). Let's make a deal: An analysis of revelations and stipulations in lonely hearts advertisements. *Journal of Personality and Social Psychology, 35,* 257-264.

Hatfield, E., Utne, M. K., & Traupmann, J. (1979). Equity theory and intimate relationships. In R. L. Burgess & T. L. Huston (Eds.), *Social exchange in developing relationships* (pp. 99-133). New York: Academic Press.

Hinde, R. A. (1974). *Biological bases of human social behavior.* New York: McGraw-Hill.

Hinde, R. A. (1984). Why do the sexes behave differently in close relationships? *Journal of Social and Personal Relationships, 1,* 471-501.

Holmes, S. J., & Hatch, C. D. (1938). Personal appearance as related to scholastic records and marriage selection in college women. *Human Biology, 10,* 65-76.

Homans, G. C. (1974). *Social behavior: Its elementary forms* (rev. ed.). New York: Harcourt Brace Jovanovich.

Huesmann, L. R., & Levinger, G. (1976). Incremental exchange theory: A formal model for progression in dyadic social interaction. In L. Berkowitz & E. Walster (Eds.), *Advances in experimental social psychology* (Vol. 9, pp. 191-229). New York: Academic Press.

Huston, T. L. (1973). Ambiguity of acceptance, social desirability, and dating choice. *Journal of Experimental Social Psychology, 9,* 32-42.

Kenrick, D. T. (1987). Gender, genes, and the social environment: A biosocial interactionist perspective. In P. Shaver & C. Hendrick (Eds.), *Review of personality and social psychology: Sex and gender* (Vol. 7, pp. 14-43). Newbury Park, CA: Sage.

Kenrick, D. T., Dantchik, A., & MacFarlane, S. (1983). Personality, environment, and criminal behavior: An evolutionary perspective. In W. S. Laufer & J. M. Day (Eds.), *Personality theory, moral development, and criminal behavior* (pp. 217-241). Lexington, MA: Lexington.

Kenrick, D. T., & Keefe, R. C. (1988). *Gender differences in age criteria for a mate increase over the life span.* Manuscript submitted for publication.

Kenrick, D. T., Montello, D., & MacFarlane, S. (1985). Personality: Social learning, social cognition, or sociobiology? In R. Hogan & W. Jones (Eds.), *Perspectives in personality* (Vol. 1, pp. 201-234). Greenwich, CT: JAI.

Kenrick, D. T., Sadalla, E. K., Groth, G., & Trost, M. R. (in press). Gender and trait requirements in a mate. An evolutionary bridge between personality and social psychology. [Special issue]. *Journal of personality.*

Kenrick, D. T., Stringfield, D. O., Wagenhals, W. L., Dahl, R. H., & Ransdell, H. J. (1980). Sex differences, androgyny, and approach responses to erotica: A new variation on the old volunteer problem. *Journal of Personality and Social Psychology, 38,* 517-524.

Kenrick, D. T., & Trost, M. R. (1987). A biosocial theory of heterosexual relationships. In K. Kelley (Ed.), *Females, males, and sexuality: Theories and research* (pp. 59-100). Albany: State University of New York Press.

Kenrick, D. T., Trost, M. R., Groth, G., & Sadalla, E. K. (1988). *Gender differences in mate selection criteria vary with different phases of courtship.* Unpublished manuscript.

Kiesler, S. B., & Baral, R. L. (1970). The search for a romantic partner: The effects of self-esteem and physical attractiveness on romantic behavior. In K. J. Gergen & D. Marlowe (Eds.), *Personality and social behavior* (pp. 155-165). Reading, MA: Addison-Wesley.

Kinsey, A. C., Pomeroy, W. B., & Martin, C. E. (1948). *Sexual behavior in the human male.* Philadelphia: Saunders.

Kinsey, A. C., Pomeroy, W. B., Martin, C. E., & Gebhard, P. H. (1953). *Sexual behavior in the human female.* Philadelphia: Saunders.

Koestner, R., & Wheeler, L. (in press). Self-presentation in personal advertisements: The influence of implicit notions of attraction and role expectations. *Journal of Personal and Social Relationships.*

LaGaipa, J. J. (1977). Interpersonal attraction and social exchange. In S. Duck (Ed.), *Theory and practice in interpersonal attraction* (pp. 129-164). New York: Academic Press.

Lancaster, J. B. (1975). *Primate behavior and the emergence of human culture.* New York: Holt, Rinehart, & Winston.

Levinger, G. (1983). Development and change. In H. H. Kelley, E. Berscheid, A. Christensen, J. H. Harvey, T. L. Huston, G. Levinger, E. McClintock, L. A. Peplau, & D. R. Peterson (Eds.), *Close relationships* (pp. 315-359). New York: Freeman.

Levinger, G., & Huesmann, L. R. (1980). An "incremental exchange" perspective on the pair relationship: Interpersonal reward and level of involvement. In K. J. Gergen, M. S. Greenberg, & R. H. Willis (Eds.), *Social exchange: Advances in theory and research* (pp. 165-188). New York: Plenum.

Levinger, G., & Snoek, J. D. (1972). *Attraction in relationships: A new look at interpersonal attraction.* Morristown, NJ: General Learning.

Lewis, R. A., Casto, R., Aquilino, W., & McGuffin, N. (1978). Developmental transitions in male sexuality. *The Counseling Psychologist, 7,* 15-19.

Loehlin, J. D., & Nichols, R. C. (1976). *Heredity, environment, and personality.* Austin: University of Texas Press.

Lumsden, C. J., & Wilson, E. O. (1981). *Genes, mind, and culture: The coevolutionary process.* Cambridge, MA: Harvard University Press.

Lynn, M., & Bolig, R. (1985). Personal advertisements: Sources of data about relationships. *Journal of Social and Personal Relationships, 2,* 377-383.

Marshall, D. S. (1971). Sexual behavior on Mangaia. In D. S. Marshall & R. C. Suggs (Eds.), *Human sexual behavior: Variations in the ethnographic spectrum* (pp. 103-162). New York: Basic Books.

Mazur, A., & Lamb, T. (1980). Testosterone, status, and mood in human males. *Hormones and Behavior, 14*, 236-246.

McDougall, W. (1908). *Social psychology: An introduction.* London: Methuen.

Messenger, J. C. (1971). Sex and repression in an Irish folk community. In D. S. Marshall & R. C. Suggs (Eds.), *Human sexual behavior: Variations in the ethnographic spectrum* (pp. 3-37). New York: Basic Books.

Mills, J., & Clark, M. S. (1982). Exchange and communal relationships. In L. Wheeler (Ed.), *Review of personality and social psychology* (Vol. 3, pp. 121-144). Beverly Hills, CA: Sage.

Murstein, B. I. (1972). Physical attractiveness and marital choice. *Journal of Personality and Social Psychology, 22*, 8-12.

Murstein, B. I. (1981). Process, filter, and stage theories of attraction. In M. Cook (Ed.), *The bases of human sexual attraction* (pp. 179-211). London: Academic Press.

Peplau, L. A., Rubin, Z., & Hill, C. T. (1977). Sexual intimacy in dating relationships. *Journal of Social Issues, 33*(2), 86-109.

Rose, R., Bernstein, I., & Gordon, T. (1975). Consequences of social conflict on plasma testosterone levels in rhesus monkeys. *Psychosomatic Medicine, 37*, 50-61.

Rose, R. M., Holaday, J. W., & Bernstein, I. (1971). Plasma testosterone, dominance rank, and aggressive behavior in male rhesus monkeys. *Nature, 231*, 366-368.

Rowe, D. C., Rodgers, J. L., Meseck-Bushey, S., & St. John, C. (1987). *Sexual behavior and deviance: A sibling study of their relationship.* Unpublished manuscript, University of Oklahoma.

Rushton, J. P. (1985). Differential *K* theory: The sociobiology of individual and group differences. *Personality and Individual Differences, 6*, 441-452.

Sadalla, E. K., Kenrick, D. T., & Vershure, B. (1987). Dominance and heterosexual attraction. *Journal of Personality and Social Psychology, 52*, 730-738.

Sadalla, E. K., & Fausal, M. (1980). *Dominance and heterosexual attraction: A field study.* Unpublished manuscript, Arizona State University.

Sarason, I. G., & Sarason, B. R. (1987). *Abnormal psychology.* Englewood Cliffs, NJ: Prentice-Hall.

Shepher, J., & Reisman, J. (1985). Pornography: A sociobiological attempt at understanding. *Ethology and Sociobiology, 6*, 103-114.

Svare, B., & Kinsley, C. H. (1987). Hormones and sex-related behavior: A comparative analysis. In K. Kelley (Ed.), *Females, males, and sexuality: Theories and research* (pp. 13-58). Albany: State University of New York Press.

Tavris, C. & Wade, C. (1984). *The longest war* (2nd ed.). San Diego: Harcourt Brace Jovanovich.

Thibaut, J. W., & Kelley, H. H. (1959). *The social psychology of groups.* New York: John Wiley.

Trivers, R. L. (1972). Parental investment and sexual selection. In B. Campbell (Ed.), *Sexual selection and the descent of man* (pp. 136-179). Chicago, IL: Aldine.

Walster, E., Aronson, V., Abrahams, D., & Rottmann, L. (1966). Importance of physical attractiveness in dating behavior. *Journal of Personality and Social Psychology, 4*, 508-516.

Walster, E., Berscheid, E., & Walster, G. W. (1973). New directions in equity research. *Journal of Personality and Social Psychology, 25*, 151-176.

Walster, E. H., Walster, G. W., & Berscheid, E. (1978). *Equity: Theory and research.* Boston: Allyn & Bacon.

Williams, G. C. (1966). Natural selection, the costs of reproduction, and a refinement of Lack's principle. *American Naturalist, 100,* 687-690.

Williams, J. E., & Best, D. L. (1982). *Measuring sex stereotypes.* Beverly Hills, CA: Sage.

Wilson, E. O. (1975). *Sociobiology: The new synthesis.* Cambridge, MA: Harvard University Press.

Behavior and Satisfaction in Marriage
PROSPECTVE MEDIATING PROCESSES

THOMAS N. BRADBURY
FRANK D. FINCHAM

Thomas N. Bradbury is a graduate student in clinical psychology at the University of Illinois at Urbana-Champaign. He is interested primarily in empirical and theoretical analyses of marriage and the application of social psychological principles to the examination of close relationships. His clinical activities are devoted to assessment, treatment, and prevention of marital discord.

Frank D. Fincham is the Associate Director of Clinical Training at the University of Illinois at Urbana-Champaign. He obtained his Ph.D. in social psychology from the University of Oxford. His doctoral research was on attribution of responsibility and led to an early career award from the British Psychological Society. Since completing his clinical training at the State University of New York at Stony Brook, he has conducted research on marital and parent-child relationships and on children's reactions to failure. His interests also include theoretical and methodological issues in the study of close relationships, the prevention and treatment of marital discord, and the sociology of knowledge.

Although considerable progress has been made in the study of close relationships, few models integrate existing research and point to new areas of inquiry. Moreover, the models that are available pertain either to discrete segments of interaction, and hence neglect many important phenomena, or they pertain to close relationships more generally, and hence lack sufficient detail at the level of interaction (Newcomb & Bentler, 1981). One purpose of this article is to offer a framework for the study of marriage that incorporates both levels of analysis. Following discussion of the historical context that has given rise to this framework, we attempt to show how such a framework can both organize existing research and identify additional topics for investigation. The chapter concludes with a summary of major themes and a discussion of the limitations of our analysis.

AUTHORS' NOTE: Address correspondence to Thomas N. Bradbury, Department of Psychology, University of Illinois at Urbana-Champaign, 603 East Daniel Street, Champaign, IL 61820. Telephone: (217) 333-0631; (217) 333-8624. We thank Anita DeLongis, Kathy Pielsticker, and three anonymous reviewers for their helpful comments on earlier versions of the chapter. This chapter was written while Frank Fincham was a Faculty Scholar of the W. T. Grant Foundation.

HISTORICAL CONTEXT

Historically, researchers have devoted most of their attention in the study of marriage to understanding marital satisfaction, and two distinct research traditions have emerged.[1] The *sociological tradition* is characterized by large-scale surveys conducted to determine the associations between demographic, personality, and familial variables and marital satisfaction. This tradition generated a large body of findings (see Burgess, Locke, & Thomes, 1971; Tharp, 1963), yet also led to the observation that "knowing the correlates of marital success actually presents the theoretical problem of explaining why these correlations exist" (Barry, 1970, p. 44).

Responding to the atheoretical nature of these data and to limitations of the self-report methods used to obtain them, Raush, Barry, Hertel, and Swain (1974) sought to explain the sociological findings by examining the overt behaviors of couples as they engaged in marital conflict in a laboratory setting. Their work, together with Stuart's (1969) extension of social learning principles to the treatment of distressed couples, was instrumental in introducing the *behavioral tradition* to the study of marital satisfaction. A spate of studies relating coded behavior in interaction to satisfaction followed (e.g., Birchler, Weiss, & Vincent, 1975; Gottman, 1979; Gottman, Markman, & Notarius, 1977; Vincent, Weiss, & Birchler, 1975), and recent reviews of this research indicate that the interactions of distressed couples, compared to those of nondistressed couples, are characterized by a higher rate of negative behaviors, more reciprocity of negative behaviors, and a greater degree of stereotypy or predictability (see Schaap, 1984).

A second research strategy in the behavioral tradition, initiated by Wills, Weiss, and Patterson (1974), examined spouses' daily ratings of satisfaction in relation to the pleasing and displeasing behaviors exhibited by their partners. It was determined that spouses' reports of partner behavior, and in particular displeasing partner behavior, accounted for a significant proportion of variance in their daily satisfaction. This finding has been replicated in subsequent studies (e.g., Barnett & Nietzel, 1979; Jacobson, Waldron, & Moore, 1980). Thus, in the behavioral tradition the two dominant paradigms have produced evidence to document an association between behavior and satisfaction in marriage.

Although research in the behavioral tradition provides important information about marriage, the need to explain established findings is once again evident. Attention is turning from strictly behavioral accounts of marriage to the study of factors that may intervene between behavior and satisfaction. In particular, the realization from laboratory studies that nonverbal behavior (e.g., facial movement, voice tone, gestures) is more powerful than verbal behavior in discriminating distressed and nondistressed couples (e.g., Gottman, 1979) has led to the view that affect may play a central role in marital interaction (e.g., Gottman & Levenson, 1984; for review see Bradbury & Fincham, 1987a). Similarly, the finding that spouses disagree over the occurrence of daily behaviors in their relationship (e.g., Jacobson & Moore, 1981) has led to consideration of the role of cognition in marriage (e.g., Berley & Jacobson, 1984; for review see Arias & Beach, 1987).

Based on these and related developments, we believe that a third tradition in the study of marital satisfaction is presently underway. In this *mediational tradition*, emphasis is upon factors that may clarify the association between behavior and satisfaction rather than upon the association itself. Indeed, few studies have appeared in recent years that focus solely upon the relation between behavior and satisfaction and, instead, attention within the behavior tradition has shifted to refining existing measures of behavior (e.g., Jacob & Krahn, 1987) and satisfaction (e.g., Huston, McHale, & Crouter, 1986) so that their association might be more clearly understood.

It is useful to contrast the evolution of the behavioral tradition with that of the mediational tradition, as doing so reveals two important differences. First, the initial decision to study behavior reflected a rejection of sociological methods (e.g., see Raush et al., 1974, p. 5). The mediational tradition, in comparison, appears to be an acceptance and expansion of the behavioral and sociological approaches, and may be appropriately referred to as an *integrative* movement. Second, with few exceptions (e.g., Krokoff, Gottman, & Roy, 1988), there has been little recognition of the possibility that sociological variables influence marital interaction. A corresponding disregard of the interplay between behavior and mediating variables is difficult to sustain, however, insofar as a couple's overt behaviors are likely to be intricately related to affective and cognitive processes.

Although the study of potential mediating variables is gaining momentum, the need to broaden the behavioral model of marriage has long been recognized (e.g., Glick & Gross, 1975; Gurman & Knudson, 1978; Hinde, 1979). Indeed, the study by Raush et al. (1974), widely cited as seminal in the behavioral tradition, was conceptualized in terms of the psychoanalytic notion of object relations schemata. Raush et al. (1974) made little effort to assess these "organized structures of images of the self and others" (p. 43), yet a variety of interesting results have since emerged from the study of factors believed to be relevant to the association between behavior and marital satisfaction. These factors include physiological arousal (e.g., Levenson & Gottman, 1983), accuracy of communication (e.g., Noller, 1980), attributions for marital problems (e.g., Fincham & Bradbury, 1988), commitment and exchange orientations (Broderick & O'Leary, 1986), and spouses' perceptions of marital communications (e.g., Gottman et al., 1976).

While encouraging, the very diversity of these studies makes salient the fact that a comprehensive understanding of the association between behavior and satisfaction has yet to be established. In the next section we offer an organizational framework, which we refer to as the contextual model, that might serve as a first approximation to a comprehensive account of the relations among behavior, satisfaction, and mediating processes in marriage.

A CONTEXTUAL MODEL OF BEHAVIOR, SATISFACTION, AND PROSPECTIVE MEDIATING PROCESSES

A primary consideration in developing a model for organizing and advancing research on marriage is the breadth of focus taken in selecting mediating processes. In discussing this issue, Hinde (1979, p. 22) noted that "If we are to come to terms with the affective/cognitive aspects of interpersonal relationships . . . we shall need additional concepts. Yet if we are too generous in introducing them we shall find ourselves swimming in a mush with nothing firm to stand on. But if we are too niggardly, we run the risk of missing important phenomena." Although we are mindful of this delicate balance, it is possible that we shall err in the overinclusive direction, with the realization that parsimony will dictate the form that our framework ultimately takes.[2]

The first component to be included in the framework is *behavior* itself. For the purpose of discussion we will assume that behaviors are exhibited alternately by a husband and wife as they interact with one another. Given that the husband has behaved at one point in time and that the wife behaves shortly thereafter, it is reasonable to inquire about the psychological processes that have intervened, or about the factors that may have given rise to the wife's action. We can infer that the wife *attends to and perceives* the behavior in some rudimentary fashion, following which may occur an *interpretation* of the husband's behavior. Evidence has accumulated to indicate that such events can have affective consequences (e.g., Weiner, 1986), suggesting that it is necessary to include *affect* in a comprehensive model of marriage. We will refer to these three processes collectively as the *processing stage*.

The foregoing sequence of events suggests that the wife's behavior will be a function of how she perceives, interprets, and responds affectively to the husband's behavior. It is important to emphasize, however, that the relations among these processes are likely to be probabilistic rather than deterministic in form. That is, for example, variance in perceptual processes will not account entirely for variance in interpretations, and the processing stage will not determine entirely the nature of the subsequent behavior. Realization of these probabilistic relations raises the question of what other factors may contribute to the wife's behavior. An answer may be found in the observation that as yet she is depicted as operating independently of prior events in the interaction and of any continuing psychological characteristics.

Accordingly, it seems appropriate to propose first that the wife's thoughts and feelings elicited by prior events influence her responses to later events. We will refer to such momentary thoughts and feelings as the *proximal context*, as they are assumed to provide an immediate environment that qualifies the processing of events. The proximal context includes thoughts and feelings prompted by events outside the relationship (e.g., weather, work) as well as those specific to the marriage. Second, an understanding of the events that intervene between the husband's behavior and the wife's subsequent behavior is aided by knowledge of the wife's stable and continuing psychological characteristics. Elements in this *distal context* include individual difference variables (e.g., personality traits, goals, or chronic mood states), preexisting relationship-relevant variables (e.g., general relationship expectations), and variables that emerge over the course of a relationship (e.g., learning histories). These variables are themselves interrelated and are likely to influence each other.

The importance of the elements in the distal context lies in their potential to influence (a) variables in the proximal context and (b) the processing stage.[3] For example, the wife's proximal context at the outset of an interaction is likely to be a function not only of her thoughts and feelings about existing circumstances, but also of more stable factors such as her chronic mood state. Similarly, an interpretation of the husband's behavior will be related to memories of his prior behaviors, her learning history in the relationship, her expectations about what sorts of behaviors are appropriate in marriage, and so on. Moreover, elements in the distal context may be modified gradually as a function of the thoughts and feelings that comprise the proximal context. For example, a husband may become more trusting of his wife on the basis of the thoughts and feelings prompted by the things she says or does in their relationship.

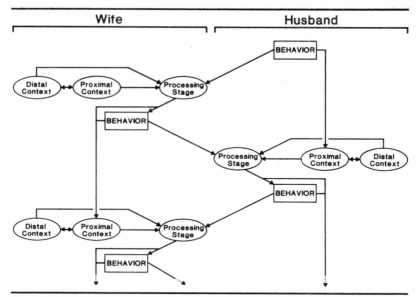

Figure 5.1 **The contextual model of marital interaction. According to the contextual model, partner behavior is processed by the spouse, that processing is influenced by the spouse's proximal context and distal context, and spouse behavior then occurs. The spouse's proximal context is updated frequently on the basis of his or her processing stage and behavior. For clarity, depiction of the model has been simplified in several ways: The processing stage includes attention and perception, interpretation, and affective responding; events between interactions (i.e., appraisals) are not included; and marital satisfaction, an important element in the distal context, is not shown. See text for further details.**

A diagram showing the relations among behavior, the processing stage, proximal context, and distal context is shown in Figure 5.1 for three interpersonal transactions. Here it can be seen that the wife's proximal context is updated frequently in an interaction. That is, the wife's processing of the husband's behavior (which is modified by the distal and proximal contexts), together with her own behavior, influence her proximal context.

In sum, according to the framework we have proposed, behaviors are enacted by a spouse, and the partner then perceives, interprets, and responds affectively to them. These processes, together with (a) residual thoughts and feelings from prior events in the interaction (i.e., proximal context) and (b) a variety of continuing psychological characteristics of the partner (i.e., distal context) guide the partner's behavioral response. The proximal context is updated as a result of each such sequence of events, and the nature of elements in the distal context may also change over time.

The above analysis provides relatively thorough coverage of the classes of variables that are likely to be involved in the exchange of behaviors in marriage. Conspicuously absent, however, is consideration of the role of marital satisfaction. To the degree that it is typically conceptualized as a relatively stable variable, it would appear most appropriate to assign satisfaction to the distal context. It follows that a spouse's marital satisfaction can be expected to influence directly the perceptual, interpretive, and affective responses to partner behavior, and to influence indirectly the spouse's behavior that follows from these three processes. A spouse's marital satisfaction may in turn be altered by both self and partner behaviors that alter the thoughts and feelings (i.e., proximal context) that arise in interaction (see a later section, *Appraisals between interactions,* for a second way in which satisfaction may be altered). In addition to suggesting a reciprocal association between behavior and satisfaction, it can be seen that these constructs are indirectly related. Indeed, it is difficult to construe the relation between behavior and satisfaction solely in direct terms, an observation that corroborates the need to extend the behavioral tradition by examining potential mediating processes.[4]

Comparison of the Contextual Model with Other Models

One useful way of evaluating the contextual model is to compare it with other models of close relationships. Doing so reveals that most existing models tend to focus either on proximal factors (e.g., Berscheid, 1983; Gottman, 1979; Gottman & Levenson, 1986; Kelley, 1985) or on distal factors (e.g., Chelune, Robison, & Kommor, 1984; Rempel, Holmes, & Zanna, 1985; Sternberg, 1986). The lack of attention given to the interplay among proximal and distal factors is consistent with the observation that existing theories in the marital domain "either effectively explain a small segment of the marital interaction, but lack the scope and range of the many factors involved, or else have the range and broad perspective, but lack detail and intricacy at the practical, dyad level of analysis" (Newcomb & Bentler, 1981, p. 92).

In contrast, the contextual model, like the model presented by Kelley et al. (1983, Chapter 2), is one of few that seeks to combine a detailed analysis of dyadic interaction in close relationships with consideration of the relatively stable factors that influence, and are influenced by, the interaction (see Levinger & Rands, 1985; Schindler & Vollmer, 1984). Although the two approaches share some common features (e.g., a focus on interaction), they differ fundamentally in the close relationships they seek to represent. Specifically, the focus of the contextual model is on marriage, whereas the Kelley et al. model concerns close dyadic relationships of all forms (e.g., between friends, spouses, co-workers, parents and children). This difference can be viewed as a trade-off between a desire to understand the marital relationship with depth and accuracy on one hand, and a desire to achieve a broadly generalizable understanding of close relationships on the other.

A related difference is that development of the contextual model was prompted in part by the well-established empirical association between behavior and satisfaction in marriage; our framework reflects an attempt to explain and expand upon this association in terms of research and theory on marriage. Thus, the contextual model is not only specific to one particular form of close relationship, but it is also derived in part from a set of studies that document a specific relation between marital phenomena. The Kelley et al. model, in contrast, apparently was not guided by existing data and is instead an effort to provide a descriptive, nontheoretical conception of "the essential phenomena of close interaction" (1983, p. xiii).

An important implication of the relative breadth of the Kelley et al. model is that it touches upon, in varying degrees of detail, all the phenomena that can be addressed in models of close relationships. This is evident in the assertion by Kelley et al. (1983, p. 64) that "all investigators, all hypotheses, and all theories relating to dyadic inter-action refer in one way or another to this broad framework or to its components." Although generalizability across relationships is an asset of the Kelley et al. model, this gain appears to come at the expense of detailed specification of important processes that occur in close relationships. The contextual model, in comparison, allows a greater degree of specificity and therefore differs in relative emphasis; it also permits identification and specification of issues relevant to the study of interaction that are not addressed explicitly by the Kelley et al. approach. Four such issues are described here.

First, the emphasis in the contextual model is primarily upon psychological factors in marriage. The Kelley et al. model includes psychological processes, yet also assigns a unique role to the environment in which a relationship occurs (e.g., weather conditions, lighting, furniture). Although we acknowledge that the physical and social environments are relevant to the study of close relationships (e.g., interaction in the laboratory may differ from interaction in the home), we maintain that consideration of the *psychological consequences* of environmental factors, as reflected in the proximal and distal contexts, is sufficient for understanding their role in relationships. Thus, unlike

Kelley et al. (1983, p. 53), we do not reject a "wholly 'psychological'" level of analysis.

Second, attention to and perception of partner behavior is an essential element of marital interaction in the contextual model and is therefore analyzed in some detail (see later section *Attention and perception*). To our knowledge, however, the Kelley et al. model does not provide a detailed description of attentional and perceptual processes.

Third, we view as important the events that occur *between* dyadic interactions, in part because they may influence spouses' evaluations of their marriage and the proximal context present at the start of subsequent interactions (see later section *Appraisals between interactions*). As in other models of marital interaction (e.g., Gottman, 1979; Gottman & Levenson, 1986), little mention is made in the Kelley et al. model of the events that occur between interactions, and no mechanism is specified by which changes in relatively stable variables can occur.

Fourth, although the distal context for the wife may be similar to that of the husband in the contextual model, it is generally held that the contexts differ for the two spouses. The analogous concept in the Kelley et al. model, that is, the causal conditions, includes variables that exist solely at the dyadic level (e.g., attitude similarity). The focus on variables that operate at the level of the interaction in the Kelley et al. model is accompanied by a relative lack of attention to individual differences. In contrast, the distal context in the contextual model operates solely at the level of the individual, indicating that individual differences are essential to this model.

The different levels of specificity in the contextual model and the Kelley et al. model appear to have implications not only for the processes they identify but also for whether the models themselves are subjected to empirical analysis. In its initial form, the contextual model included a series of testable research propositions (Bradbury & Fincham, 1987b), and research guided by the framework has recently appeared (Bradbury & Fincham, 1988; Sillars, Wilmot, & Hocker, in press). To our knowledge, little research has been guided explicitly by the Kelley et al. model since its publication, a factor that may be due to the level of specificity at which it was proposed.

To conclude, although the two approaches bear certain similarities, there are fundamental differences between the contextual model and the Kelley et al. model in the degree to which various issues are emphasized. The purposes for which these approaches were formulated are different and the level at which various processes are specified differ in the two models. As a consequence, we believe that important phenomena will be overlooked to the extent that the two approaches are assumed to be equivalent.

APPLICATION OF THE CONTEXTUAL MODEL

The framework we have offered serves to illustrate the incomplete nature of research conducted in the sociological and behavioral traditions. Data from the sociological tradition derive predominantly from attempts to relate variables in the distal context to marital satisfaction, another variable in the distal context. The attempt to explain why particular variables were associated with marital satisfaction led investigators in the behavioral tradition to examine an additional component of the framework, namely, the overt behaviors exhibited by spouses in interaction. As noted, research on marital behavior and satisfaction suggested the need to consider factors that might mediate their association; this step in the progression toward understanding marital satisfaction is reflected in the processing stage that occurs following partner behavior, and in the proximal and distal contexts that modify it. In the remainder of the chapter we use the framework as a vantage point from which to evaluate research in the mediational tradition and to suggest potentially fruitful avenues of future inquiry.

Relevance to Existing Mediational Research

Several research strategies have emerged for examining prospective mediating processes in the association between behavior and marital satisfaction. Three of these strategies are used here to illustrate the utility of the proposed framework for evaluating existing research. They involve the "talk table" paradigm, comparison of inside and outside perspectives on interaction, and physiological indices of affect. We anticipate that other marital research could be analyzed in a similar manner.

Talk table studies. The talk table procedure was devised to define operationally the rewards and costs posited by social exchange theory and to "provide a first approximation to the schema that Raush et al. proposed" (Gottman, 1979, p. 218). With this procedure, spouses are asked to sit at either side of a table and to speak one at a time, usually while discussing a marital difficulty. After speaking, a spouse rates the intended impact or *intent* of the sent message, following which the partner rates the perceived *impact* of the message. The partner then speaks and rates the intent of the message, the spouse rates the perceived impact, and the couple alternates in this way through their discussion. Intent and impact ratings are made privately on a 5-point scale ranging from "super positive" to "super negative." Discrepancies between the intent of the messages sent by one spouse and their impact as rated by the other spouse are then examined in satisfied and dissatisfied couples. Results from talk table studies typically show that both groups send messages with positive intent, but that the messages of distressed spouses have a negative impact. A discrepancy between intent and impact thus distinguishes the interactions of distressed couples (see Gottman et al., 1976; Markman, 1981; Schachter & O'Leary, 1985).

In terms of the contextual model, the talk table requires spouses to report on one aspect of the processing stage (i.e., the impact of the partner's message), to speak, and then to report on one aspect of their proximal context (i.e., the intent of their own message). Two issues become apparent when the talk table paradigm is viewed from this perspective. First, because spouses rate the impact that partner messages have on them and the intent behind their own messages, the talk table places greater emphasis on self-perception than on partner-perception. The contextual model suggests, in contrast, that the inferences made about *partner* behavior are at least as important as self-perceptions. To examine the inferences made in response to partner behavior, the talk table strategy requires modifications such that a spouse judges the intent of a partner behavior ("He said that to hurt me"), rather than its impact ("What he just said makes me feel bad"). The spouse could then send a message and rate its intended impact (i.e., actual intent) as in the original talk table, and discrepancies between a spouse's actual intent and the partner's perception of the spouse's intent could be explored. We do not mean to imply that the existing impact rating is unimportant, but perceptions of partner intent may be equally important in understanding marital interaction.

Second, analysis of ratings from the talk table involves the discrepancy between the intent of one spouse in sending a message and the impact of that message as rated by the partner. This approach therefore emphasizes important and often neglected phenomena that occur *between* spouses. However, a different analytic strategy could shed light on the intraindividual processes that are highlighted by the framework we have outlined. In particular, one could examine the association between the spouse's first response to a given partner behavior (e.g., perceived impact, as in the original talk table) and that same spouse's subsequent (a) behavior or (b) rating of intent in sending a message. Applied across distressed and nondistressed couples, this approach could provide information about how the processing stage influences later events within an individual, at different levels of marital satisfaction. To our knowledge, intraindividual events in marital interaction have yet to be investigated in this manner.

Impetus for pursuing an intraindividual level of analysis comes from the need to understand the cycles of negative reciprocity that are known to occur in the interactions of distressed couples. To date, attempts to understand intraindividual factors relevant to negative affect reciprocity have been indirect. For instance, the process of *cognitive editing*, whereby a spouse's negative thoughts and feelings shown while listening to the partner *do not* lead to a negative behavioral response, has been inferred on the basis of coded behavior (Gottman, 1979). An intraindividual analysis of talk table data would permit a more direct examination of this mediational process. In addition, it might be hypothesized that distressed spouses are more likely to interpret partner behavior as being motivated by negative intent and, as a consequence, feel justified to respond behaviorally in kind. Interpretations, as well as other pertinent processes identified in the framework, could be assessed readily with an appropriately modified talk table procedure.

Inside versus outside perspectives. As noted in the introduction, an emphasis on cognitive processes in marriage was spurred by data that questioned the assumption that spouses generally agree on the behaviors that occur in their relationship. As Jacobson and Moore (1981, p. 276) stated, "The fact that two spouses living in the same environment perceive such different worlds suggests that in functional terms, spouses are operating in vastly different environments. . . . How spouses in a marital relationship perceive and process information relevant to the relationship . . . and the factors that influence these cognitive events potentiate the development of . . . a richer understanding of the characteristics of marital distress." Thus, refutation of the assumption that spouses were accurate observers aided in opening up a new domain of research in marriage.

With this as their starting point, Floyd and Markman (1983) sought to compare spouse's perceptions of their partner's interaction behaviors with undergraduate coders' perceptions of the same behaviors. They argued that spouses would provide an inside perspective on their interaction, whereas trained coders would provide an outside criterion against which spouse's perceptions could be meaningfully compared (see Christensen & Nies, 1980; Margolin, Hattem, John, & Yost, 1985). Both sets of observers rated behaviors from conflict discussions on a five-point scale ranging from very negative to very positive. It was found that nondistressed spouses, as well as distressed husbands, rated partner behavior as more positive than it was rated by outside coders; distressed wives displayed the opposite tendency as they rated partner behavior as less positive than did outside coders.

In discussing their results, Floyd and Markman (1983) underscored the importance of cognition in marriage by noting that "the pattern of insider/outsider differences suggests that cognitive/perceptual factors for the spouses were determining the differences rather than systematic objective observer bias. The results suggest that *cognitive* factors may have systematic influences on spouse's evaluations of their interactions" (p. 456). The potential significance of such factors is best illustrated by considering the sources of influence that most likely affected the ratings from the inside and outside perspectives. From the inside perspective, it seems likely that spouse's ratings of partner behavior emerged from the sequence depicted in Figure 5.1. That is, thoughts and feelings from previous events in the interaction serve as the proximal context for a partner behavior and, as a function of elements in the proximal and distal contexts (e.g., history of the relationship, feelings of satisfaction with the marriage), the behavior elicits perceptual, interpretive, and affective responses. From the outside perspective, the rating of partner behavior probably draws upon coders' stereotypes of how men and women behave in close relationships and lay conceptions of what constitutes a positive or negative behavior in a close relationship, both of which are elements in the distal context.

This comparison reveals that the two perspectives differ dramatically, and it becomes understandable how they might lead to different impressions of the interaction. The inside perspective involves, for example, perceptual and interpretive processes that are not available to the outside coders, thus supporting Floyd and Markman's (1983) suggestion that cognitive factors underlie the observed differences. Although this is a useful suggestion, it is probably incomplete. In particular, the two perspectives are likely to diverge in many other ways, raising the possibility that differences arise because of other factors, including affective processes. For instance, spouse's judgments of partner behavior may be influenced by affect via (a) the proximal context, which reflects transient thoughts and feelings about the interaction; (b) the distal context, which comprises such factors as marital satisfaction and stable affective response tendencies; and (c) the affective response to the partner behavior itself, which is proposed to follow the initial perception. Thus, in our opinion, discrepancies between inside and outside perspectives are not surprising, and explanation of the discrepancies cannot be limited to cognitive factors.

In sum, application of the contextual model indicates that the perceptual and cognitive features that are prominent in studies of inside and outside perspectives are likely to be accompanied by affective responses. The framework therefore may afford a more comprehensive approach to marriage whereby affective and cognitive processes are viewed as interrelated in a reciprocal association with one another and with ongoing behavior.

Affect and physiology in marital interaction. Among the most important findings to result from behavioral research on marital interaction is that distressed and nondistressed couples are more powerfully discriminated on the basis of their nonverbal behaviors than on the content of their speech. For example, Gottman (1979) discovered that these groups did not differ in the overall extent of verbal disagreement, yet distressed couples were ten times more likely than nondistressed couples to express disagreement with nonverbal behavior. These and related data led Levenson and Gottman (1983, p. 588) to surmise that "patterns of observable affect and affect exchange that typify dissatisfied marriages would be accompanied by parallel patterns of physiological response."

To examine in greater detail the role of physiological indices of affect in marriage, Levenson and Gottman (1983) assessed the physiology (e.g., heart rate, sweating) of spouses as they discussed a marital difficulty. They found that 60% of the variance in couples' satisfaction was accounted for by physiological *linkage*, defined as the physiological interrelatedness of a husband and wife over the course of their interaction. Specifically, lower marital satisfaction was related to higher physiological linkage.

Having demonstrated a concurrent relation between physiological indices of affect and marital satisfaction, Levenson and Gottman (1985) then sought to determine whether changes in satisfaction could be predicted from the same set of physiological measures. Three years after their laboratory interaction, 19 of the original 30 spouses provided self-reports of their marital satisfaction. In addition to a series of interesting gender effects, greater declines in satisfaction were predictable from higher levels of physiological arousal (e.g., faster heart rate, more sweating) at the time of the interaction. Particularly surprising was the finding that decreases in satisfaction were a function of levels of arousal measured in the five-minute baseline period *before the interaction began*, as the spouses sat silently facing one another in anticipation of their conflict.

From the perspective of the contextual model, this study can be construed as an attempt to relate marital satisfaction to physiological changes that accompany the processing stage, the subsequent updating of the proximal context, and the influence of the proximal context on the processing stage. In discussing their findings, Levenson and Gottman (1985) maintained that the predictive power of the pre-interaction levels of physiology resulted from the fact that spouses knew that they would soon be interacting with one another and were thinking about past events in their relationship. They reasoned that "over time, a couple develops a set of expectations about the prospect of interacting that is grounded in their past interactive experience. . . . We believe it is these pleasurable or displeasurable expectations that account for the arousal differences we have observed during baseline periods" (p. 92). Thus, as might have been predicted from our framework, an explanation of the longitudinal findings was best achieved by invoking elements of the distal context (i.e., expectations and learning histories) and by hypothesizing that they exerted an impact on the proximal context, the interaction, and associated physiology.

In the same way that reconsideration of Floyd and Markman's (1983) study made salient the role of affective processes in the examination of ostensibly cognitive variables, so too does reexamination of Levenson and Gottman's (1985) investigation highlight the importance of (a) cognitive variables in understanding affective responses and of (b) distal variables in the study of proximal variables and the processing stage. Again, insofar as it is designed to provide a comprehensive account of important overt and covert events in marriage, the framework we have outlined may prove heuristic in identifying mediating processes that may not have been otherwise considered in the conceptualization and study of marital phenomena.

Summary. The foregoing discussion illustrates some of the progress already made in the mediational tradition. By analyzing three research strategies we have tried to show that seemingly disparate findings can be understood and organized in terms of a common framework, and that application of the framework can extend what is now known. Thus, our analysis points to the relevance of factors that were not considered in the original discussion of these findings and makes apparent the need to incorporate measures of mediating variables in such research. Although the extension of existing work is worthwhile, a more exacting test of our conceptual scheme lies in its ability to identify avenues not yet pursued systematically within the mediational tradition, and it is to this issue that we now turn.

Directions for Future Research

The model outlined earlier points to several directions for research, thus raising the problem of which issues to address and which to exclude. The issues discussed here represent a compromise between those that appear most promising on one hand, and those that can be described adequately in the remaining pages.

Appraisals between interactions. The framework we have outlined is an attempt to describe the events that occur as a husband and wife talk with one another. However, spouses do not spend all their time interacting, and while apart it is likely that they experience a variety of feelings and think about past discussions, the quality and future of their marriage, and about issues in the relationship that concern them. It is necessary therefore to accommodate phenomena that occur between interactions in conceptual accounts of marriage. We will refer to these phenomena as *appraisals* and, because the partner is not necessarily present when these thoughts and feelings occur, it is posited that they pertain primarily to elements in the distal context.

Central to the study of marriage are those factors that lead to changes in one element of the distal context, marital satisfaction. In Figure 5.1, the line drawn from the proximal context to the distal context implies that, within an interaction, particular thoughts and feelings may lead to changes in satisfaction. For example, a husband's revealing that he has had an extramarital affair may cause a wife to believe that she is no longer happy in her marriage. However, it seems more likely that variation in satisfaction comes about gradually as a function of appraisals between interactions. For example, while alone a husband may think to himself, "She really isn't paying much attention to me anymore," a realization that he finds inconsistent with his conception of a satisfying marriage. A belief of this sort may enter into subsequent interactions, either implicitly (e.g., it may lead the husband to attend selectively to those statements by his wife that confirm the belief) or explicitly (e.g., he may tell his wife that he is feeling this way so that they might come to a mutual understanding of the issue), and over time satisfaction may change accordingly.[5]

This proposal has at least three implications for future research. First, the relation between events that occur within an interaction and those that occur following an interaction could be examined. A few studies have begun to look at the role of distal variables (e.g., marital satisfaction, expectations) and processing-stage variables (e.g., impact ratings of spouse behavior) in predicting the immediate outcome of interaction (e.g., Koren, Carlton, & Shaw, 1980; Weiss, 1984). A valuable extension of these studies would entail assessment (a) of a broader array of distal variables, (b) in an unstructured format (e.g., with a "think-aloud" task), (c) at intervals hours or days after the initial interaction. Second, the appraisal process could be explored by measuring spouses' thoughts and feelings as they occur in natural settings. Procedures for *in vivo* assessment are now available for this purpose (e.g., Hormuth, 1986) and could be used to discern patterns in couple's day-to-day fluctuations in satisfaction and the interactions and appraisals that accompany them. Third, the relation between the appraisal process and the nature of subsequent interactions could be investigated. Over long periods of time such an interplay is likely to be involved in establishing the learning history of a couple. However, because it may be difficult to detect gradual changes of this sort, the thoughts and feelings that occur immediately preceding an interaction may be a more viable starting point. The data by Levenson and Gottman (1985) suggest the need to examine such phenomena and, in terms of the contextual model, they may be critical determinants of the initial proximal context within which an interaction occurs.

Attention and perception. A common strategy in marital therapy is to teach spouses to attend more to the positive behaviors and less to the negative behaviors emitted by their partner (e.g., Stuart, 1980). As suggested earlier, the significance of attentional and perceptual processes is likely to stem from their hypothesized role in interpretations of partner behavior, which in turn are expected to influence affective and behavioral responding. Surprisingly little research has been conducted on the attentional and perceptual characteristics of spouses in inter-action, yet this line of inquiry holds considerable potential for under-standing the dysfunctional patterns of behavior observed in distressed couples. For example, it is of clinical as well as theoretical relevance to ascertain whether the tendency to reciprocate negative behaviors is a function of perceptual or interpretive processes. In the former case interventions might be designed to modify how spouses extract information from the stream of partner behavior, whereas in the latter case spouses might be taught to interpret in a more benign manner the information that is extracted. In all probability, of course, these operations are likely to be highly complex, and as a first step toward their understanding we speculate below on how attention and perception may be related to partner behavior and may be qualified by elements of the distal and proximal contexts.

First, variation in perception is likely to be related to properties of the behaviors available to be perceived. Extrapolating from research in social psychology, it might be inferred that those behaviors which are particularly intense and negative will draw spouses' attention (e.g., Fiske, 1980; see Bradbury & Fincham, 1987b). This may account for the fact that reciprocation of negative behaviors is more likely than reciprocation of positive behaviors in marital interaction (Schaap, 1984). Further, an explanation for why negative reciprocity is more common in distressed than nondistressed couples might be derived from testing the hypothesis that, all else being equal, a distressed spouse is more likely to attend to the negative rather than to the positive component of the partner's behavior. This hypothesis might be tested by providing spouses with ambivalent partner statements ("I really appreciate your helping out with the kids, yet I wish you could try to be a little more consistent when you discipline them") and assessing their responses to them and their recall of them.

A second factor that is likely to determine the perceptions of spouses is their expectations regarding partner behavior. Expectations are posited as an element in the distal context, and it is well documented that distressed couples hold general expectations about marriage that are more unrealistic than those held by nondistressed couples (e.g., Eidelson & Epstein, 1982). It would not be surprising, therefore, if distressed spouses also developed specific negative expectations about their partners' behavior, a process that emphasizes the dynamic relation among elements in the distal context. Again drawing upon social psychological research, there is evidence to suggest that people's perceptions and impressions of behavior in interaction are guided by the behaviors that they are led to expect, and that expectations are related to knowledge of a person's past behavior (see Higgins & Bargh, 1987; McArthur, 1981). Although caution must be exercised when extending this work to the marital realm, it follows that if a wife has learned to expect her husband to be aggressive and uncompromising in interaction, she may attend selectively to those aspects of his behavior that support her expectations. Because spouses may behave in accordance with the events they anticipate, rather than in response to unanticipated aspects of partner behavior, there may be a disproportionate tendency to attend to and reciprocate those partner behaviors that are expected. In this way, the distal context may exert an impact on attentional and perceptual processes that promotes reciprocity of negative behaviors in distressed couples.

The proximal context is a third factor that may impinge upon attentional and perceptual processes in marital interaction. One component of the proximal context is the level of physiological arousal of spouses as they discuss their marital difficulties. In a study mentioned earlier, Levenson and Gottman (1983) found that the interactions of distressed couples are characterized by a greater degree of physiological arousal than are those of nondistressed couples. This finding, coupled with the proposition that higher levels of arousal can lead to a restriction in the range of stimuli to which an individual is able to attend (Easterbrook, 1959), suggests that distressed spouses are operating on the basis of less information than are nondistressed spouses. This may mean in turn that they are responding to only the most salient aspects of their partner's behavior (e.g., negative and intense statements) and, as a consequence, are quite likely to exhibit and reciprocate negative behavior. Thus, by circumscribing the range of incoming stimuli, the physiological component of the proximal context may be detrimental to effective problem-solving.

Interpretations. Unlike the study of attention and perception, several investigations have been conducted on the interpretations, and particularly the causal attributions, that spouses make for events in their marriage. A concurrent association between attributions and marital satisfaction has been documented (for reviews see Bradbury & Fincham, in press-a; Fincham & Bradbury, in press-a), and longitudinal evidence indicates that, at least for wives, attributions are predictive of changes in satisfaction over a 12-month period (Fincham & Bradbury, 1987a).

The general pattern of results to emerge from this literature is that the attributions of distressed spouses, compared to those of nondistressed spouses, are more likely to minimize the impact of positive behaviors (e.g., "He bought me flowers because he wanted to look good in front of his co-workers") and accentuate the impact of negative behaviors (e.g., "He criticized me because he doesn't care about how I feel"). Such attributions are likely to maintain marital distress. In addition to this basic effect, attributions have been related to such distal variables as unrealistic expectations and perceived efficacy in solving relationship problems (Fincham & Bradbury, 1987a, 1987b).

Despite these advances, the possibility that attributions may serve to mediate the association between behavior and satisfaction in marriage has not been widely acknowledged. Little attention has been devoted to the processes that give rise to attributions in interaction (see Holtzworth-Munroe & Jacobson, in press) or to the consequences that attributions for partner behavior have for a spouse's behavioral responding (see Fincham & Bradbury, in press-b). As a result, the present understanding of marital attributions is limited largely to mindful attributions that are reported publicly, whereas the contextual model suggests that implicit, mindless attributions and attributions that remain private also may be important in interaction (see Bradbury & Fincham, in press-b for a discussion of these types of attribution).

At least two directions for research become apparent when attributions are viewed as potential mediators of the association between behavior and marital satisfaction. Most obviously, there is a need to examine the implications of attributions for behavior. A first step toward doing so might involve correlating couples' explanations for their primary marital difficulty with the behaviors they exhibit in discussing this problem, with the hypothesis that distress-maintaining attributions will relate to higher rates of negative behavior and greater propensities to reciprocate negative behavior (see Fincham & Bradbury, in press-a). Support for this hypothesis would then justify closer inspection of the attribution-behavior relationship at a finer level. One possible means of doing so, noted earlier, would involve altering the talk table paradigm so that attribution judgments are requested after partner behaviors; the attributions could then be examined in regard to the spouse's subsequent behavior.

Second, it is not presently known whether the types of attributions that have been studied are more appropriately designated as elements in the distal context or as interpretive events. Thus, it would be valuable to know the degree to which variance in marital attributions is a function of either discrete stimuli (e.g., partner behavior), trait-like tendencies to make certain attributions rather than others, or a combination of these factors. An adaptation of the talk table procedure could be informative once again, as attributions that occur as the interaction proceeds (i.e., interpretations) could be compared with those that are stable across time and marital situations (i.e., distal elements). To the extent that attributions were found to be relatively trait-like, the question would then arise as to what occurs in the interpretive stage in marital interaction, and what sorts of information in the distal context are drawn upon when they are made.

Summary. To complement our earlier analysis of research on possible mediating processes, several topics were identified and discussed that have yet to be examined within the mediational tradition. The argument was made that, because important events occur outside marital interaction, the model we have proposed should be expanded to accommodate the appraisals that spouses make before and after their discussions. We then considered the importance of attentional and perceptual factors that occur within an interaction and went on to examine the contribution of research on attributions to an understanding of the interpretations that spouses make for partner behavior. Questions remain about the specific role of attributions in the contextual model, yet the demonstrated impact of attributions on marital satisfaction would appear to justify their inclusion in theoretical accounts of marriage.

CONCLUSION

The central purpose of this chapter is to recognize formally the emergence of a *mediational tradition* in the study of marital satisfaction.

This movement, which evolved from earlier eras where sociological and behavioral variables were the primary focus, is characterized by research designed to clarify processes that may mediate the association between satisfaction and behavior in marriage. In an effort to give coherence and direction to this developing area, we described a contextual model that serves as a framework for organizing and conceptualizing mediating processes in marital interaction. After elaborating upon the components of this model, we applied it to existing research within the mediational tradition, with the intent of demonstrating how a comprehensive scheme of this sort can (a) make apparent the common elements of a seemingly diverse group of studies and (b) indicate how present research can be extended to address additional mediating factors. Having done so, we then identified three promising domains for future investigation by drawing upon the contextual model itself, research in social psychology, and marital studies not yet fully recognized as relevant to the association between behavior and satisfaction.

Limitations of our analysis derive from the untested validity of the contextual model and from the necessarily restricted range of topics that we have selected for its illustration. Continued advances in the mediational tradition may reveal that the distinctions we have drawn do not represent adequately the processes we have sought to illuminate, and the topics we have chosen to focus upon may prove to be less important than those we have excluded. Nevertheless, we offer this formulation as a means to organize within a common framework seemingly disparate lines of marital research, mindful of the fact that "it is necessary to formulate each piece of knowledge in a manner that enables it to be incorporated alongside others" (Hinde, 1979, p. 6).

NOTES

1. The history of research on marital satisfaction is much more complicated than we have portrayed it here. To our knowledge, a definitive treatment of this literature has not been written, and interested readers are encouraged to examine original sources for further information (see also Fincham & Bradbury, in press-a).

2. Owing to space limitations, it is not possible to present the model in its complete form. For related discussions, see Bradbury and Fincham, 1987b, Bradbury and Fincham, 1988, and Fincham & Bradbury, in press-a.

3. The possibility must be maintained that the distinction between proximal and distal factors may be more appropriately viewed as a continuum rather than as a dichotomy, an issue that warrants further empirical and theoretical development.

4. This conception of marital satisfaction does not preclude the possibility that satisfaction can be viewed as a state-like appraisal of the quality of marriage, thus suggesting that satisfaction also may be an element in the proximal context.

5. We emphasize here how marital satisfaction, as an element in the distal context, might change over time as a function of the appraisals that occur between interactions. A similar perspective might be taken on other variables in the distal context. For example, personality characteristics are known to have a profound effect on the quality of marriage (e.g., Kelly & Conley, 1987) and it seems likely that over time close relationships exert some influence on the personalities of their participants (Hinde & Stephenson-Hinde, 1986). The appraisal process represents a mechanism by which such changes may occur.

REFERENCES

Arias, I., & Beach, S.R.H. (1987). The assessment of social cognition in the context of marriage. In K. D. O'Leary (Ed.), *Assessment of marital discord* (pp. 109-137). Hillsdale, NJ: Lawrence Erlbaum.

Barnett, L. R., & Nietzel, M. T. (1979). Relationship of instrumental and affectional behaviors and self-esteem to marital satisfaction in distressed and nondistressed couples. *Journal of Consulting and Clinical Psychology, 47*, 946-957.

Barry, W. A. (1970). Marriage research and conflict: An integrative review. *Psychological Bulletin, 73*, 41-54.

Berley, R. A., & Jacobson, N. S. (1984). Causal attributions in intimate relationships: Toward a model of cognitive-behavioral marital therapy. In P. Kendall (Ed.), *Advances in cognitive-behavioral research and therapy* (Vol. 3, pp. 1-60). New York: Academic Press.

Berscheid, E. (1983). Emotion. In H. H. Kelley, E. Berscheid, A. Christensen, J. H. Harvey, T. L. Huston, G. Levinger, E. McClintock, L. A. Peplau, & D. R. Peterson, *Close relationships* (pp. 110-168). New York: Freeman.

Birchler, G. R., Weiss, R. L., & Vincent, J. P. (1975). Multimethod analysis of social reinforcement exchange between maritally distressed and nondistressed spouse and stranger dyads. *Journal of Personality and Social Psychology, 31*, 349-360.

Bradbury, T. N., & Fincham, F. D. (1987a). Assessment of affect in marriage. In K. D. O'Leary (Ed.), *Assessment of marital discord* (pp. 59-108). Hillsdale, NJ: Lawrence Erlbaum.

Bradbury, T. N., & Fincham, F. D. (1987b). Affect and cognition in close relationships: Towards an integrative model. *Cognition and Emotion, 1*, 59-87.

Bradbury, T. N., & Fincham, F. D. (1988). Individual difference variables in close relationships: A contextual model of marriage as an integrative framework. *Journal of Personality and Social Psychology, 54*, 713-721.

Bradbury, T. N., & Fincham, F. D. (in press-a). *Attributions in marriage: Review and critique. Psychological Bulletin.*

Bradbury, T. N., & Fincham, F. D. (in press-b). Assessing spontaneous attributions in marital interaction: Methodological and conceptual considerations. *Journal of Social and Clinical Psychology.*

Broderick, J. E., & O'Leary, K. D. (1986). Contributions of affect, attitudes, and behavior to marital satisfaction. *Journal of Consulting and Clinical Psychology, 54*, 514-517.

Burgess, E. W., Locke, H. J., & Thomes, M. M. (1971). *The family.* New York: Van Nostrand Reinhold.

Chelune, G. J., Robison, J. T., Kommor, M. J. (1984). A cognitive interactional model of intimate relationships. In V. J. Derlega (Ed.), *Communication, intimacy, and close relationships* (pp. 11-40). New York: Academic Press.

Christensen, A., & Nies, D. C. (1980). The spouse observation checklist: Empirical analysis and critique. *The American Journal of Family Therapy, 8*, 69-79.

Easterbrook, J. A. (1959). The effect of emotion on cue utilization and the organization of behavior. *Psychological Review, 66*, 183-201.

Eidelson, R. J., & Epstein, N. (1982). Cognition and relationship maladjustment: Development of a measure of dysfunctional relationship beliefs. *Journal of Consulting and Clinical Psychology, 50*, 715-720.

Fincham, F. D., & Bradbury, T. N. (1987a). The impact of attributions in marriage: A longitudinal analysis. *Journal of Personality and Social Psychology, 53*, 510-517.

Fincham, F. D., & Bradbury, T. N. (1987b). Cognitive processes and conflict in close relationships: An attribution-efficacy model. *Journal of Personality and Social Psychology, 53*, 1106-1118.

Fincham, F. D., & Bradbury, T. N. (1988). The impact of attributions in marriage: Empirical and conceptual foundations. *British Journal of Clinical Psychology, 27*, 77-90.

Fincham, F. D., & Bradbury, T. N. (in press-a). Cognition in marriage: A program of research on attributions. In D. Perlman & W. Jones (Eds.), *Advances in personal relationships* (Volume 2). Greenwich, CT: JAI.

Fincham, F. D., & Bradbury, T. N. (in press-b). The impact of attributions in marriage: An experimental analysis. *Journal of Social and Clinical Psychology*.

Fiske, S. T. (1980). Attention and weight in person perception: The impact of negative and extreme behavior. *Journal of Personality and Social Psychology, 38*, 889-908.

Floyd, F. J., & Markman, H. J. (1983). Observational biases in spouse observation: Toward a cognitive/behavioral model of marriage. *Journal of Consulting and Clinical Psychology, 51*, 450-457.

Glick, B. R., & Gross, S. J. (1975). Marital interaction and marital conflict: A critical evaluation of current research strategies. *Journal of Marriage and the Family, 37*, 505-512.

Gottman, J. M. (1979). *Marital interaction: Experimental investigations*. New York: Academic Press.

Gottman, J. M., & Levenson, R. W. (1984). Why marriages fail: Affective and physiological patterns in marital interaction. In J. C. Masters & K. Yarkin-Levin (Eds.), *Boundary areas in social and developmental psychology* (pp. 67-106). New York: Academic Press.

Gottman, J. M., & Levenson, R. W. (1986). Assessing the role of emotion in marriage. *Behavioral Assessment, 8*, 31-48.

Gottman, J. M., Markman, H., & Notarius, C. (1977). The topography of marital conflict: A sequential analysis of verbal and nonverbal behavior. *Journal of Marriage and the Family, 39*, 461-477.

Gottman, J. M., Notarius, C., Markman, H., Banks, S., Yoppi, B., & Rubin, M. E. (1976). Behavior exchange theory and marital decision making. *Journal of Personality and Social Psychology, 34*, 14-23.

Gurman, A. S., & Knudson, R. M. (1978). Behavioral marriage therapy: I. A psychodynamic-systems analysis and critique. *Family Process, 17*, 121-138.

Higgins, E. T., & Bargh, J. A. (1987). Social cognition and social perception. *Annual Review of Psychology, 38*, 366-425.

Hinde, R. A. (1979). *Toward understanding relationships*. London: Academic Press.

Hinde, R. A., & Stevenson-Hinde, J. (1986). Relationships, personality, and the social situation. In R. Gilmour & S. Duck (Eds.), *The emerging field of personal relationships* (pp. 63-76). Hillsdale, NJ: Lawrence Erlbaum.

Holtzworth-Munroe, A., & Jacobson, N. S. (in press). Toward a methodology for coding spontaneous causal attributions: Preliminary results with married couples. *Journal of Social and Clinical Psychology*.

Hormuth, S. E. (1986). The sampling of experiences *in situ*. *Journal of Personality, 54*, 262-293.

Huston, T. L., McHale, S. M., & Crouter, A. C. (1986). When the honeymoon's over: Changes in the marriage relationship over the first year. In R. Gilmour & S. Duck (Eds.), *The emerging field of personal relationships* (pp. 109-132). Hillsdale, NJ: Lawrence Erlbaum.

Jacob, T., & Krahn, G. (1987). The classification of behavioral observation codes in studies of family interaction. *Journal of Marriage and the Family, 49*, 677-687.

Jacobson, N. S., & Moore, D. (1981). Spouses as observers of the events in their relationship. *Journal of Consulting and Clinical Psychology, 49*, 269-277.

Jacobson, N. S., Waldron, H., & Moore, D. (1980). Toward a behavioral profile of marital distress. *Journal of Consulting and Clinical Psychology, 48*, 696-703.

Kelley, H. H. (1985). Affect in interpersonal relations. In P. Shaver (Ed.), *Review of personality and social psychology* (Vol. 5, pp. 89-115). Beverly Hills, CA: Sage.

Kelley, H. H., Berscheid, E., Christensen, A., Harvey, J. H., Huston T. L., Levinger, G., McClintock, E., Peplau, L. A., & Peterson, D. (1983). *Close relationships*. New York: Freeman.

Kelly, E. L., & Conley, J. J. (1987). Personality and compatibility: A prospective analysis of marital stability and marital satisfaction. *Journal of Personality and Social Psychology, 52*, 27-40.

Koren, P., Carlton, K., & Shaw, D. (1980). Marital conflict: Relations among behaviors, outcomes, and distress. *Journal of Consulting and Clinical Psychology, 48*, 460-468.

Krokoff, L. J., Gottman, J. M., & Roy, A. K. (1988). The blue-collar couple: A re-evaluation. *Journal of Social and Personal Relationships, 5*, 201-221.

Levenson, R. W., & Gottman, J. M. (1983). Marital interaction: Physiological linkage and affective exchange. *Journal of Personality and Social Psychology, 45*, 587-597.

Levenson, R. W., & Gottman, J. M. (1985). Physiological and affective predictors of change in relationship satisfaction. *Journal of Personality and Social Psychology, 49*, 85-94.

Levinger, G., & Rands, M. (1985). Compatibility in marriage and other close relationships. In W. Ickes (Ed.), *Compatible and incompatible relationships* (pp. 309-331). New York: Springer-Verlag.

Margolin, G., Hattem, D., John, R. S., & Yost, K. (1985). Perceptual agreement between spouses and outside observers when coding themselves and a stranger dyad. *Behavioral Assessment, 7*, 235-247.

Markman, H. (1981). Prediction of marital distress. A 5-year follow-up. *Journal of Consulting and Clinical Psychology, 49*, 760-762.

McArthur, L. Z. (1981). What grabs you? The role of attention in impression formation and causal attribution. In E. T. Higgins, C. P. Herman, & M. P. Zanna (Eds.), *Social cognition: The Ontario Symposium* (pp. 201-246). Hillsdale, NJ: Lawrence Erlbaum.

Newcomb, M. D., & Bentler, P. M. (1981). Marital breakdown. In S. Duck & R. Gilmour (Eds.), *Personal relationships: 3. Personal relationships in disorder* (pp. 57-94). New York: Academic Press.

Noller, P. (1980). Misunderstandings in marital communication: A study of couples' nonverbal communication. *Journal of Personality and Social Psychology, 39*, 1135-1148.

Raush, H. L., Barry, W. A., Hertel, R. K., & Swain, M. A. (1974). *Communication, conflict, and marriage.* San Francisco: Jossey-Bass.

Rempel, J. K., Holmes, J. G., & Zanna, M. P. (1985). Trust in close relationships. *Journal of Personality and Social Psychology, 49,* 95-112.

Schaap, C. (1984). A comparison of the interaction of distressed and nondistressed married couples in a laboratory situation: Literature survey, methodological issues, and an empirical investigation. In K. Hahlweg & N. S. Jacobson (Eds.), *Marital interaction: Analysis and modification* (pp. 133-158). New York: Guilford.

Schachter, J., & O'Leary, K. D. (1985). Affective intent and impact in marital communication. *American Journal of Family Therapy, 13,* 17-23.

Schindler, L., & Vollmer, M. (1984). Cognitive perspectives in behavioral marital therapy: Some proposals for bridging theory, research, and practice. In K. Hahlweg & N. S. Jacobson (Eds.), *Marital interaction: Analysis and modification* (pp. 309-324). New York: Guilford.

Sillars, A. L., Wilmot, W. W., & Hocker, J. C. (in press). Communication strategies in conflict and mediation. In J. Wiemann & J. Daly (Eds.), *Communicating strategically: Strategies in interpersonal communication.* Hillsdale, NJ: Lawrence Erlbaum.

Sternberg, R. J. (1986). A triangular theory of love. *Psychological Review, 93,* 119-135.

Stuart, R. B. (1969). Operant interpersonal treatment for marital discord. *Journal of Consulting and Clinical Psychology, 33,* 675-682.

Stuart, R. B. (1980). *Helping couples change.* New York: Guilford.

Tharp, R. G. (1963). Psychological patterning in marriage. *Psychological Bulletin, 60,* 97-117.

Vincent, J. P., Weiss, R. L., & Birchler, G. R. (1975). A behavioral analysis of problem-solving in distressed and nondistressed married and stranger dyads. *Behavior Therapy, 6,* 475-487.

Weiner, B. (1986). *An attributional theory of motivation and emotion.* New York: Springer-Verlag.

Weiss, R. L. (1984). Cognitive and behavioral measures of marital interaction. In K. Hahlweg & N. S. Jacobson (Eds.), *Marital interaction: Analysis and modification* (pp. 232-252). New York: Guilford.

Wills, T. A., Weiss, R. L., & Patterson, G. R. (1974). A behavioral analysis of the determinants of marital satisfaction. *Journal of Consulting and Clinical Psychology, 42,* 802-811.

6

Emotional Communication in Personal Relationships

A DEVELOPMENTAL-INTERACTIONIST VIEW

ROSS BUCK

Ross Buck is Professor of Communication Sciences and Psychology at the University of Connecticut. He received his M.A. from the University of Wisconsin, Madison and his Ph.D. from the University of Pittsburgh. He was a Research Associate at the University of Pittsburgh Medical School and taught at Carnegie-Mellon University before coming to Connecticut. He has been a Visiting Scholar at Harvard University and the Aphasia Research Unit of the Boston Veterans Administration Hospital, and a Visiting Fellow at Wolfson College, Oxford in 1988. His books include *Human Motivation and Emotion* (1976, Second edition, 1988) and *The Communication of Emotion* (1984).

By their very nature, feelings have an irrational quality—which doesn't mean, however, that they are necessarily inappropriate or irrelevant. The irrational stems from sources in the personality that lie deeper than the roots of reason. The irrational is always opposed to the reasonable because the irrational speaks for the body, while the reasonable speaks for society. (Alexander Lowen, *The Betrayal of the Body*, 1967, p. 9)

A DEVELOPMENTAL-INTERACTIONIST VIEW OF EMOTION

This chapter approaches personal relationships with a conceptual scheme that seeks to integrate the cognitive approach taken by most social psychologists with the notion of spontaneous emotional communication. Specifically, I argue that the *body* must be viewed as a source of structured information in the attribution process. This bodily information is of various sorts, and includes drives, affects, and physical symptoms. The child must learn to deal with this internal bodily environment just as he or she must learn to deal with the external environment, but this is a complex process from a social learning point of view because the internal information accessible to the child is not accessible to others. For example, it is relatively easy to learn about the

AUTHOR'S NOTE: The author is grateful to the University of Connecticut Research Foundation and the National Institutes of Mental Health for the support of research reported in this chapter, and to Michael Argyle for his comments and suggestions.

color red because red objects are simultaneously accessible to both the child and the socialization agent. Learning about feelings like joy and anger involves the response of the socialization agent to the expressions of the child, providing a "looking glass" by which the child comes to label and understand the feelings (see Cooley, 1902). This *social biofeedback* process takes place within the context of a personal relationship, and the quality of this process, I suggest, determines much about the quality of the relationship.

This point of view is based upon a developmental interactionist theory of emotion. This theory takes the basic insight of the Schachter and Singer (1962) theory, that emotion involves an interaction of cognitive and physiological mechanisms, but developmental-interactionist theory introduces two fundamental changes. First, the notions of "physiological" and "cognitive" are recast into notions of special-purpose processing systems structured by evolution (phylogeny) and general-purpose processing systems structured by individual experience (ontogeny). Second, the theory emphasizes that this interaction occurs in a developmental context such that the individual learns about the "internal environment" of feelings and desires engendered by the special-purpose processing systems much as the individual learns about events in the external environment. Specifically, the special-purpose processing systems are seen to be primary motivational-emotional systems (Primes) that include reflexes, instincts, drives, and affects. The Primes constitute sources of structured information internal to the body just as the external physical/social environment is an external source of structured information. The Primes are accessible to the individual via subjective experience (termed Emotion III), an internal readout of motivational/emotional information that evolved in ways analogous to the external, expressive-social readout (termed Emotion II; see Buck, 1980, 1985).

One learns to understand and label this internal information—to "come to terms with one's feelings," so to speak—through a process of *emotional education.* One's success or failure in this process results in a greater or lesser degree of emotional competence analogous to competence in dealing with external reality. The emotional education process proceeds in great part in the context of personal relationships in what is literally a social biofeedback process.

This chapter explores the implications of the developmental-interactionist theory of emotion for understanding personal relationships. The theory regards emotional expression and communication to be the essential link between phenomena at the social level of analysis (i.e., personal relationships) and phenomena at the physiological level of analysis (i.e., autonomic, endocrine, and immune system functioning). It is through emotional communication that the personal relationship influences the emotional life of the individual, and it is through emotional communication that personal relationships are created and cemented.

The first part of this chapter summarizes my position on the nature and importance of emotional communication. It presents the notion of structured bodily information and defines spontaneous communication. It is suggested, following Darwin, that spontaneous communication underlies social organization, and Panksepp's (1981) theory that attachment is based upon opiate mechanisms is considered. The implication is that humans may be literally "addicted to love": that close personal relationships are associated with the release of endogenous opiates.

The second part presents and defines formally the processes by which emotion becomes regulated socially. The *accessibility dimension* involves the fact that subjective experience and spontaneous expression are differentially accessible to the responder and to others. The *education of attention* is a concept from Gibsonian perceptual theory (Gibson, 1966, 1979). It is applied here to structured internal bodily information as opposed to structured information in the external environment, as is the case in Gibson's theory. The social biofeedback process is then defined, as is the notion of emotional education. The latter argues that humans differ from animals in that we have language; and that humans must develop a linguistically structured "naive theory of emotion" just as they develop other sorts of naive theories that get them through life. The process of coming to a linguistically structured understanding of emotion is emotional education, and in humans it is the ultimate result of the social biofeedback process.

The final part of the chapter applies this thinking to the notion of personal and social relationships, arguing that these serve as the context within which a linguistically structured understanding of emotion occurs. Within the context of specific personal relationships, we develop *rules* of emotional experience and expression just as we develop other sorts of rules governing relationships. Because of this rule development, personal relationships come to function as emotional regulators for the individual. Thus, spontaneous emotional communication simultaneously serves functions of *social coordination* and *self-regulation*, and these processes occur in the context of the rules developed in specific personal relationships.

THE NATURE OF EMOTIONAL COMMUNICATION

Rediscovery of the Body

Subjective experience. In the original Schachter and Singer (1962) formulation, the physiological side of the cognitive-physiological interaction was provided by sympathetic nervous system arousal (experimentally induced by the injection of epinephrine). It was reasoned that cognitive information and labels regarding this relatively undifferentiated arousal state were responsible for qualitative differences in emotion. This theory was applied not only to emotion, but to hunger as well, in Schachter's (1970) theory of obesity: obese persons were thought to "label" their hunger in terms of external food-related cues rather than internal metabolic signals.

In recent years it has become clear that the physiological factors were oversimplified in the original formulation, and that mechanisms exist within the body to provide *structured* information to the central nervous system regarding bodily functioning. In other words, we have direct access to certain kinds of important information internal to the body just as we have direct access to certain kinds of important information external to the body. The new understanding of the biological mechanisms underlying the control of eating, for example, forced a reformulation of the externality theory of eating (Rodin, 1981).

The Gibsonian ecological theory of perception describes how mechanisms evolve to "pick up" information directly, "in the light, in the air, on the skin" (Gibbs, 1985, p. 114). The same reasoning can be applied to information *within* the skin: it simply makes sense that if an organism has evolved to have knowledge of the external milieu, it must also have knowledge of certain important aspects of the internal milieu as well. It would not be useful to an organism to have knowledge of food if it did not also have knowledge of its need for food.

Knowledge by acquaintance versus description. This internal knowledge is a direct, immediate subjective experience of feelings and desires. Being knowledge, it constitutes a kind of cognition, but it is an automatic, holistic, prerational sort of "hot" cognition as opposed to "cold," analytic, sequential information processing. This direct sort of cognition is what has been termed knowledge-by-acquaintance in epistemological theories (Russell, 1948) and syncretic cognition in Tucker's (1981) analysis of right versus left hemisphere functioning. Cold cognition in contrast is knowledge-by-description, or analytic cognition. Cognitive theories in psychology are typically concerned with cold cognition.

   This distinction between two sorts of cognition is, I think, essential for understanding the relationship between emotion and cognition. Emotion is often distinguished from cognition, but in reality emotion involves a kind of cognition: a direct, immediate, syncretic experience of feelings and desires. The brain "knows" how to experience anger and fear, happiness and sadness, hunger and thirst, warmth and coldness.

   The notion of the reality of subjective experience seems at first glance to be incompatible with objective science, since it seems impossible to study subjectivity objectively. However, there have been advances in the understanding of the biological bases of behavior that make possible the objective study of neurochemical mechanisms that appear to be closely associated with subjective experience. In particular, the recent work on the neuropeptides, such as the endogenous opiates or endorphins, provides an objective basis for the study of (at least) pleasure, pain, anxiety, and hunger (see Buck, 1988).

   Implications for attribution theory. This new work on the physiological level is forcing a rediscovery of the body on the part of social scientists. For example, it has important consequences for the Schachter and Singer (1962) formulation, as it indicates that there is much more to emotional experience than sympathetic nervous system arousal. It also has important implications for attribution theory, as it indicates the presence of a kind of mechanism of behavior control that is not considered in conventional formulations. Attribution theory distinguishes between internal or personal causes of behavior that are under voluntary control, and external or situational causes of behavior that are not under voluntary control. This new perspective suggests that there must be causes of behavior that are internal to the organism, but are not under voluntary control. These constitute *bodily* sources of the causation of behavior that are beyond the voluntary control of the individual, yet inextricably bound to the individual. An extreme example of such behavior is uncontrollable aggression brought about by a brain tumor, or by brain stimulation (Mark & Ervin, 1970).

Spontaneous Versus Symbolic Communication

   Spontaneous communication. I suggest that the communication process involves two simultaneous streams of information that are based upon different sending and receiving mechanisms. *Spontaneous communication* is direct and biologically based in both its sending and receiving aspects. That is, it is based upon innate tendencies to display certain kinds of motivational/emotional information and to respond appropriately to those displays when one notices them in others,

Spontaneous communication is in no way intentional. It is composed of signs rather than symbols, where symbols have arbitrary relationships with their referents and signs are *externally accessible aspects* of their referents. Since the sign cannot occur in the absence of the referent, it cannot convey false information. Therefore, spontaneous communication is always veridical and therefore nonpropositional. Its content consists of motivational/emotional states—signs of feelings and desires (see Buck, 1984, 1985).

Symbolic communication. Symbolic communication is learned and socially based. It is at some level intentional. It is composed of symbols, and its content consists of propositions, of statements that can be false. It should be noted that "nonverbal communication" may be either spontaneous or symbolic. It is spontaneous *only* when it is a direct and veridical expression of actual motivational/emotional states. If display rules or facial management techniques are employed, as when we try to look happy at a party even when we are miserable, this "nonverbal" communication is symbolic.

Emotion and Social Regulation

Darwin (1872) argued that emotional communication evolved to serve functions of social organization. We display information about socially relevant things: about courting status and dominance; about happiness, sadness, fear, surprise, and anger. Social species, such as canids (wolves, dogs), plains-dwelling baboons, chimpanzees, and human beings have more complex displays than do less social species such as mandrills and orangutans. Indeed, it can be argued that the basic social agenda for any species is set by the nature and variability of its innately organized system of spontaneous emotional communication.

The fact that the spontaneous emotional communication system is innately based does not mean that learning is not important. As Harlow demonstrated in his studies of rhesus monkeys, social learning is absolutely necessary if the individual is to *learn how to use* appropriately its innately based communication abilities in social contexts (see Harlow & Mears, 1983; Miller, Caul, & Mirsky, 1967). This research is in fact an excellent example of how the interaction between special-purpose processing systems (the innately based abilities) and general-purpose processing systems (learning how to use these abilities) occurs in a developmental context.

Might as Well Face It: We're Addicted to Love

The basic nature of love. The foundation of all social behavior is attachment. Psychoanalytic theorists, beginning with Freud, have suggested that attachment begins with infant's relationship to the mother. In effect, the mother is the original object of love, and subsequent objects of love are seen to be substitutes for the original. This notion of a primal symbiotic need for union with the mother has received support from intriguing and well-controlled studies that demonstrate that the subliminal presentation of a symbiotic message ("Mommy and I are one" or "Daddy and I are one") has significant positive effects in many persons (Silverman & Weinberger, 1985).

Mammalian infants come from an environment in which they are, literally, attached to the mother within the womb and are born into a world where this attachment must continue for a time if they are to survive. Harlow and his colleagues demonstrated the importance of contact comfort in the early establishment of attachment bonds. In social animals such as wolves or rhesus monkeys, the growing infant must transfer its original attachment to the mother to other animals in the group. This transfer seems to occur during play. As the infant grows and gains motor skills, the mother usually begins to resist unrestricted attachment behavior, and the youngster turns naturally to its peers. In rough and tumble play the growing youngster learns to communicate with peers about matters basic to social organization—about dominance, submission, and courting. After puberty, these communication abilities form the basis of the social order. This transition occurs, however, in the context of a basic attachment to the peers that in turn seems based upon the earlier relationship with the mother. If these personal relationships are disrupted, as in Harlow's deprivation experiments, the social abilities of the individual are deeply affected (Harlow & Mears, 1983).

The biology of love. It may be that there is a feature common to all attachment—that between mother and infant, between immature peers, between adult males and females—that appears in humans as well as other social animals. It may be that attachment is based upon neurochemical systems involving the endogenous opiates, or endorphins. This hypothesis is based upon the work of Jaak Panksepp on distress calls in young animals. Panksepp reasoned that the distress call occurs when the object of attachment is absent, so that in learning more about the biological systems underlying distress calls, we can learn something very basic to the biology of attachment.

Panksepp (1981, 1986) has found that the distress call is related to the presence and absence of endorphins. The endorphins are peptide neurohormones that have effects similar to those of morphine, the active ingredient of opium and heroin. One of these effects is analgesia:

Morphine is a painkiller because it interferes with substance P, another peptide neurohormone that carries pain messages from the body periphery to the brain. Another action of morphine involves the inhibition of respiration. Respiratory failure is a common cause of death in heroin overdose; the individual literally stops breathing. A third action of morphine is a subjectively experienced euphoria: the "high" that abusers of opium, heroin, and other morphine-related drugs strive to experience. This all-encompassing pleasure replaces all natural pleasures, including the pleasures derived from attachment to others. Morphine addicts do not love: Their need for social attachment is replaced by their need for the drug.

The fetus in the womb is liberally bathed in endorphins. It is possible that the endorphins function to inhibit respiration in the unborn fetus, and also protect it from the pain of birth. It is also possible that the fetus is in a euphoric state induced by the endorphins that becomes the prototype for love.

Panksepp (1981, 1982) argued that the brain's endorphins play a central role in the physiological substrates for attachment. Very low nonanalgesic doses of morphine reduce distress vocalizations in many species (Panksepp, 1986), and at this low dose range morphine seems to "substitute for mother" in a dose-dependent fashion: the more morphine, the fewer distress calls (Panksepp, 1981, p. 299). Also, the morphine antagonist naloxone, which blocks the action of the endorphins, causes distress calls even when the mother is present. Panksepp suggested that the presence of endorphins at functionally important brain sites induces a natural "high" associated with attachment, and that their absence induces a "panic" that is signalled by distress calls.

The endorphinergic systems in the brain are as "basic" as the systems mediating eating and drinking, extending from limbic system structures (particularly the septal area), through the hypothalamus, into the midbrain. The evolutionary age of these structures implies that the endorphins have been involved in social attachment through much of vertebrate evolution; indeed, they have been linked with schooling behavior in fish (Karaliers, 1981). Panksepp (1981, 1982) suggested that the social attachment mechanism evolved from a mechanism originally designed to control pain, and that the loss of the object of a strong attachment may actually be associated with a kind of generalized, unlocalizable pain.

Panksepp (1986) also suggested that there are analogies between love and morphine addiction in human beings that are due to their common basis in the endorphinergic neurochemical systems. The presence of the loved one is associated with a euphoric "high" due to the natural release of endorphins, and the absence of the loved one may be analogous to morphine withdrawal. Also, continued association with the loved one may produce a phenomenon analogous to morphine tolerance: The euphoria previously produced by the loved one may not occur, leading to certain tendencies toward philandering that are well-established features of human behavior.

The rhetoric of love. Although the endorphins may provide the basis of social attachment in human beings as well as in other animals, the internal information provided by the endorphins is organized and understood linguistically in humans. Thus, although the biological foundations of love are common to all human beings, each culture and society may develop definitions of what love is and rules about the circumstance under which love occurs and is expressed. This understanding is often communicated to the members of a culture in songs and stories that instruct them when to love and whom to love and not to love. This is the rhetoric of love, which reflects linguistic cultural traditions.

These definitions and rules may also be specific to given personal relationships, and may vary from relationship to relationship. The six basic love styles identified by Lee (1973/1976) and developed into a multidimensional scale by Hendrick and Hendrick (1986) describe ways in which the primal feelings of attachment may be differentiated as the child grows into adulthood and learns different sets of rules that cover different sorts of personal and social relationships. It may be, nevertheless, that all of these rest ultimately upon attachment and the endorphins.

THE SOCIAL REGULATION OF EMOTION

This section formally defines four processes important in the process by which emotion becomes regulated socially: the accessibility dimension, the education of attention, the social biofeedback process, and emotional education.

The Accessibility Dimension

The accessibility dimension involves the fact that different sorts of motivational/emotional responses are differentially accessible to the responder and the socialization agent, so that they must be subjected to different sorts of social learning experience (Buck, 1971). *Accessibility* is defined as the extent to which a behavior is normally apparent via sensory cues (Buck, 1984). Goal-directed behaviors are accessible to both the responder and the socialization agent, subjective experiences are accessible to the responder but not the socialization agent, expressive nonverbal behaviors are more accessible to the socialization agent than they are to the responder, and physiological responses (automatic, endocrine, immune system) responses are normally inaccessible to anyone without special equipment.

The Education of Attention

A response may be accessible to the individual, but that does not mean that the individual will necessarily attend to that response. The organism is bombarded by many stimuli, both internal and external, and must learn how most efficiently to direct its attention to the most relevant stimuli. This learning process is the education of attention (Buck, 1984).

The concept of the education of attention is taken from the Gibsonian ecological theory of perception (Gibson, 1966, 1979), but is applied here to the direct perception of events occurring *within the body*: of feelings, desires, and physical symptoms of various sorts. Pennebaker (1983) has shown how attention to physical symptoms varies with attention to external events. For example, people cough more during boring moments of a lecture, presumably because they are then more likely to notice minor throat irritations. I suggest that a great range of emotional experience is always available to the individual in the form of gentle desires and moods: We can always attend to our present level of drives involving warmth or coldness, sexual arousal, hunger, and thirst; and affects involving happiness, sadness, fear, anger, and so on. However, like the feel of our shoes, we *attend* to this internal information only when it is strong and pressing (i.e., when the shoes are uncomfortable), or when our attention is consciously drawn to it.

There is evidence that different persons learn to direct their attention toward different stimuli. M. A. Wenger described the case of a student from India who had studied Yoga, who was markedly superior to American students in relaxing his muscles. In the context of his culture, he had learned to pay attention to internal bodily processes that Americans learn to ignore (Wenger & Bagchi, 1961).

One learns to direct one's attention in one way or another in part by observing the behaviors of social models—i.e., parents, peers, teachers, and models in mass media. Models presented via media are often more informative in some ways than are other persons, in that drama can make accessible thought processes, desires, and feelings that are usually not accessible in other persons. One also learns to direct one's attention in the context of interactive situations involving a person with whom one has a personal or social relationship. This learning involves the social biofeedback process (Buck, 1988).

The Social Biofeedback Process

I propose that the child comes to understand his or her feelings and desires via a social biofeedback process in which the child's spontaneous expressions are responded to by others. The notion of social biofeedback is quite literal. A biofeedback device works by making normally inaccessible physiological responses accessible to the responder, so that they can in many cases come under voluntary control. The device measures the physiological response and gives the responder feedback, which may be gradually associated with the complex of relevant bodily information. In other words, "the subject discovers the relationship of some aspect of his (or her) *consciousness* or subjective awareness to that aspect of his (or her) *physiological* activity indicated by the feedback signal" (Kamiya, 1968, p. 56).

I propose that spontaneous expression makes certain physiologically based activities *accessible to other persons*, so that they can respond, giving feedback to the expresser. It therefore makes possible a natural social biofeedback process in which the subject learns about the subjective aspects of his or her own feelings and desires (emotions and motives) via feedback from others. The subjective aspect of feelings and desires is accessible to the responder (i.e., a child, C) but not the socialization agent (i.e., a parent, P). P does, however, have access to C's spontaneous facial expressions, gestures, postures, and tones of voice. I suggest that when an emotional state occurs, certain neurochemical systems are activated, leading (separately and independently) to subjective experience and to spontaneous expressions. For example, if when unable to build a desired structure with blocks, C screams and throws a block at P, I assume that independent of this display C is subjectively experiencing a state associated with neurochemical activity in the vicinity of the amygdalae, posterior hypothalamus, and midbrain central gray. P does not have access to this experience but certainly does have access to the display. P's response to C will be important in several respects, including the elaboration of the personal relationship between and P and C. More immediately, P will fulfill a role analogous to that of a biofeedback device.

The response of P to C's display constitutes feedback that will be associated with C's subjective experience. If P says, for example, that blocks can be frustrating and make you angry, but that you must not throw your blocks at people, C will gain a wealth of information about the subjectively experienced state: that it is called anger, is a common response to frustration, but that it cannot be uncontrollably expressed. On the other hand, if P says that C is a bad girl, that good girls do not act that way, and that Santa Claus may bring sticks and stones at Christmas, C learns quite a different lesson. She may well come to associate the subjective experience of this state with being a bad girl, and feel anxious and guilty when the state is aroused.

Emotional Education

The result of observing social models and participating in the social biofeedback process is emotional education, in which the responder learns to label and understand events "within the skin," that is, feelings and desires. In effect, the responder constructs a "naive theory of emotion" from his or her subjective experience of bodily states, the feedback from others that is associated with these subjective experiences, and the relevant behaviors of social models. In humans this naive theory is linguistically organized, having the properties of logical consistency and comprehensiveness that are essential aspects of such organization. What results is a (more or less) logically organized view of a biologically organized phenomenon.

Emotional education must influence the sorts of personal relationships that the individual feels comfortable engaging in, and these relationships in turn must influence the continuing course of emotional education. This process may be compared to the process by which political views are shaped by social relationships and in turn shape future social relationships (Newcomb, 1963). For example, the girl who is consistently labeled as "bad" when being aggressive may have difficulty with a person who expects her to be assertive. In general, the individual may tend to be most comfortable in those relationships that reinforce previous patterns of emotional education, even when those relationships from another point of view may appear to be maladaptive. Thus, an individual who has suffered abuse as a child may choose to enter abusive relationships as an adult, because it is consistent with past experience. The individual may literally learn to love the abuse.

RELATIONSHIPS AS EMOTIONAL REGULATORS

There has long been evidence that the presence or absence of other people has physiological effects upon the individual, and that these effects can be particularly striking if one has a close personal relationship with the other. This section examines the role played by personal and social relationships in the emotional life of the individual.

The Other as a Biofeedback Device

Over time, relationships increasingly become structured by rules, and this applies to rules of emotional experience and expression as much as it applies in other realms. It is axiomatic that as one goes from more impersonal "social" relationships to more intimate "personal" relationships, there are changes in the information used to relate to the other and in the rules governing behavior vis-à-vis the other. Specifically, social relationships use general information about such things as age, sex, and physical attractiveness, while personal relationships use information intrinsic to the relationships that would not be available if the relationships did not exist. Similarly, social relationships are governed by general rules of politeness that tend to limit intimacy, while personal relationships have rules specific to the relationship that regulate intimacy in a way appropriate to the relationship (Argyle, Henderson, & Furnam, 1985).

As a relationship becomes more personal, the rules governing emotional experience and expression become more specific and intrinsic to the relationship. Expressive displays to which the other responds quickly and reliably become controlled by display rules, while expressive behaviors that are ignored by the other are less controlled and may thus "leak" the individual's true feelings (Ekman & Friesen, 1969). This is, in effect, an education of attention, where the individual's attention is drawn to those aspects of his or her own display that are responded to by the other. Also, this interpersonal feedback functions as social biofeedback, so that certain relatively inaccessible physiological responses are rendered more accessible because of their association with the other's response. Thus, through spontaneous communication the personal relationship functions as a social biofeedback device that is focused upon some physiological responses but not others.

For example, given a relationship between a subject S and an other O: As the relationship between S and O becomes more personal, O becomes a more reliable, although not necessarily more valid, source of social biofeedback to S; and S in turn becomes a more reliable source to O. S and O are increasingly able to predict how the other will respond to different sorts of emotional expressions, and they learn to label and understand their subjective emotional response (emotional education) in a way that may be carried over into other situations. In effect, *rules about emotion* develop that are specific to the personal relationship in question, but that also may have a general impact upon the ways that S and O label and understand their feelings. These rules can have *bioregulatory* implications for the persons involved, because S's ability to predict the response of O, and to understand S's own subjective emotional response, may increase S's ability to cope with stressful events. S will know what kinds of emotional responses are appropriate in that particular situation, and will not feel confused and helpless about how to respond (Reardon & Buck, in press).

The bioregulatory functions of personal relationships may explain why personality patterns associated with physical illnesses—the Type-A behavior pattern associated with cardiovascular disease, the Type-C behavior pattern associated with cancer, and the alexithymic personality associated with psychosomatic disorder—all involve problems in emotional communication (Buck, 1988). These functions may also explain why the presence of strong personal relationships is associated with resistance to physical stress and disease and why bereavement is associated with a decrease in such resistance (Hofer, 1984).

Thus, in the context of a given personal relationship, O becomes a more reliable feedback device, in that S comes to have more specific expectations about the feedback that will result from certain expressions. It should be emphasized again that O will *not* necessarily become a more *valid* feedback device: There may be some people who, for example, might consistently respond to female expressions of anger as if it were "bad behavior," or to male expressions of caring as "weakness" when there is no justification for such a response.

The emergence of rules about emotional experience and expression is one process by which the relationship comes to serve bioregulatory functions for the individual. The individual comes to rely upon the expected response of the other as a guide to emotional expression and for the interpretation of emotional experience, and this may engender feelings of competence in the emotional realm. This is not to say that the relationship is necessarily beneficial to the individual when other criteria are considered. For example, the other may encourage a distorted view of emotional expression and experience, as in the second example of the interchange between C and P considered previously. Regardless of, and sometimes because of these distortions, C may become greatly dependent upon P.

Expressiveness and Social Attraction

There is evidence that more expressive people are seen as more interpersonally attractive. Sabatelli and Rubin (1986) presented the videotaped expressions of persons watching emotionally loaded color slides to raters who judged the person's warmth and likability. More expressive persons were rated as more warm and likable, independent of their physical attractiveness. Together with other evidence (e.g., Bayes, 1972; Shrout & Fiske, 1981), this finding suggests that people who provide much interpersonal nonverbal information are perceived, at least initially, more favorably. I suggest that this favorable impression is due to the fact that such persons provide much social biofeedback.

Empathy

Traditional approaches. The study of the ability to perceive accurately the qualities of other persons has been variously called accuracy in person perception, social sensitivity, and empathy. It is one of the oldest areas of research in social psychology, with attempts to measure this ability going back to the 1920s. The story of this research effort is very largely a story of failure. A bewildering array of seemingly valid measures of accuracy in person perception were constructed, but no generally accepted measure prevailed. The early research in person perception ended in the mid-50s when Hastorf and Bender (1952), Cronbach (1955) and others pointed out serious problems in the typical methodology used in these studies.

More recently, studies of emotional sensitivity or nonverbal receiving ability have been constructed in attempts to measure the ability to perceive accurately affect in other persons. Measures such as the Brief Affect Recognition Test (BART, Ekman & Friesen, 1974), the Communication of Affect Receiving Ability Test (CARAT, Buck, 1976), Profile of Nonverbal Sensitivity (PONS, Rosenthal et al., 1979), and Situations Interpretation Task (SIT, Archer & Akert, 1977) have been proposed that escape the methodological problems of the early person perception research. However, the relationships among these instruments, and even between different versions of the same instrument, have been disappointing. Thus despite over 50 years of effort, there is still no generally accepted measure of emphatic abilities (see Buck, 1983, 1984).

It is important to inquire about the reasons for this half-century of failure, so that past mistakes will not be repeated. I suggest that the problems lie in the basic conceptualization of empathy: of viewing what is essentially an interactive phenomenon as an "ability" that resides within the individual. Psychologists tend to approach phenomena with the individual as the unit of analysis, which is appropriate if the phenomenon in question is truly a quality of the individual. I submit that it is a fundamental mistake to regard empathy as a skill that resides within the individual and that is testable by conventional psychometric techniques. Instead, empathy is an aspect of a *communication* process, and any communication process is inherently dyadic, for it implies both a sender and a receiver. The qualities of the individual as a receiver cannot be divorced from the qualities of the individual as a sender, or from the sending and receiving qualities of the partner in the interaction.

More specifically, in ordinary life empathy operates in a transactional context in which one's own expressions can affect the other's behavior. By being expressive, a person encourages the other to reciprocate, so that an expressive person in effect goes through life leaving a trail of emotional expression in his or her wake, while a nonexpressive person leaves the reverse. Also, in ordinary life one has a wide choice in deciding to what aspects of the environment one will attend. There are many potential sources of information: the situational context, the symbolic communication behavior of the other, the spontaneous behavior of the other, and so forth. People who habitually ignore spontaneous expressive behavior to concentrate on symbolic communication should be low in emotional sensitivity, but if *instructed* to pay attention to spontaneous cues in the context of a test of emotional sensitivity, they may do well.

An alternative view. I have suggested a view of empathy in which the individual's ability to gain information from others is primarily a matter of (1) the expressiveness of the individual, which encourages the other to be expressive, and (2) learning to attend to spontaneous cues in the behavior of the other via the education of attention (Buck, 1983, 1984). In other words, the most controllable way to be a good receiver is by being expressive to encourage others to be expressive, and to attend to the other's expressions when they occur.

The contention that spontaneous expressiveness is a particularly important aspect of empathy is supported by studies using Kenny's (1981) social relations model. This model allows dyadic data to be broken into individual sending ability, individual receiving ability, and unique dyadic effects. Studies employing the social relations model have suggested that sending abilities contribute much variance to communication accuracy scores and receiving abilities do not (Sabatelli, Buck, & Kenny, 1986).

Expressiveness in schizophrenia. An interesting example of the effects of the expressiveness in an interactive situation has been reported by Rainer Krause, Evlyne Steimer, and their colleagues. They filmed the facial behavior of subjects engaged in a political discussion, and subsequently analyzed the expressions by the Facial Affect Coding System (FACS, Ekman & Friesen, 1975). One interactant was either a normal person, a hospitalized schizophrenic, an outpatient schizophrenic, or a patient with psychosomatic disorder. The other interactant was normal. Steimer, Krause, Sanger, & Wagner (in press) have found substantially less facial behavior in the *normal* interactant while talking to a patient, particularly a hospitalized schizophrenic, than when talking to another normal individual. This was the case even though the normal interactant did not know or suspect when the partner was schizophrenic: Any "strangeness" experienced during the conversation was attributed to the laboratory rather than the other person.

Schizophrenics are often described as being unexpressive and having "flat affect." A common explanation is that schizophrenics are poor receivers: they certainly do poorly on conventional measures of social sensitivity. However, Krause (1987) suggested an opposite explanation: Schizophrenics are so extremely *sensitive* to emotional cues that their feelings tend to be controlled by the expressions of others. He sees the schizophrenic's lack of expression as a protective device, functioning to "turn off" affect expression in others, so that the patient will not be overwhelmed. It may be that the results of conventional tests suggesting a lack of emotional sensitivity on the part of schizophrenics may actually reflect their inability to be *insensitive*.

Expressiveness and empathy. The argument that empathy is an interactive phenomenon implies that it should be measured in a interactive setting. For example, the sensitivity of subjects vis-à-vis one another could be assessed in a round-robin design and analyzed by the social relations model (Kenny & Nasby, 1980). However, there are occasions when this approach is impractical and an individual assessment of empathy is required. If the present view of empathy is correct, spontaneous expressiveness constitutes one of the best measures of empathy at the individual level. It reflects the tendency of the person to encourage emotional expression in others.

It should be noted that unless spontaneous expressiveness is measured when the individual is alone and unaware of being observed, the subject may use expression management techniques consistent with the rules associated with the personal or social relationship that is salient at the time (Ekman & Friesen, 1975). The results can be quite misleading, in that they will not reflect the general expressive tendencies of the individual. Thus I suggest that, paradoxically, the best individual measure of empathy is one taken when the subject is alone and unaware of being observed.

CONCLUSIONS

This chapter has presented a view of the functions played by emotional relationships from the point of view of developmental-interactionist theory. Emotional expression and communication are seen to be the link between phenomena at the social and the biological levels of analysis: It is through emotional expression that biologically structured bodily systems become accessible socially, and it is through the expressive feedback from others that the bodily systems become socially regulated. These processes take place within the context of personal and social relationships: Emotional communication is important in the establishment of these relationships, and the nature of the relationships that have been established plays an essential role in the emotional education process.

Regarding Lowen's quote given at the beginning of this chapter, I agree that feelings stem from bodily sources that "lie deeper than the roots of reason," but hope that the irrational is not always opposed to the reasonable, and certainly do not agree with the implication that the irrational is opposed to society. Indeed, I suggest that the roots of society are to be found in quite irrational emotional communication.

REFERENCES

Archer, D., & Akert, R. M. (1977). Words and everything else: Verbal and nonverbal cues in social interpretation. *Journal of Personality and Social Psychology, 35,* 443-449.

Argyle, M., Henderson, M., & Furnam, A. (1985). The rules of social relationships. *British Journal of Social Psychology, 24,* 125-139.

Bayes, M. A. (1972). Behavioral cues of interpersonal warmth. *Journal of Counsulting and Clinical Psychology, 39,* 333-339.

Buck, R. (1971, April). *Differences in social learning underlying overt-behavioral, subjective, and physiological responses to emotion.* Paper presented at the meeting of the Midwestern Psychological Association, Detroit.

Buck, R. (1976). *Human motivation and emotion.* New York: John Wiley.

Buck, R. (1980). Nonverbal behavior and the theory of emotion: The facial feedback hypothesis. *Journal of Personality and Social Psychology, 38,* 811-824.

Buck, R. (1983). Recent approaches to the study of nonverbal receiving ability. In J. Weimann & R. Harrison (Eds.), *Nonverbal communication: The social interaction sphere* (pp. 209-242). Beverly Hills, CA: Sage.

Buck, R. (1984). *The communication of emotion.* New York: Guilford.

Buck, R. (1985). Prime theory: An integrated view of motivation and emotion. *Psychological Review, 92,* 389-413.

Buck, R. (1988). *Human motivation and emotion* (2nd ed.). New York: John Wiley.

Cooley, C. H. (1902). *Human nature and the social order.* New York: Scribner's.

Cronbach, L. J. (1955). Processes affecting scores on "understanding of others" and "assumed similarity." *Psychological Bulletin, 52,* 177-193.

Darwin, C. (1959). *Expression of the emotions in man and animals.* New York: Philosophical Library. (Original work published 1872).

Ekman, P., & Friesen, W. V. (1969). Nonverbal leakage and clues to deception. *Psychiatry, 32,* 88-105.

Ekman, P., & Friesen, W. V. (1974). Nonverbal behavior and psychopathology. In R. J. Friedman & H. M. Katz (Eds.), *The psychology of depression: Contemporary theory and research.* New York: John Wiley.

Ekman, P., & Friesen, W. V. (1975). *Unmasking the face.* Englewood Cliffs, NJ: Prentice-Hall.

Ekman, P., & Friesen, W. V. (1978). *The facial action coding system (FACS): A technique for the measurement of facial action.* Palo Alto, CA: Consulting Psychologists Press.

Gibbs, J. C. (1985). The problem of knowledge, still: A review of (Liben's Piaget and the Foundations of Knowledge). *Merrill-Palmer Quarterly, 31,* 111-115.

Gibson, J. J. (1966). *The senses considered as perceptual systems.* Boston: Houghton-Mifflin.

Gibson, J. J. (1979). *The ecological approach to visual perception.* Boston: Houghton-Mifflin.

Harlow, H. F., & Mears, C. E. (1983). Emotional sequences and consequences. In R. Plutchik & H. Kellerman (Eds.), *Emotion: Theory, research, and experience: Vol. 2. Emotions in early development* (pp. 171-198). New York: Academic Press.

Hastorf, A. H., & Bender, I. E. (1952). A caution respecting the measurement of empathic ability. *Journal of Abnormal and Social Psychology, 45,* 575-576.

Hendrick, C., & Hendrick, S. (1986). A theory and method of love. *Journal of Personality and Social Psychology, 50,* 392-402.

Hofer, M. A. (1984). Relationships as regulators: A psychobiologic perspective on bereavement. *Psychosomatic Medicine, 46,* 183-198.

Kamiya, J. (1968). Conscious control of brain waves. *Psychology Today* 1 (11), 56-60.

Karaliers, M. (1981). Schooling behavioral in fish: An opiate-dependent activity. *Behavioral and Neural Biology, 33,* 379-401.

Kenny, D. A. (1981). Interpersonal perception: A multivariate round robin analysis. In M. Brewer & B. Collins (Eds.), *Scientific inquiry and the social sciences* (pp. 288-309). San Francisco: Jossey-Bass.

Kenny, D. A., & Nasby, W. (1980). Splitting the reciprocity correlation. *Journal of Personality and Social Psychology, 38,* 249-256.

Krause, R. (in press). Empirical research on the affect system: Relevance for psychoanalytic theory and technique. In H. Dahl, H. Thoma, & H. Kachele (Eds.), *Psychoanalytic process research strategies.* Heidelberg: Springer.

Lee, J. A. (1973). *The colors of love: An exploration of the ways of loving.* Don Mills, Ontario: New Press.

Lowen, A. (1967). *The betrayal of the body.* New York: Collier.

Mark, V., & Ervin, F. V. (1970). *Violence and the brain.* New York: Harper & Row.

Miller, R. E., Caul, W. F., & Mirsky, I. A. (1967). Communication of affects between feral and socially isolated monkeys. *Journal of Personality and Social Psychology, 7,* 231-239.

Newcomb, T. (1963). Stabilities underlying changes in interpersonal attraction. *Journal of Abnormal and Social Psychology, 66,* 376-386.

Panksepp, J. (1981). Hypothalamic integration of behavior. In P. Morgane & J. Panksepp (Eds.) *Handbook of the hypothalamus. Vol. 3., Part B. Behavioral studies of the hypothalamus* (pp. 289-431). New York: Marcek Dekker.

Panksepp, J. (1982). Toward a general psychobiological theory of emotions. With commentaries. *The Behavioral and Brain Sciences, 5,* 407-467.

Panksepp, J. (1986). The neurochemistry of behavior. *Annual Review of Psychology, 1986, 37,* 77-107.

Pennebaker, J. W. (1983). Physical symptoms and sensations: Psychological causes and correlates. *Social Psychophysiology*, 543-564.

Reardon, K. K., & Buck, R. (in press). Emotion, reason, and communication in coping with cancer. *Health Communication*.

Rodin, J. (1981). Current status of internal-external hypothesis for obesity: What went wrong? *American Psychologist, 36*, 361-372.

Rosenthal, R., Hall, J. A., DiMatteo, M. R., Rogers, P. L., & Archer, D. (1979). *Sensitivity to nonverbal communication: The PONS test*. Baltimore: Johns Hopkins University Press.

Russell, B. (1948). *Human knowledge: Its scope and limits*. New York: Simon & Schuster.

Sabatelli, R., Buck, R., & Kenny, D. (1986). A social relations analysis of nonverbal communication accuracy in married couples. *Journal of Personality, 54*, 513-525.

Sabatelli, R., & Rubin, M. (1986). Nonverbal expressiveness and physical attractiveness as mediators of interpersonal perceptions. *Journal of Nonverbal Behavior, 10*, 120-133.

Schachter, S. (1970). Some extraordinary facts about obese humans and rats. *American Psychologist, 26*, 129-144.

Schachter, S., & Singer, J. (1962). Cognitive, social and physiological determinants of emotional state. *Psychological Review, 69*, 379-399.

Shrout, P. E. & Fiske, D. W. (1981). Nonverbal behaviors and social evaluations. *Journal of Personality, 49*, 115-128.

Silverman, L. H., & Weinberger, J. (1985). Mommy and I are one: Implications for psychotherapy. *American Psychologist, 40*, 1296-1305.

Steimer, E., Krause, R., Sanger, C., & Wagner, G. (in press). Mimisches verhalten schizophrener patienten und ihrer gesprachspartner. (Facial behavior of schizophrenic patients and their speaking partners). *Zeitschrift für Klinische Psychologie*.

Tucker, D. M. (1981). Lateral brain function, emotion, and conceptualization. *Psychological Bulletin, 89*, 19-46.

Wenger, M. A., & Bagchi, B. K. (1961). Studies of autonomic functions in practitioners of yoga in India. *Behavioral Science, 6*, 312-323.

7

The Influence of Gender
on Same-Sex Friendships

DRURY SHERROD

Drury Sherrod is associated with the Claremont Colleges in Claremont, California, where he has served on the faculties of Pitzer College, Scripps College, and the Claremont Graduate School. He has published a social psychology textbook and numerous articles on environmental stress, self-perception, and social behavior. His current research focuses on social support and friendship, and his most recent publications have dealt with the stress-protective role of social support and the nature of friendship in the lives of women and men.

Two recent television commercials exemplify the apparent differences in the forms and functions of women's and men's friendships. In the first commercial, two female friends gaze intently into each other's eyes across a small round table as they pause to enjoy a cup of premium coffee. While a breeze ruffles lace curtains and coffee steams temptingly in china cups, one woman leans toward the other in a gesture of familiar intimacy. She slides her upturned palm across the linen-covered table and says with feeling, "Oh, Joan, thanks for listening." Her friend squeezes the open hand and responds comfortingly, "Susan, what are friends for?"

The corresponding commercial with male friends depicts an entirely different scene. This time the product is an imported beer, and six or seven men work side by side in boisterous camaraderie, painting a friend's sailboat. At break time, they drag their hands across paint-smeared tee-shirts, wipe their brows and slump down on the deck. The owner of the boat reaches into a cooler, pulls out an ice cold can of beer, and hoists it before the group. As his friends roar with pleasure, the host shrugs and grins. "Hey, what are friends for?"

In these two commercials, the answer to the question "what are friends for?" clearly depends on the sex of the friends. Yet beneath the easy images of the TV screen, how different are friendships of women and men? What do self-reports and observed differences in behavior and tone indicate about the underlying emotional intimacy for same-sex friendships? Moreover, what is an acceptable standard of comparing emotional intimacy across gender, if women and men may define intimacy in different terms? Finally, what accounts for differences in women's and men's friendships? These are the questions to be explored in this chapter, in an analysis of the relationship between friendship and gender.

APPROACHING RESEARCH ON FRIENDSHIP AND GENDER

A review of research on friendship and gender encounters several thorny conceptual and methodological problems, not the least of which is the limitations of gender as an explanatory construct. Summing up a decade's research on gender, Deaux (1984) cautioned against over-interpreting the effects of gender as a subject variable, and Wright (in press a; in press b) has applied this warning to the effects of gender on friendship. Wright argues that although the modal differences in women's and men's friendships are clear and robust, the statistically significant differences are often quite small, the variability within sexes is large, the differences between sexes may be associated with other confounding subject variables, and beyond the differences the friendships of women and men exhibit many basic similarities. Nevertheless, as the research discussed below will indicate, the modal differences in women's and men's friendships are quite consistent, as Wright himself points out (in press-b), and not necessarily inconsequential, particularly in later life when males typically claim fewer close friends than do females (Fischer & Oliker, 1983; Dickens & Perlman, 1981) and some men have no close male friends at all (Levinson, 1978).

A second conceptual problem in comparing the friendships of women and men is the possible nonequivalence in the meaning of friendship and intimacy to each sex. Although women and men identify similar goals and values in friendship, particularly in long-standing friendships (e.g., Wright, 1982), the research reviewed below suggests that each sex generally defines and enacts friendship differently. Consequently, research that relies on a single method to assess intimacy in both sexes may not necessarily tap the same experiential dimension in each sex (e.g., McCarthy, 1981).

Methodologically, research on friendship typically relies on written self-reports, for example, of disclosure, social support, conversational content, or shared activities. Not only are self-reports about sex-appropriate behavior notoriously subject to reporting biases, as Deaux (1984) notes, but ubiquitous sex-role stereotypes can even bias the accuracy of people's private judgments about their own behavior. In order to escape the possibility of these reporting biases, research should employ multiple operations, including behavioral observations in addition to self-reports. With these caveats in mind, let us turn to the research on women's and men's same-sex friendships.

THE NATURE OF SAME-SEX FRIENDSHIPS

To understand the nature of same-sex friendships, investigators have often compared friendship with other forms of love. From Aristotle, to Michel de Montaigne, to modern researchers (e.g., Davis & Todd, 1982; Sternberg, 1986), close friendships have been characterized as embodying the intimacy of romantic and familial love, but usually lacking the passion of the former and the involuntary aspects of the latter. For example, in descriptive research conducted by Davis and Todd (1982), people viewed both close friends and lovers as enjoying, accepting, respecting, helping, and confiding in each other, although lovers were thought to display a degree of passion, pleasure and mutual preoccupation that even the closest friendships lacked. Similarly, in Sternberg's triangular theory of love (1986), both lovers and close friends are seen as sharing the "intimacy" component of love, although close friends lack the "passion" component, and unless friendships have endured over time, they also lack the "decision/commitment" component. In support of this theory, Sternberg and Grajek (1984) factor analyzed subjects' ratings of various loving relationships (e.g., parent, sibling, lover, same-sex close friend) and found that the passion and decision/commitment components are indeed unique to certain types of relationships, but the intimacy component forms a common core across various loving relationships, including romantic partner and close friend.

Although intimacy in Sternberg's view is a continuous variable, friendship researchers have conventionally divided the dimension into several subcategories for the purposes of analysis, ranging from low to high intimacy and bearing familiar labels such as "casual friends," "close friends," and "best friend" (e.g., Caldwell & Peplau, 1982; Davis & Todd, 1985; Wright, 1969, 1985). Most of the research discussed below employs such categories to compare the nature of women's and men's friendships.

Definitions of Friendship Across Gender

A necessary beginning to a comparative study of friendship is to determine whether friendship means the same thing to each sex. Several studies have asked women and men what they want from a friend, and the reports of each sex are similar in many ways. College-age adults of both sexes value friendship highly, and both women and men say they want intimate same-sex friends (Caldwell & Peplau, 1982; Rose, 1985). Furthermore, both women and men rank empathy and altruism as more important to their friendships than mere companionship (Fox, Gibbs, & Auerbach, 1985; Gibbs, Auerbach, & Fox, 1980), and both women and men name "trust" as the quality they value most in a friend (Bell, 1981b). Moreover, when college students rated their long-term best friendships, both women and men saw their friendships as equally intimate and interdependent (Wright, 1982). Therefore, in terms of their values and goals regarding friendship, women and men are quite similar.

Despite these similarities, however, when people are asked to define their expectations of a close friend more specifically, reliable differences emerged in the modal responses of each sex. For example, in a study based on in-depth interviews, both women and men defined a friend as "someone you could talk to about anything"; yet when the interviewers probed further, the "anything" for men tended to be topics such as sports, politics, and business, while for women it was more likely to be feelings and problems (Fox, Gibbs, & Auerbach, 1985). Similarly, in a study of best-friendship patterns among college students in St. Louis, females tended to seek a best friend who could be a "confidante," someone to help them "grow as persons"; males were more likely to seek a best friend with similar interests, someone "to have fun with" (Yoon, 1978).

Caldwell and Peplau (1982) found similar differences among a sample of college students in Southern California when they asked young women and men detailed questions about their friendships. What do friends do when they are together? What do they talk about? What is the basis of best friendships? Given the choice between "doing some activity" or "just talking" with their best friend, over three times as many women as men chose just to talk, while almost twice as many men as women preferred some activity. Like their counterparts in St. Louis, the majority of young women wanted a best friend who "feels the same way about things," while the majority of young men sought a best friend who "likes to do the same things." Furthermore, when these students listed three things that formed the basis of a best friendship, women were more likely than men to list talking, while men were more likely to mention an activity.

Thus, while women and men seek the same abstract qualities in a best friend—intimacy, acceptance, trust, and help—the specific expectations of best friendship differ consistently in each sex. The typical woman tends to look for an intimate confidante, someone who shares the same feelings, while the typical man tends to seek a partner for activities, someone who shares his interests. However, because these conclusions are based on potentially biased self-reports, it is important to validate them against research findings dealing with other types of verbal responses, as well as overt and nonverbal behaviors. The following sections review research in each of these areas.

Self-Disclosure and Friendship

Many researchers interested in friendship have compared the friendships of women and men in terms of self-disclosure. Based not only on Jourard's Self-Disclosure Questionnaire (Jourard, 1971) but also on a variety of research paradigms, females in general have been found to disclose significantly more intimate information about themselves to same-sex friends than males do (Cozby, 1973; Reis, Senchak, & Solomon, 1985). This gender difference increases still further when responses to the most intimate items on the self-disclosure questionnaire are analyzed separately (Morgan, 1976). Moreover, when a close friendship lacks intimate self-disclosure, women are more disturbed than men, and women feel more lonely than do men when close friends fail to disclose intimate information (Solano, 1982). Yet there are several exceptions to this pattern, and the finding that male friends are generally less self-disclosing than female friends does not necessarily indicate that men's friendships are less intimate than women's; rather, it suggests that men in general may not express intimacy through self-disclosure.

Exceptions to the gender difference in self-disclosure reflect both dispositional and situational influences. For example, androgynous males report that they disclose as much to their best male friend as traditional or androgynous women disclose to a best friend, and much more than traditional men disclose to a best friend (Lavine & Lombardo, 1984). Similarly, "nonconventional" males (based on clinical assessment of their "well being and desire for change") say they disclose more to their best male friends than "conventional" males, and they are as disclosing as are nonconventional females to their best women friends (Bell, 1981a). Other exceptions to the modal gender difference in self-disclosure reflect situational factors. For instance, in a laboratory first-encounter situation males revealed more intimate information about themselves to a female stranger than females disclosed to a male, although first encounters between two men were less disclosing overall than those between two women (Derlega, Winstead, Wong, & Hunter, 1985). A related laboratory study, which compared women's interactions with opposite- versus same-sex intimates, found women to be more disclosing to a male intimate than to a female intimate (Fischer & Sollie, 1986). Similarly, a target person's sex influenced women's and men's disclosure in another laboratory observation study, along with other situational factors such as the type of emotions being expressed and the discloser's role in the conversation, but even given the importance of these situational influences, males were still less verbally expressive overall than were females (Dosser, Balswick, & Halverson, 1986). Finally, the importance of situational variables is further emphasized by a study that found no difference in self-disclosure between pairs of women and pairs of men, but whose interpretation is clouded because the specific nature of each pair's relationship is not described (Hacker, 1981).

Despite these exceptions, the modal gender difference in self-disclosure has been found repeatedly in studies of women's and men's conversations with same-sex friends. For example, when Caldwell and Peplau (1982) asked subjects to list the kinds of subjects they talked about with their close same-sex friends, many more women than men listed topics such as feelings, problems and people. As a check against the biases inherent in written self-reports, when these researchers asked their subjects to role-play a conversation with a close friend, they found that men expressed less enthusiasm, offered less support, talked less about relationships, and asked much less about feelings than did women.

Other research supports this gender difference in conversational content. In New York, when college students supplied written narratives of their last two interactions with same-sex best friends, judges rated the females' interactions as significantly more intimate than the males' interactions (Reis, Senchak, & Solomon, 1985). In Massachusetts, when middle-aged women and men rated how frequently and how deeply they had discussed a list of conversational topics with a same-sex close friend, the only topic on which males exceeded females was sports (Aries & Johnson, 1983). And in New Jersey (Davidson & Duberman, 1982), when women and men in their twenties and thirties kept detailed accounts of conversations with their best friends, the men were found to talk mainly about topical issues, such as work, sports, movies or politics, while the women talked about these issues too, but also about personal problems, as well as their relationship with each other. However, regardless of the actual differences in the conversations of these women and men, both sexes said they felt completely open and trusting with their best friend.

The same disparity between actual disclosure and perceived intimacy has also been found in studies of adolescent boys and girls. While both sexes say that they feel equally free to reveal personal information to their same-sex best friends, and both sexes believe they know their best friends intimately, when adolescents are asked how much they actually disclose to one another, girls usually reveal more intimate information than boys do (Diaz & Berndt, 1982).

In sum, although dispositional and situational factors influence women's and men's patterns of self-disclosure, in general women report that they talk more intimately with their friends than men do. However, most of these studies are based on information gathered through some form of questionnaire, diary or self-report, and they are subject to the reporting biases discussed earlier. Therefore, before considering the implications of this modal difference in verbal intimacy, it is helpful to examine whether the verbal differences are reflected in affective expressions and nonverbal behaviors in same-sex friendships.

Affective and Nonverbal Expressions of Intimacy

Despite the often-noted distinction that women's friendships are "expressive," while men's are "instrumental" (Dosser, Balswick, & Halverson, 1986; Lewis, 1978; Wright, in press a), until recently little specific research had probed beyond verbal measures of intimacy to assess the expressive or nonverbal dimension of women's and men's friendships. One recent attempt (Williams, 1985) sought to relate gender to a 20-item emotional intimacy scale and found, as predicted, that the best friendships of women were more emotionally intimate than the best friendships of men. However, the emotional intimacy scale, whose items were "derived from the literature," included both verbal items (e.g., "I often confide in my friends about my dreams for the future.") as well as non-verbal items (e.g., "It would embarrass me to hug my best friend."), and the two classes of items were not analyzed separately. Another study (Naurus & Fischer, 1982) focused only on males and measured emotional "expressivity" in terms of responses to a seven-item scale assessing ease of communication and a six-item scale assessing global confidence-sharing. Based on these general self-report measures, none of the males was viewed as inexpressive, although androgynous men scored higher than sex-typed and undifferentiated men, and all males shared fewer confidences with a best same-sex friend than with a spouse. In related research, the same investigators (Fischer & Naurus, 1981) found androgynous men and women to rate their same-sex friendships as more emotionally intimate than other subjects did, although again males overall rated their same-sex friendships as less intimate than women rated theirs.

Another approach to assessing perceived intimacy in same-sex friendships, also employing written self-reports, is based on the

Rochester Interaction Record at the University of Rochester. In these studies, female and male college students recorded every interaction with another person that lasted ten minutes or longer, for a period of up to two weeks, and the results paralleled the modal gender differences obtained in studies of self-disclosure and conversational content. Women rated their same-sex social interactions as significantly more intimate than men rated their same-sex interactions, even when the ratings involved the students' best friends (Nezlek, Wheeler, & Reis, 1983; Reis, Senchak, & Solomon, 1985; Wheeler & Nezlek, 1977; Wheeler, Reis, & Nezlek, 1983).

A similar pattern of results was obtained in another self-report study, which investigated the development of same-sex friendships among a sample of college students in Oregon, although in this study each sex seemed to express intimacy in a different mode (Hays, 1984, 1985). For example, women reported more physical affection and somewhat more verbal intimacy with their close same-sex friends than did men, but men reported more intimate "companionship" with their close same-sex friends.

A different research tradition has compared the expressive behavior of women and men in single-sex groups, both in the lab and in the field, and since these groups qualify as "casual friendships," this research is relevant to our review. In one study, Aries (1976) observed five hour-and-a-half sessions of all-male and all-female groups of students at an Ivy League university and noted marked differences across gender: Males quickly developed a stable dominance hierarchy, while females tended to share the dominant role; males spoke to the group as a whole, as if to command attention, while females talked more to specific others, as equals; males also expressed more sarcasm, putdowns, and laughter, telling stories of superiority, humiliation, and aggression, while females stuck to the topic longer and talked more intimately, revealing more about their feelings, homes, and families. Similar patterns of expressive behavior have also been noted in naturally occurring groups of adolescent and preadolescent girls and boys (Fine, 1980; Savin-Williams, 1980).

Another research strategy has focused on the role of nonverbal expression in same-sex friendships. In the New Jersey study cited above (Davidson & Duberman, 1982), the researchers asked women and men, "Do you and your friend seem to understand each other with a minimum of talking, using mostly gestures and facial expressions?" To this question 82% of the women said they frequently relied on nonverbal cues in understanding their friends, compared to only 28% of the men.

According to the research reviewed in this section, women and men differ systematically in their ratings and expressions of emotional intimacy in same-sex friendships. In general, compared to men's friendships, women perceive their friendships as more emotionally intimate; women say they are more attuned to subtle nuances in each other's behavior; women are more likely to express intimacy through verbal and physical means; and in groups women behave in more self-revealing ways. However, again there are exceptions to these modal gender differences, for androgynous males described their same-sex friendships as more emotionally expressive and more intimate than those of other males. Yet, because the bulk of this research relies on self-reports, these findings may be biased to the extent that males are reluctant to describe their friendships with other men as "intimate." Furthermore, the actual meaning of intimacy in male friendship is still unclear, nor is it clear how satisfied males are with the level and type of intimacy they find in their typical friendships with other men. Research reviewed in the next section, on social support, begins to answer these questions, as it focuses on the consequences of close friendships in the lives of women and men.

Social Support, Stress Reduction, and Gender

Social support may be defined as the perceived availability of others to help meet a variety of human needs. In numerous recent studies, people who perceive a high degree of support from others have reported greater emotional and physical well being than people with a low degree of support, especially during times of stress (Cohen & Wills, 1985). Research also suggests that women perceive more social support— especially emotional support—to be available from their friends than men do (Burda, Vaux, & Schill, 1985; Sherrod, Cohen, & Clark, 1986; Stokes & Wilson, 1984; Vaux, 1985; Wright, 1985). However, exactly how social support affects women and men is unclear; in part because researchers have defined and measured social support differently, and because few studies have evaluated actual social support transactions and their consequences in the lives of women and men (Gottlieb, 1985).

Of the few studies that have examined social support processes as a function of gender, two found that "confidante support" (the availability of someone to confide in) reduced depression for adult women who had recently experienced a high degree of stress, but not for men (Cleary & Mechanic, 1983; Henderson, Byrne, Duncan-Jones, Scott, & Adcock, 1980), and a third found that, compared to boys, adolescent girls sought more support from their friends and were more satisfied with the support they received (Burke & Weir, 1978). On the other hand, one of these same studies (Henderson et al., 1980) also found that "social integration" (an index of embeddedness in a wide range of social relationships) reduced depression for both women and men, but particularly for men who had recently experienced a high degree of stress. In our own longitudinal research with a student sample at Carnegie Mellon University, we found that social support—independent of personality and social skills—reduced depression for both women and men who had recently experienced a high degree of stress (Cohen, Sherrod, & Clark, 1986; Sherrod, Cohen, & Clark, 1986). Furthermore, we found that three different types of social support—"tangible support" (material aid), "appraisal support" (confiding about problems), and "belonging support" (companionship)—were equally beneficial to both women and men in terms of reducing depression. Finally, two studies have determined that the sources of social support are particularly important to women, for women perceive more support to be available from close friends than from casual friends (Davidson & Packard, 1981; Wright, 1985); comparable data are unavailable for males.

Although these studies are inconsistent about whether particular forms of social support affect women and men differently, the research indicates that the perception of support from friends is beneficial to both sexes. In other words, even though most men rate their friendships as less intimate than do women—at least in terms of self-disclosure and emotional expressiveness—men's friendships nevertheless serve to buffer stress and reduce depression in the same way that women's friendships do. But how should we interpret this finding? This is the question we will consider further in the next section.

Gender Differences in Paths to Friendship

One way to explain the benefits that both women and men derive from friendships is to view the social support findings as evidence that men's friendships are in fact as intimate as women's friendships, despite the differential ratings of each sex. From this perspective, the consistent modal gender difference in intimacy ratings of close friendships may be explained in two ways: Either males fail to report accurately the true intimacy of their friendships because high intimacy is inappropriate for the male sex role, or males express intimacy through different dimensions than self-disclosure and emotional expressiveness, and the true nature of male friendships has thus escaped detection.

In fact some data are consistent with this latter explanation. Camarena and Sarigiani (1985) compared the friendships of adolescent girls and boys and found, as expected, that girls' friendships exceeded boys' in emotional closeness. Yet, when the measure of emotional closeness was broken down into two components—self-disclosure and shared activities—the researchers found that girls' friendships were considerably more intimate than boys' on a measure of self-disclosure, but only slightly more intimate on a measure of shared activities. Although we cannot extrapolate directly from adolescents to adults, Hays (1985) similarly found that college females perceived their same-sex friendships to be more emotionally expressive than did men, while males viewed their same-sex friendships as involving more intimate companionship than did women.' Moreover, as we discussed earlier, men tend to expect companionship and shared interests from a friend, while women tend to look for a confidante and shared feelings. Thus there is clearly some support for the view that females and males typically achieve intimacy via different paths.

Yet there is also support for an alternative explanation of the modal gender difference in intimacy ratings of same-sex friendships. The alternative view holds that men do not misreport the true intimacy of their friendships, nor do they achieve intimacy through a different path than women, but that men simply do not seek the same degree of intimacy from same-sex friendship that women seek. From this perspective, men are satisfied with less intimacy than women because they prefer less intimacy than women. A recent experiment by Reis, Senchak, and Solomon (1985) lends strong credence to this perspective. These researchers hypothesized four potential explanations for the finding that men's friendships were less intimate than women's: (1) that males hold different criteria for what constitutes intimacy; (2) that males are reluctant to attach the label "intimate" to their encounters with other males; (3) that males lack the ability to express intimacy; and (4) that males are so selective in same-sex interactions that they can experience real intimacy only with a best friend. However, the researchers rejected each of these explanations, concluding (1) that males do employ the same criteria as females when they judge a videotaped interaction between two men; (2) that males do not simply avoid the label "intimate" when describing their same-sex interactions, for independent judges also rated males' written records of their interactions as less intimate than women's accounts; (3) that when men are required to conduct an intimate conversation, they are indeed as capable as women, according to ratings of independent judges; and (4) that male interactions are less intimate than women's, even when the interaction is restricted to best friends. Overall, these researchers concluded that the gender difference in same-sex intimacy reflects not simply divergent pathways to intimacy within each sex, but a genuine preference among males for less intimate interactions with same-sex friends than women prefer.

Putting together the research cited in this section with that from previous sections, we can reach two tentative conclusions: first, that the typical male generally prefers less intimacy in same-sex friendships than the typical woman prefers; and second, that when the typical male does achieve a high level of intimacy with another man, he usually follows a different path than a woman, one that emphasizes activities and companionship over self-disclosure and emotional expressiveness.

Before considering some possible explanations for the apparent differences in women's and men's friendships, it would be helpful to pause and review some of the difficulties in interpreting and comparing findings in this area of research. Perhaps the most glaring problem is an overreliance on self-reports, as we have mentioned. It is the rare study that observes actual behavior in the laboratory or field, and given the real possibility of sex-role biases in self-reports, there is a great need for multiple operationalism in measurement procedures. The self-reports also have been hampered by a wide variety of scales and measures, sometimes containing only a few global items derived from the researcher's intuitions and sometimes including overlapping items in measures of independent and dependent variables (e.g., a measure of androgyny and a measure of intimacy may both include items assessing emotional expressiveness). In addition, studies have employed such an array of target persons and types of relationships when assessing intimacy that comparisons across studies is often impossible. For example, in the studies reviewed above, the target persons have included an idealized friend, a best friend, a close friend, a spouse or romantic partner, a same-sex and an opposite-sex intimate, the person one is closest to, someone who will accompany the subject to the laboratory, a stranger in the laboratory and an unspecified same-sex or opposite-sex other. Finally, very few studies have examined the effects of specific situational variables or the specific processes through which each sex expresses intimacy. Nevertheless, the modal gender differences in same-sex friendships are clear enough and consistent enough to warrant consideration of their possible causes.

POSSIBLE CAUSES FOR GENDER DIFFERENCES IN SAME-SEX FRIENDSHIPS

The modal gender differences in women's and men's same-sex relationships can be explained in various ways (Sherrod, 1987). In this section we will consider four possible influences on the observed differences in women's and men's friendships. The four approaches include the economic/historical, the biological, the psychoanalytic, and the socialization perspectives.

The Economic/Historical Perspective

According to Gergen (1973), many of the phenomena of social psychology are valid within specific cultures and historical periods but cannot be generalized across culture and time, and gender differences in close friendships may be one of these phenomena. In order to determine the universality of gender differences in friendship, we would need to compare similar classes of data across history and across cultures. Although various cultures have celebrated the virtues of friendship, particularly classical Greece and Renaissance Europe, it is virtually impossible to find the sort of comparative data our "archival experiment" would require. For one thing, according to Peter Stearns, editor of the *Journal of Social History*, there is no existing social history of friendship (P. Stearns, personal communication, February 13, 1984) as there is of marriage and the family (e.g., Stone, 1977) or even of sexual behavior (e.g., Foucault, 1978), for the data are simply unavailable. Unlike the bonds of marriage, birth and kinship, friendships were not documented in courthouse files, village records, or family Bibles. Furthermore, when the historical record happens to exist in the occasional letter, diary, or literary account, the record invariably pertains to the friendships of men, not of women, for women's friendships were so little noted that women's ties remained obscure until very recent times (Seiden & Bart, 1975).

Historically, male friendships were heralded during two distinct periods of western culture. During the Classical Age of Greek society, and during the European Renaissance, male friendships were considered the highest form of love (e.g., Dover 1978; Flaceliere, 1962; Mills, 1937). The same case can be made for traditional peoples in contemporary non-Western cultures, where the anthropologist Robert Brain (1976) has described friendship and its rituals among the tribal people of Africa, South America and Oceania. Noting that most male anthropologists have ignored the 50% of their samples who happen to be women, Brain observes that social roles in traditional societies are rigidly defined by gender, and both women and men expect intimate social bonds to develop within their own sex as well as with the opposite sex. For example, Brain describes numerous cultures in which males ceremonially formalize their friendship bonds as lifetime "comrades," "blood brothers," or even symbolic "spouses." Compared with the research on modern American male friendships, these cross-cultural patterns and literary portrayals of friendship in other periods suggest that the typical male's friendships in modern America are less intimate than men's friendships have been in other cultures and other periods.

Although the paucity of sources makes similar comparisons for women's friendships nearly impossible, feminist scholars are beginning to fill in the gaps in the record of women's lives. For example, the literary critic Bernikow (1980) and the historian Smith-Rosenberg (1975) have produced evidence indicating that women's friendships were no less intimate in the past than they are today. In traditional cultures, despite the relative scarcity of cross-cultural data on women's lives, Brain (1976) has observed that women's same-sex ties appear to be as intimate as those in our own society.

According to the economic/historical perspective, among the many factors that may have operated to diminish the intimacy of men's friendships in our own culture are the spread of capitalism and the Industrial Revolution (e.g., Illich, 1982; Stone, 1977). Corresponding changes in marriage and the family provided sources of intimacy that men had formerly obtained only from same-sex friends (Leites, 1982; Stone, 1977), while the emerging commodity value of male labor replaced cooperative relationships between men with competitive relationships (Illich, 1982). At the same time that men's lives were changing in response to economic forces, women remained relatively powerless, continuing to rely on other women as their prime source of emotional support (e.g., Smith-Rosenberg, 1975). Thus the economic/historical perspective provides a possible explanation for the decline in the intimacy of men's friendships in our own culture.

The Psychoanalytic Perspective

Other theorists have traced the differences in women's and men's experience of intimate friendships not to sweeping economic and historical changes but to dispositional traits resulting from the psychodynamics of early childhood. Feminist psychoanalytic theorists such as Nancy Chodorow (1978) and Dorothy Dinerstein (1976) have reinterpreted male and female Oedipal conflicts in light of the mother-child relationship, and this perspective, derived from object relations theory, speaks directly to women's and men's experience of friendships.

According to Chodorow, girls' and boys' gender identities develop at three crucial stages: (1) the pre-Oedipal stage, when mothers relate to boys and girls in distinctly different ways; (2) the Oedipal stage, when boys and girls encounter different types of Oedipal conflicts; and (3) the post-Oedipal stage, when males and females resolve their Oedipal conflicts in different ways. Because of the differences at these three stages, Chodorow argues, girls develop more permeable, less rigid ego boundaries than boys. In Chodorow's words, (1978, p. 169) "The basic feminine sense of self is connected to the world, the basic masculine sense of self is separate."

In the pre-Oedipal period, because mothers are thought to "over-identify" with their daughters but perceive their sons as a male opposite, mothers bond less tightly with their sons than with their daughters, and boys pass through the pre-Oedipal period more quickly than girls. Boys then defend against this loss of the pre-Oedipal relationship by developing firmer, more differentiated ego boundaries than girls, while a girl's lack of separateness between self and mother leads to more permeable ego boundaries and a built-in basis for empathy that boys lack.

When girls enter the Oedipal stage they are thought to encounter different types of conflicts than boys. While boys switch their identification from mother to father in order to defend against castration anxiety, girls, in contrast, never quite surrender their mother as an internal love object. Because a father is usually not a primary caretaker, he is a less satisfying love object for a young girl than is a mother. Consequently, girls tend to oscillate between mother and father as love objects and, as a result, girls develop a more complex inner relational world than boys, retaining an emotional attachment to other women even as they develop a sexual attachment to men.

Finally, girls do not resolve their Oedipal conflicts as thoroughly as boys are thought to. Because a boy's Oedipal conflict is more intense than a girl's, boys have a greater need to repress their Oedipal conflicts, turn outward to the nonfamilial world, and develop firm ego boundaries. In contrast, because a girl's Oedipal conflict is weaker than a boy's, girls do not turn away from the family, repress their Oedipal attachments, or develop as firm ego boundaries as do boys. As a result, women remain preoccupied with ongoing relationship issues, while men tend to deny relationships and connections, instead preferring a more fixed and simpler world.

Because of these differing Oedipal processes, in Chodorow's view women are thought to become vulnerable, disclosing, and attentive in same-sex friendships, while men's concern with separateness and individuation leads them to invest less time and energy in developing and maintaining intimate relationships, particularly with other men. From this perspective, the same dynamics that bind women together serve to drive men apart, and the differences in the typical adult friendships of each sex are the residues of childhood conflicts.

The Biological Perspective

Evidence from many sources suggests that males, particularly prepubertal and adolescent males, tend to behave more aggressively than females, and that this aggressive behavior is most frequently directed toward other males (e.g., Eagly & Steffen, 1986; Hyde, 1984; Rohner, 1976). Some theorists have interpreted this evidence as support for the theory that intramale aggression is biologically mediated (e.g. Maccoby & Jacklin, 1974), while others have disputed the role of biological influences (e.g., Bleier, 1984; Fausto-Sterling, 1985). If males in fact have some biologically mediated tendency to behave aggressively toward other males, and if this tendency is most pronounced in childhood when sex-role behavior is acquired, then this tendency could help account for typical male behavior in same-sex friendships. However, several problems cloud the research on biological mediators of aggression.

The first problem is simply defining what constitutes aggression. In research on animals, aggression is defined as fighting; in research on children, aggression is loosely defined as "rough-and-tumble play;" and in research on adults, particularly prisoners, aggression has been defined as "violent crimes." Exactly how these diverse criteria relate to competitiveness and dominance in male friendships is debatable. Second, much of the testosterone research has been conducted on rats and monkeys, species whose behavior is more directly controlled by hormones. Third, when research on human beings appears to link hormones with aggression, the samples have been small and the observations have sometimes been potentially biased and lacking in adequate controls. Finally, even if clear links could be established between testosterone and aggression in humans, human behavior is far more controlled by culture and cognition than by hormones.

Yet the case for male aggression does not rest entirely on disputed biological research and unnatural laboratory environments. Observations of nonhuman primates in the wild as well as observations in a variety of human cultures support the view that young males exhibit more aggression than young females, and that this aggression is generally directed toward other males. For example, among monkeys and apes in the wild, adolescent males spend most of their time at the periphery of the group jockeying for dominance over peers, while adolescent females usually remain close to home, often in the company of adult females rather than peers (Savin-Williams, 1980). Similar patterns are found in many human cultures (Fine, 1980). For example, in traditional African societies, gangs of young boys wander far from home and play imaginary war games; in Mongolia bands of boys steal cattle and sheep and pretend to go on long caravans; in Native American cultures, groups of boys set off on imaginary war parties and stalked their foes for days at a time. In contrast, girls in traditional cultures usually remain within the household, learning adult roles from their mothers and older women, and playing in pairs and small groups rather than in gangs, as boys do.

If biology predisposes males toward greater intragender aggression than females, then biology may contribute to the modal gender differences observed in same-sex friendships by helping to set the conditions under which young boys learn to relate to each other. In an atmosphere of competition and dominance, boys are unlikely to acquire or to value skills of intimacy, vulnerability, and self-disclosure; as a result, friendships among adult males may reflect corresponding deficits.

The Socialization Perspective

The final perspective argues that modal differences in women's and men's friendships reflect differential socialization of girls and boys. This perspective is represented in the work of Jeanne Block (1982), who asserts that our social institutions encourage boys to develop "wings," while we expect girls to put down "roots." Wings without roots, she says (Block, 1982, p. 190), can lead males to become "unfettered, adventurous souls—free spirits who, however, may lack commitment, civility, and relatedness"; in contrast, roots without wings, can produce females who are "prudent, dependable, nurturing, but tethered individuals—responsible beings who may lack independence, self-direction, and a sense of adventure." Block cites four categories of research to demonstrate her thesis.

Parents' attitudes and values. When parents are asked to describe their approach to child-rearing, boys' parents—both mothers and fathers—emphasize achievement and competition, while girls' parents stress warmth and closeness (Block, 1979). Similarly, surveys of parents' attitudes find that parents expect their sons to be independent, self-reliant, ambitious, and strong willed, among other traits, while daughters are expected to be unselfish, loving, well-mannered, and kind (Hoffman, 1977).

Parents' behavior. Almost from birth, boys are held more, aroused more, responded to more contingently, and given richer, more varied stimulation than girls, all of which may provide boys with a stronger sense of self-efficacy than girls and predispose boys toward a more active engagement with the world (Margolin & Patterson, 1975). Furthermore, parents, and particularly fathers, give boys more freedom and less supervision, set higher standards, encourage greater achievement, and provide different kinds of reinforcements than for girls (Saegart & Hart, 1976). As a result, boys and girls grow up in systematically different social environments, which may leave girls more embedded in social and familial networks, while sending boys out into the world to develop competence and mastery.

Teachers' behavior. According to Block (1982), several studies have found that nursery school teachers give boys more attention and encouragement than girls, and that teachers are particularly discouraging to high-achieving girls. In Block's view, this pattern of discouragement and negative reinforcement for females' intellectual activities may help account for males' consistently greater confidence in school settings, higher self-concepts, and greater mastery of problem solving behaviors.

Childrens' games. Even children's games help shape differences in boys' and girls' behavior (Lever, 1978). Boys' games typically occur in larger groups, have more rules, are more complex, require more player interdependence, feature more explicit goals, and are more competitive than girls' games. Team sports account for many of these differences, but even sedentary games differ for each sex. Overall, 65% of boy's games have been rated as competitive, as compared to only 37% of girls' games.

Like the psychoanalytic perspective, the socialization perspective sees females as embedded in family and social networks, while males are propelled onto an independent path beyond the family and social relationships. Because of these comprehensive differences in socialization, the same-sex friendships of the average male are instrumental and side-by-side, while same sex female friendships are expressive and face-to-face (Wright, 1982).

Comparing the Theories

Although each of these theories can be advanced to account for the observed gender differences in same-sex friendships, some are more compatible with the data than others. At the least, biological influences on men's same-sex relationships must be viewed against the considerable variation and exceptions to modal friendship patterns within each sex, as well as the high value placed on intimate male friendships in many cultures. If biology is a determinant of same-sex intimacy, its contribution appears to be clearly less significant than other factors.

While the economic-historical perspective is consistent with historical trends, it offers little supporting data, and in its broad sweep it is difficult to falsify. To the extent that it is explanatory, it is a version of role theory, with economic forces viewed as the determinant of social roles. The most interesting test of this perspective will be whether the changes it predicts in friendships occur as greater numbers of women compete with each other in work roles traditionally occupied by males.

The psychoanalytic and socialization perspectives make essentially identical predictions about women's and men's orientation toward intimate relationships, though the two theories postulate different causes. However, the psychoanalytic perspective would seem to have a harder time accounting for observed situational variability in the expression of intimacy, as well as for the divergent pathways by which each sex approaches intimacy. Overall, the socialization perspective is more capable of explaining both the similarities and the modal differences in women's and men's friendships, as well as the data on situational variability, and it is consistent with the role theory underpinnings of the economic historical approach. The task for the socialization perspective is to provide a better accounting of the specific processes through which each sex acquires expectations of intimacy in same sex friendships and through which each sex selects and enacts appropriate behaviors.

Because of the many unanswered questions, research on gender and friendship is a particularly fruitful area for researchers interested in close relationships. Areas of fruitful exploration include: examining the specific expectations and meaning of intimate friendship in each sex; moving beyond global self-reports to determine gender-specific behaviors that characterize intimate friendships; comparing the friendships of theory-relevant subpopulations such as working women and men, lesbians and gay males, children of traditional and nontraditional parents, and different races and classes; investigating neglected topics such as cross-sex friendships, conflict and jealousy in same-sex friendships, and the competing demands of a best friend, a romantic partner, and family members; evaluating the degree, type, and satisfactoriness of social support provided by same-sex friendships; and exploring how friendships are developed, maintained, and terminated among women and men. At the current stage, research on friendship is less advanced than research on romantic love, perhaps reflecting our own culture's preoccupation with romantic ties rather than the bonds of same-sex friends, bonds that for most human beings throughout most of history have provided life's most emotionally meaningful relationships.

REFERENCES

Aries, E. J. (1976). Interaction patterns and themes of male, female, and mixed-sex groups. *Small Group Behavior, 7*, 7-18.

Aries, E. J., & Johnson, F. L. (1983). Close friendship in adulthood: Conversational content between same-sex friends. *Sex Roles, 9*, 1183-1196.

Bell, R. R. (1981a). Friendships of women and men. *Psychology of Women Quarterly, 5*, 1981.

Bell, R. (1981b). *Worlds of friendship.* Beverly Hills, CA: Sage.

Bernikow, L. (1980). *Among women.* New York: Harper.

Bleier, R. (1984). *Science and gender: A critique of biology and its theories on women.* New York: Pergamon.

Block, J. (1979). Another look at sex-differentiation in the socialization behavior of mothers and fathers. In J. Sherman & F. K. Denmark (Eds.), *Psychology of women: Future directions of research* (pp. 71-101). New York: Psychological Dimensions.

Block, J. (1982). Psychological development of female children and adolescents. In P. W. Berman & E. D. Ramey (Eds.), *Women: A developmental perspective* (pp. 188-229). Bethesda, MD: National Institutes of Health.

Brain, R. (1976). *Friends and lovers.* New York: Basic Books.

Burda, P. C., Vaux, A., & Schill, T. (1985). Social support resources: Variations across sex and sex role. *Personality and Social Psychology Bulletin, 10*, 119-126.

Burke, R., & Weir, T. (1978). Sex differences in adolescent life stress, social support, and well being. *Journal of Psychology, 98*, 277-288.

Caldwell, M., & Peplau, L. A. (1982). Sex differences in same-sex friendship. *Sex Roles, 8*, 721-731.

Camarena, P. H., & Sarigiani, P. A. (1985, August). *Gender pathways to intimacy in early adolescence.* Paper presented at the Annual Convention of the American Psychological Association, Los Angeles.

Chodorow, N. (1978). *The reproduction of mothering.* Berkeley: University of California Press.

Cleary, P. D., & Mechanic, D. (1983). Sex differences in psychological distress among married women. *Journal of Health and Social Behavior, 24*, 111-121.

Cohen, S., Sherrod, D., & Clark, M. (1986). Social skills and the stress-protective role of social support. *Journal of Personality and Social Psychology, 50*, 963-973.

Cohen, S., & Wills, T. A. (1985). Stress, social support, and the buffering hypothesis. *Psychological Bulletin, 98*, 310-357.

Cozby, P. (1973). Self-disclosure: A literature review. *Psychological Bulletin, 70*, 73-91.

Davidson, L. R., & Duberman, L. (1982). Friendship: Communication and interactional patterns in same sex dyads. *Sex Roles, 8*, 809-822.

Davidson, S., & Packard, T. (1981). The therapeutic value of friendship between women. *Psychology of Women Quarterly, 5*, 495-510.

Davis, K. E., & Todd, M. J. (1982). Friendship and love relationships. *Advances in descriptive psychology. Vol. 2.* Greenwich, CT: JAI.

Davis, K. E. & Todd, M. J. (1985). Assessing friendship: Prototypes, paradigm cases and relationship description. In S. Duck & D. Perlman (Eds.), *Understanding personal relationships: An interdisciplinary approach* (pp. 17-38). Beverly Hills, CA: Sage.

Deaux, K. (1984). From individual differences to social categories: Analysis of a decade's research on gender. *American Psychologist, 39*, 105-116.

Derlega, V. J., Winstead, B. A., Wong, P. T. P., & Hunter, S. (1985). Gender effects in an initial encounter: A case where men exceed women in disclosure. *Journal of Social and Personal Relationships, 2*, 25-44.

Diaz, R. M., & Berndt, T. J. (1982). Children's knowledge of a best friend: Fact or fancy? *Developmental Psychology, 18*, 787-794.

Dickens, W. J., & Perlman, D. (1981). Friendship over the life-cycle. In S. Duck & R. Gilmour (Eds.), *Personal relationships 2: Developing personal relationships* (pp. 91-122). London: Academic Press.

Dinerstein, D. (1976). *The mermaid and the minotaur: Sexual arrangements and human malaise.* New York: Harper.

Dosser, D. A., Balswick, J. O., & Halverson, C. F. (1986). Male inexpressiveness and relationships. *Journal of Social and Personal Relationships, 3* 241-258.

Dover, K. J. (1978). *Greek homosexuality.* Cambridge, MA: Harvard University Press.

Eagly, A. H., & Steffen, V. J. (1986). Gender and aggressive behavior: A meta-analytic review of the social psychological literature. *Psychological Bulletin, 100*, 309-330.

Fausto-Sterling, A. (1985). *Myths of gender: Biological theories about women and men.* New York: Basic Books.

Fine, G. A. (1980). The natural history of pre-adolescent male friendship groups. In H. C. Foot, A. J. Chapman, & J. R. Smith (Eds.), *Friendship and social relations in children* (pp. 234-268). Chicester, England: John Wiley.

Fischer, C., & Oliker, S. (1983). A research note on friendship, gender, and the life cycle. *Social Forces, 62*, 124-133.

Fischer, J. L., & Naurus, L. R. (1981). Sex roles and intimacy in same and other sex relationships. *Psychology of Women Quarterly, 5*, 444-455.

Fischer, J. L., & Sollie, D. L. (1986). Women's communication with intimates and acquaintances. *Journal of Social and Personal Relationships, 3*, 19-30.

Flaceliere, R. (1962). *Love in ancient Greece.* New York: Crown.

Foucault, M. (1978). *The history of sexuality.* New York: Random House.

Fox, M. F., Gibbs, M., & Auerbach, D. (1985). Age and gender dimensions of friendship. *Psychology of Women Quarterly, 9*, 489-502.

Gergen, K. J. (1973). Social psychology as history. *Journal of Personality and Social Psychology, 26*, 309-320.

Gibbs, M., Auerbach, D., & Fox, M. F. (1980). A comparison of male and female same-sex friendships. *International Journal of Women's Studies, 3*, 261-272.

Gottlieb, B. H. (1985). Social support and the study of personal relationships. *Journal of Social and Personal Relationships, 2*, 351-375.

Hacker, H. M. (1981). Blabbermouths and clams: Sex differences in self-disclosure in same-sex and cross-sex friendship dyads. *Psychology of Women Quarterly, 5*, 385-401.

Hays, R. B. (1984). The development and maintenance of friendship. *Journal of Social and Personal Relationships, 1*, 75-98.

Hays, R. B. (1985). A longitudinal study of friendship development. *Journal of Personality and Social Psychology, 48*, 909-924.

Henderson, S., Byrne, D. G., Duncan-Jones, P., Scott, R., & Adcock, S. (1980). Social relationships, adversity, and neurosis: A study of associations in a general population sample. *British Journal of Psychiatry, 136*, 574-583.

Hoffman, L. W. (1977). Changes in family roles, socialization, and sex differences. *American Psychologist, 32*, 644-657.

Hyde, J. S. (1984). How large are gender differences in aggression? A developmental meta-analysis. *Developmental Psychology, 20*, 722-736.

Illich, I. (1982). *Gender.* New York: Pantheon.

Jourard, S. (1971). *Self-disclosure.* New York: John Wiley.

Lavine, L. O., & Lombardo, J. P. (1984). Self-disclosure: Intimate and non-intimate disclosures to parents and best friends as a function of Bem sex-role category. *Sex Roles, 11*, 735-744.

Leites, E. (1982). Love, friendship and sexuality in some Puritan theories of marriage. *The Journal of Social History, 15*, 383-408.

Lever, J. (1978). Sex differences in the complexity of children's play and games. *American Sociological Review, 43*, 471-483.

Levinson, D. (1978). *The seasons of a man's life.* New York: Ballantine.

Lewis, R. (1978). Emotional intimacy among men. *Journal of Social Issues, 34* (1), 109-121.

Maccoby E. E., & Jacklin, C. N. (1974). *The psychology of sex-differences.* Stanford, CA: Stanford University Press.

Margolin, G., & Patterson, G. R. (1975). Differential consequences provided by mothers and fathers for their sons and daughters. *Developmental Psychology, 11*, 537-538.

McCarthy, B. (1981). Studying close relationships. In S. W. Duck & R. Gilmour (Eds.), *Personal relationships I: Studying personal relationships* (pp. 63-85). London: Academic Press.

Mills, L. J. (1937). *"One soul in bodies twain:" Friendship in Tudor literature and Stuart drama.* Bloomington, IN: Principia.

Morgan, B. S. (1976). Intimacy of disclosure topics and sex differences in self-disclosure. *Sex Roles, 2*, 161-166.

Naurus, L. R., & Fischer, J. L. (1982). Strong but not silent: A reexamination of expressivity in the relationships of women and men. *Sex Roles, 8*, 159-168.

Nezlek, J., Wheeler, L., & Reis, H. T. (1983). Studies of social participation. In H. T. Reis (Ed.), *Naturalistic approaches to studying social interaction* (pp. 57-73). San Francisco: Jossey-Bass.

Reis, H. T., Senchak, M., & Solomon, B. (1985). Sex Differences in the intimacy of social interaction: Further examination of potential explanations. *Journal of Personality and Social Psychology, 48*, 1204-1217.

Rohner, R. P. (1976). Sex difference in aggression: Phylogenetic and enculturation prespectives. *Ethos, 4*, 57-72.

Rose, S. (1985). Same- and cross-sex friendships and the psychology of homosocialty. *Sex Roles, 12*, 63-74.

Saegart, S., & Hart, R. (1976). The development of sex-differences in the environmental competence of children. *Child Development, 46*, 459-653.

Savin-Williams, R. C. (1980). Social interactions of adolescent females in natural groups. In H. C. Foot, A. J. Chapman, & J. R. Smith (Eds.), *Friendship and social relations in children* (pp. 130-158). Chicester, England: John Wiley.

Seiden, A. M., & Bart, P. B. (1975). Woman to woman: Is sisterhood powerful? In N. Glazer-Malbin (Ed.), *Old Family/New Family* (pp. 297-331). New York: Van Nostrand.

Sherrod, D. (1987). The bonds of men: Problems and possibilities in close male relationships. In H. Brod (Ed.), *The making of masculinities; The new men's studies* (pp. 213-240). Boston: Allen & Unwin.

Sherrod, D., Cohen, S., & Clark, M. (1986). Social support, gender, and friendship. Unpublished manuscript, Claremont Graduate School.

Smith-Rosenberg, C. (1975). The female world of love and ritual: Relations between women in nineteenth-century America. *Signs: Journal of Women in Culture and Society, 1*, 1-29.

Solano, C. H. (1982). Loneliness and patterns of self-disclosure. *Journal of Personality and Social Psychology, 43*, 524-531.

Sternberg, R. J. (1986). A triangular theory of love. *Psychological Review, 93*, 119-135.

Sternberg, R. J., & Grajek, S. (1984). The nature of love. *Journal of Personality and Social Psychology, 47*, 312-329.

Stokes, J., & Wilson, D. G. (1984). The inventory of socially supportive behaviors: Dimensionality, prediction, and gender differences. *American Journal of Community Psychology, 12*, 53-70.

Stone, L. (1977). *The family, sex, and marriage in England: 1500-1800.* New York: Harper.

Vaux, A. (1985). Variations in social support associated with gender, ethnicity, and age. *Journal of Social Issues, 41* (1), 89-110.

Wheeler, L., & Nezlek, J. (1977). Sex differences in social participation. *Journal of Personality and Social Psychology, 35*, 742-754.

Wheeler, L., Reis, H. T., & Nezlek, J. (1983). Loneliness, social interaction, and sex roles. *Journal of Personality and Social Psychology, 45*, 943-953.

Williams, D. G. (1985). Gender, masculinity-femininity, and emotional intimacy in same-sex friendship. *Sex Roles, 12*, 587-600.

Wright, P. H. (1969). A model and a technique for studies of friendship. *Journal of Experimental Social Psychology, 5*, 295-309.

Wright, P. H. (1982). Men's friendships, women's friendships, and the alleged inferiority of the latter. *Sex Roles, 8*, 1-20.

Wright, P. H. (1985). The acquaintance description form. In S. Duck & D. Perlman (Eds.), *Understanding personal relationships: An interdisciplinary approach* (pp. 39-62). Beverly Hills, CA: Sage.

Wright, P. H. (in press-a). Gender differences in adult's same and cross-gender friendships. In R. Adams & R. Blieszner (Eds.), *Perspectives on later life friendships.* Beverly Hills, CA: Sage.

Wright, P. H. (in press-b). Interpreting research on gender and friendship: A case of moderation and a plea for caution. *Journal of Social and Personal Relationships.*

Yoon, G. H. (1978). The natural history of friendship: Sex differences in best-friendship patterns. *Dissertation Abstracts, 39*, (3-B), 1553.

8

Trust in Close Relationships

JOHN G. HOLMES
JOHN K. REMPEL

John G. Holmes received his Ph.D. from the University of North Carolina at Chapel Hill, where he worked with Stacy Adams and John Thibaut. He has been a member of the Psychology Department at the University of Waterloo since 1972. His earlier research focused on the process of social conflict in interpersonal relations, negotiations and organizations. His current interests include conflict, trust and the appraisal process in close relationships, and theories of self-regulation.

John K. Rempel received his Ph.D. from the University of Waterloo in 1987. He is currently a postdoctoral fellow at the University of Texas at Austin. His primary research interests include the study of trust and attributional processes in close relationships.

Issues of trust have their origins in the dialectic between people's hopes and fears as close relationships develop. The desire for increased closeness raises the specter of giving more to the relationship and becoming more dependent on the partner. These feelings of dependency underline the risks of counting on the other to be responsive to one's needs and to fulfill one's hope for the relationship. The state of ambivalence created by this approach/avoidance conflict leads people to evaluate the partner's behavior for signs that might reduce the uncertainty they are experiencing. For some, a sense of security is achieved and their confidence in the partner's motives quells the sound of competing inner voices. For others, nagging doubts linger and any sense of inner peace remains an elusive goal, perhaps because a residue of caution remains from the unfinished business of past relationships. For others yet, the dilemma of trust may be resolved temporarily, only to appear again at some later juncture when events conspire to remind them of the risks of depending on another.

In this chapter we will examine the development and impact of trust in the context of close relationships. We will begin with a definition of

AUTHORS' NOTE: Preparation of this chapter was facilitated by a grant from the Social Sciences and Humanities Research Council of Canada. We benefited a great deal from discussions with a number of individuals, including John Darley, Harold Kelley, George Levinger, Dale Miller, and Michael Ross. Correspondence should be addressed to the first author at the Department of Psychology, University of Waterloo, Waterloo, Ontario N2L 3G1, Canada.

trust and a discussion of its roots in individuals' interpersonal histories. We will go on to explore the development of trust in intimate relationships, emphasizing how its foundations are colored by the seminal experiences that mark different stages of interdependence. We will then consider the various states of trust that can evolve and their consequences for people's emotions and perceptions in established relationships. Our goal is to create a portrait of how trust comes to be reflected in the phenomenological experience of individuals in close relationships.

THE CONCEPT OF TRUST

Deutsch (1973) defined trust as "confidence that one will find what is desired from another, rather than what is feared" (p. 149). In close relationships, trust reflects confident expectations of positive outcomes from an intimate partner. The specific nature of the outcomes people expect becomes an important issue if we adopt a definition of this kind. Expectations can be framed at varying levels of generality (Holmes, 1981). People can expect specific behaviors such as a morning kiss, and they can also expect abstract motivational orientations such as "undying love." As expectations become more abstract, they have potential implications for an increasingly broad range of the partner's behaviors. We suspect that central values and concerns such as trust are represented by abstract expectations that subsume a variety of more specific beliefs and feelings.

People's expectations relevant to trust center on their perceptions of their partner's attitude toward the relationship, on the perceived quality and intensity of the affective bond. It is important to people not only that they be loved but that they be loved in the right way, for the qualities they believe an ideal partner would value in them (Rempel, Holmes, & Zanna, 1985; Sternberg & Barnes, 1985). Expectations that form the very core of trust are those that focus on the partner's responsiveness to needs in situations of dependency. To earn trust, partners must be perceived as motivated to moderate their own self-interest in order to respond to people's needs at times when others are most relying on their good intentions (Holmes, 1981). The willingness to sacrifice self-interest in relationships is important for a variety of reasons (e.g., Clark & Mills, 1979; Kelley, 1979), and we suggest it plays a critical role in the development of trust. In summary, attitudes of trust reflect people's abstract positive expectations that they can count on partners to care for them and be responsive to their needs, now and in the future.

Dispositions to Trust or Distrust Others

Discussions of trust inevitably raise the issue of the extent to which chronic personal tendencies to trust or distrust others influence the capacity to develop feelings of confidence in specific relationships. A number of recent studies are consistent with the view that chronic tendencies have at least some impact. For instance, Hazan and Shaver (1987) classified individuals' orientations to relationships on the basis of Ainsworth's (1979) descriptions of three major styles of attachment in infants—secure, anxious/ambivalent, and avoidant. People's categorizations of their own (adult) styles related both to memories of the nature of their relationships with parents and to their experiences of love. Of particular note, secure individuals described themselves as having more trust, less fear of closeness, and fewer emotional extremes. Anxious/ ambivalent individuals reported the strongest desire for reciprocation of feelings and for union with their partners, and more intense jealousy and emotional highs and lows.

Levitz-Jones and Orlofsky (1985) developed dispositional categories based on Erikson's (1963) stage theory of identity. Their depictions of high-intimacy status, merger, and pseudointimate (self-reliant) people correspond closely to the syndromes presented by Hazan and Shaver. They also found that the latter two groups reacted more strongly to issues of potential separation or dependency. The authors speculated that the anxiety experienced by these groups reflects similar underlying concerns about whether attachment figures can be relied on to be responsive when needed, even though their styles are so phenotypically different.

The perspective offered in these two studies is a healthy antidote to the naive view that trust can be recognized by the intensity of attachment displayed and the degree to which intimates depend on each other. In fact, Holmes (1987) found that trust correlated negatively with both a scale designed to measure people's desire for extreme intimacy and merger (those who "love too much") and a scale measuring fears of closeness (at least for men). It correlated positively with a preference for some autonomy in relationships, but not with the defensive self-sufficiency of avoidant individuals. Thus trust tends to be negatively associated with more extreme motivations for affiliation or autonomy, which in our opinion are ways of *coping* with the issue of unresolved uncertainty.

The authors of the above studies were careful to note that their concurrent or retrospective measures do not permit a direct test of claims about the chronicity of interpersonal tendencies across time or different relationships. Generally speaking, efforts to predict trust in specific close relationships from measures of generalized trust have been unsuccessful (e.g., Johnson-George & Swap, 1982; Larzelere & Huston, 1980). This may reflect the fact that researchers have typically used scales developed by Rotter (1967) and Wrightsman (1972) that focus rather exclusively on beliefs about people's honesty in their communications. In any case, we are inclined to adopt a functional perspective that frames the issue more in terms of a person-situation interaction. From this perspective, a tendency to be trusting is seen as a contingency rule, a preferred adaptation if features of relationships warrant it. If we think in terms of a *readiness* to trust, we also avoid creating an unrealistic caricature of the trusting individual as a blind optimist (Erikson, 1963). If anything, there is some evidence to suggest that distrusting individuals adjust less effectively to the features of particular relationships than do trusting individuals. People who distrust the motives of others tend to have more rigid and narrow expectations and to provoke the very reactions they fear (Kelley & Stahelski, 1970; Miller & Holmes, 1975).

THE DEVELOPMENT OF TRUST IN CLOSE RELATIONSHIPS

Recent theories on the development of close relationships have focused on the growth of interdependence between partners as the critical feature that helps to explain the particular issues that surface at different phases of development (e.g., Levinger, 1983). This perspective has not been used in most depictions of the growth of trust. It fits especially well with our view that trust evolves out of successfully confronting increasing concerns about dependency as relationships develop. In this section then, we will consider the processes related to the growth of trust in the context of the different stages of interdependence that people experience as their relationships progress. First though, we need to be more specific in our analysis of the types of information about the partner that are relevant to feelings of trust.

The Process of Uncertainty Reduction

The development of trust is perhaps best described as a process of uncertainty reduction. The ultimate goal is to reach confident conclusions about the strength and quality of the partner's attachment to the relationship. In this process, people will be strongly motivated to code behavior for signs of this attachment. Rempel, Holmes and Zanna (1985) proposed that the most basic type of information relevant to the development of trust concerns the partner's behavioral *predictability*. People build their trust from the fabric of the interactions they experience. If the partner's behavior appears volatile and unpredictable, expectations will be more frequently violated, causing anxiety and attributional ambiguity. In contrast, a stable, positive orientation on the partner's part contains messages about the couple's convergent interests and the partner's commitment to shared norms (Kelley & Thibaut, 1978). It is interesting to note that attachment theorists consider behavioral consistency to be a critical ingredient of responsiveness on the part of caregivers, one that helps to create a sense of security (Sroufe, 1983).

As the focus shifts from behavior to the reasons behind it, people will interpret consistency in the partner's behavioral profile in terms of more general dispositional qualities. Theorists have considered one component of trust to be a specific set of trait attributions that center on the partner's tendency to be a responsive person. The relevant constellation of personal qualities resembles a *dependability* prototype (Rempel et al., 1985). In essence, a partner would be seen as more trustworthy if he or she were the type of person who could be counted on to be honest, reliable, cooperative, and essentially benevolent (Johnson-George & Swap, 1982; Larzelere & Huston, 1980; Rempel et al., 1985). People's confidence in such trait inferences reflects their experiences in a limited set of situations involving personal risk and vulnerability, where trust is a salient concern. Note that a partner who is consistently rewarding and virtuous in character may nevertheless fail to instill any sense of security about the future of the relationship. This can occur because the quality of the partner's responsiveness needs to be seen as uniquely tied to his or her feelings of attachment to the relationship. The issue concerns not only whether the other is capable of being "nice," but perceptions that the partner is acting that way because he or she "cares." In summary, people's convictions about a partner's *attachment* will be displayed in interpersonal attributions, explanations for responsive behavior that focus on the partner's special connection to them (Holmes, 1981; Newman, 1981).

People's judgments of a partner's predictability, dependability, and attachment are open to a wide range of influences. A sense of confidence may be achieved at one stage in the relationship, only to dissipate at a later stage when increased interdependence exposes personal concerns and aspects of the partner's attitudes that had not come into focus. In this section we will first explore the development of trust in the early stages of relationships when interdependence tends to be restricted to a selective sample of positive domains.

The Early Stages

For many people, the early stages of a romantic relationship are a blur of experience, made opaque by a rush of unreflective positive feeling toward a partner. The initial focus is on the rewarding qualities that make the relationship feel worthwhile (Eidelson, 1980; Rusbult, 1983). Decisions to move further into the relationship may initially be made in an implicit, unself-conscious manner, governed by the pull of mutual attraction and the stirrings of passion. People often experience these first waves of passionate love as being "swept away." Events conspire to feed their hopes and fantasies about the potential of the relationship. These hopes are projected onto the partner, filling in the gaps of an image constructed from fragments of information. The image may go largely unchallenged at this stage because experiences are colored by self-presentation, selective positive interactions, and inter-dependence at more superficial, less conflictual levels.

At this early stage, trust is often little more than a naive expression of hope. The projection of intense feelings, bolstered by reciprocal displays of affection from partners, creates a sense of optimism that typically belies the lack of hard evidence. Larzelere and Huston (1980) reported that trust tends to be high and strongly related to love for couples at the exclusively dating stage. Similarly Sternberg (1986) described fatuous love, and Hendrick and Hendrick (1986) described Eros, as passion accompanied by a mutual sense of commitment and common destiny without a core of sustained intimacy to support such longings. Dion and Dion (1973) reported that love and a sense of trust went hand in hand even during the more volatile infatuation period experienced by low self-esteem individuals. Thus it appears that for some, the earliest expressions of confidence in a romantic partner may be "blind faith" in an idealized image they have created.

For a variety of reasons, this portrayal does not fully capture the development of trust in the romantic period of relationships. The foundations of trust may indeed be fragile from an analytical perspective. People's understanding of their partners is often severely limited by the extent of interdependence they have experienced. On the other hand, it is important to identify the process that does promote such strong feelings of trust in people whose relationships are progressing well. Our general hypothesis is that trust evolves out of dealing successfully with concerns about dependency as love grows.

The reciprocal reassurance process. As people move further into relationships, an awareness develops that the more they allow themselves to care, the more they have to lose. Their rising hopes and their personal investments in the future of the relationship make them increasingly dependent on the ultimate designs of the partner. They come to rely on the many benefits that the partner can provide, the rewards they anticipate from increased closeness as the relationship develops. People also become vulnerable to exploitation and rejection. The risk is that their investments will be lost and the experience will prove to be an empty promise if the depth of their affections is not reciprocated. At times it may feel to people as if their personal worth is on the line, that they are waiting for a judgment to be passed on them. This situation of dependency is likely to engender anxiety and to cause people to try to reduce their uncertainty by evaluating the partner's behavior for signs of caring.

People are likely to need continued reassurance about the partner's intentions as they increase the stakes by moving further into the relationship. Consistent with this theme, Kelley and Thibaut (1978) depicted the formation of trust as an exchange of actions or messages that gradually reduces uncertainty and increases mutual assurance that the relationship will endure. The process is keyed to attributions about risk taking. Confidence in a partner increases when his or her behavior involves some sacrifice of self-interest or acceptance of risk (Pruitt, 1965; Swinth, 1967). Acceptance of risk by a partner implies that he or she must go further than simply validating the person's expressions of attachment by responding in kind. Rather, the partner must at times take the more vulnerable position of being further out on a limb. This involves displaying a response meaningfully greater than is immediately justified by the person's prior behavior. Thus, trust grows in an upward spiral, anchored by perceptions of a balanced reciprocation process.

The normal flow of this process can be endangered if partners "come on too strong." The risk is that people will become reactive to excessive expectations now thrown on their shoulders, or a level of dependency that has outstripped their own involvement. The balance can also be upset if partners are seen as dragging their feet, unless the hesitation is interpreted as indicating personal insecurities that essentially equalize the risks accepted by both parties (Kelley & Thibaut, 1978). For instance, people may find themselves in the role of the pacesetter in disclosing feelings of caring, but rationalize it by concluding that the partner incurs extra costs because he or she finds it hard to communicate emotions.

One might surmise that uncertainty about whether affections will be reciprocated would prime people's fears and provide an effective counterweight to their rising hopes. Instead, the anxieties engendered by the specter of rejection may feed the emotions that shape the romantic experience (Berscheid, 1983). Blau (1964) even suggested that people should be hesitant to quiet their partners' apprehensions, lest they diminish the tension that fuels the passion. Rather, a rough balance in the escalating cycle of reassurance offers temporary relief from the longings for reciprocation, without dampening their source.

If this process is unfolding successfully, feelings of both love and trust are strengthened together. The signs of *increasing* attachment on the part of the partner are central to the development of trust. They are likely to be interpreted as diagnostic of the partner's investment in the relationship itself, rather than as evidence of other factors such as the partner's dispositional qualities. Trust in the partner depends not only on these attributions about the strength and quality of attachment, but also on perceptions that the other's involvement is comparable to one's own. Our hunch is that when the mutual reassurance process is going smoothly, the calculus of the equation will be both imprecise and not very explicit. We suspect that ambiguity is likely to be resolved in favor of assumed similarity in feelings, as we suggested earlier.

However, the boundaries of wishful thinking can only be stretched so far, and perceptions of unequal involvement commonly occur. Concerns about trust will be surfaced for the person in the more dependent position, because the potential for rejection then becomes very salient. People's personal resources for dealing with feelings of insecurity will be challenged, though a psychological retreat in the face of such vulnerability is likely. The need for added reassurance may exceed what the partner is willing to give, especially if there was substance to the perception of unequal caring. Thus the hypothesis is that the growth of trust depends heavily on the experience of increasing reciprocal attachment, and once the process is seriously interrupted, relationships are at risk of failing.

Several lines of research are consistent with this view. The perception that love is not fully reciprocal is probably the best single predictor of the dissolution of dating relationships (Brehm, 1985; Hill, Rubin & Peplau, 1976; Walster, Walster, & Traupmann, 1978). In a similar vein, Berscheid and Fei (1977) reported that people who were insecure about their partner's feelings toward them said they were not sure they were in love, even though they admitted being dependent on the other person. In contrast, expressions of love and feelings of security went hand in hand. It appears that trust in the partner's intentions enables people to diminish psychologically the risk of moving further into the relationship, allowing emotions to crystallize in a way that lets people more fully acknowledge feelings of being "in love."

Equal involvement as insurance against risk. Evidence of equal and growing involvement strengthens trust directly by reducing uncertainty about the state of the relationship. Another important function is served by equal involvement, quite apart from the messages conveyed about people's feelings. It is experienced as a form of insurance, providing some security in the face of mounting risks (Holmes, 1981). We suggested earlier that the growth of trust depends on each person's willingness to demonstrate caring by taking risks in disclosing their feelings and responding to the other's needs at some personal cost. A rough balance in the bearing of such risks offers some protection because the partner is equally dependent and vulnerable and is venturing investments similar to one's own. Paradoxically, the reciprocal dependence that this process implies serves both as a temporary substitute for trust and as a secure base for its development.

These concerns about equal involvement motivate people to focus on the balance in patterns of social exchange in their relationships. During the periods when concerns are strongest, people will maintain reciprocity in their contributions over shorter periods of time because of the reassurance and security it provides. As confidence in the partner's attachment grows and feelings of vulnerability diminish, people will be less motivated to ensure balanced exchange in the shorter term. Essentially, the patterns of reciprocity function to address relationship issues over and above the economics of exchange. As the underlying issues recede in importance, the impetus for maintaining the patterns is removed. We are not implying that fairness or equity in social exchange becomes irrelevant as trust grows. Rather, people are then able to set aside the constraints of shorter-term reciprocity and have confidence that over time, partners will be responsive to their needs.

Altman and Taylor (1973) proposed a similar model in their description of the role of self-disclosure in the "social penetration process." They argued that the development of trust is tied to short-term reciprocity in intimate communications in the early stages of relationships, but that the safety net it provides becomes less necessary as trust is strengthened. Several studies have supported their hypothesis, finding less concern with momentary imbalances in self-disclosure in more established relationships (Derlega, Wilson, & Chaiken, 1976; Morton, 1978). Consistent with the present perspective, Altman and Taylor viewed the desire for reciprocity as reflecting needs for reassurance about the partner's intentions, rather than more direct concerns about the economics or fairness of social exchange.

Several recent studies on social exchange also concluded that people become more flexible about rules of reciprocity as their relationships progress. In research on dating couples, Lloyd, Cate, and Benton (1982) found that a general sense of equity or fair exchange was more strongly related to satisfaction at earlier rather than later stages in relationships. Schmidt, Kelley, and Fujino (1987) examined the outcome patterns preferred by dating couples across a wide range of decision situations. People in shorter-term relationships tended to show concerns with equality, expressed through efforts to minimize the differences between their respective costs or benefits. In contrast, people in serious, longer-term relationships showed an increased preference for maximizing the joint welfare of the pair, even though it might involve a temporary imbalance in outcomes.

Clark and her colleagues have presented an apparently contrasting picture of the reciprocity issue in studies of social exchange in particular encounters (e.g., Berg & Clark, 1985). In these experiments people showed an abrupt transition to a "communal" orientation very early in relationships. Partners benefited one another in direct response to their needs, with no apparent expectation of receiving comparable benefits in return. The authors concluded that people appear to have a shared understanding of this "romantic script."

Conformity to the script becomes a language for communicating one's good intentions and interest in the relationship. Conversely, if behavior is seen as part of an explicit process of quid pro quo, the value of contributions is undermined. In attributional terms, the partner's expected benefits from reciprocity weaken perceptions that his or her responsive behavior is diagnostic of caring (Holmes, 1981). Thus "local" reciprocity in particular interactions where exchange issues are salient impedes the development of trust. In contrast, a pattern of reciprocity *across* time and situations promotes trust, because a balance in behavior indicative of caring reduces concerns about equal involvement. The need to follow the communal script is most likely to compete with the need to follow rules of reciprocity in the earlier states of relationships. The challenge for people is to tolerate uncertainty to a point where the time frame for reciprocity is sufficiently extended that their motives for being responsive are not called into question.

Summary. As romantic love develops, feelings of trust largely reflect people's confidence that partners' feelings are similar to their own. Signs of mutuality in affection are used to pace people's hopes and quell their fears about dependency. If the process of reciprocal reassurance successfully diminishes perceptions of uncertainty and risk, trust develops a core through dyadic experience that goes well beyond blind assumptions about the partner's emotional investment in the relationship.

The Accommodation Stage

In our analysis of romantic love, we have suggested that couples focus heavily on the issue of reciprocal caring. Our assumption is that implicit evaluations of compatibility and interaction outcomes certainly occur, but that for successful couples an "economy of surplus" exists that makes such appraisals a secondary concern (Levinger, 1979). Often, however, appraisals are made in situations that are not representative of the sample of situations people will confront as their level of inter-dependence increases. As relationships progress, people's lives become more tightly interconnected, resulting in interdependence in a greater number of domains and at deeper levels (e.g., Levinger, 1983). In the process, people learn that their interests and preferences are sometimes opposed. Moreover, conflicts of interest occur not only at behavioral levels, but at the level of personal styles and attitudes as well. Thus people not only find themselves disagreeing on what movie to see, but perhaps also about the values the movie portrays and the right to make choices independent of the partner.

As partners begin to see each other in a more realistic light, feelings of ambivalence are likely to surface. Eidelson (1980) suggested that during this period the demands of interdependence often conflict with chronic concerns about closeness and autonomy. In fact, a number of studies found that as relationships became more serious, the incidence of interpersonal conflict, negativity, and ambivalence increased, and that this pattern was independent of the amount of love couples reported (Braiker & Kelley, 1979; Driscoll, Davis & Lipetz, 1972; Kelly, Huston, & Cate, 1985). Thus as a consequence of increased interdependence, people come to understand that the sense of harmony they once experienced may be in part illusion. They also come to realize that if their relationships are to grow, they must be willing to sacrifice personal interests to accommodate the needs of their partners.

As negative aspects of relationships come into focus, both the risks and costs of greater involvement are more fully exposed. We contend that people's agendas then become more explicitly evaluative and that their concerns cause them to turn to a *prospective analysis* of their relationships. Costs of further involvement are counted and compared to the promise of increasing rewards in the future (Huesmann & Levinger, 1976; Kelley & Thibaut, 1978). People's appraisals go beyond perceptions of the quality of the partner's attachment to include an assessment of the implications that increasing interdependence might have for each individual's particular concerns. The benefits of mutual goal facilitation are weighed against the costs of compromising aspects of personal identity, such as losing a sense of autonomy in the relationship. In other words, the specter of increased dependency sharpens people's concerns about whether they are in the *right* relationship and whether they can ultimately trust the partner to act in ways that would be compatible with their particular needs.

Other risks become more salient as well. Like a social trap, increased involvement raises the stakes, ensures greater dependency on the partner, and makes turning back increasingly difficult. People become more explicitly aware that their hopes have begun to ride on the relationship and that rejection or failure could prove to be very painful. For these reasons, they need to consolidate their sense of what the partner is ultimately capable and willing to provide and they also need to establish the worth of the relationship in their lives in a way that does not simply deny the negative elements (Holmes, 1981; Kelley & Thibaut, 1978). Thus, people's decisions to move further into their relationships become increasingly tuned to their subjective forecasts of what the future holds. A transition occurs to a more controlled orientation in which people's evaluations of their prospects become more extended in time and serve to *regulate* the depth of their involvement.

In this period trust starts to develop a separate core from love, a core that is forged from diagnostic experiences specific to concerns about the future of the relationship. The results of a number of studies seem consistent with the notion that trust has foundations in the accommodation process that do not always overlap with factors that promote love. Driscoll et al. (1972), Dion and Dion (1976), and Larzelere and Huston (1980) all found only a low correlation between love and trust for couples in this phase, especially when compared to married couples. The latter authors also reported that the low correlation represents a significant shift from the strong association we noted earlier for less committed couples.

Negotiating terms of endearment. What then, is unique about experiences that relate specifically to trust? How does the process of accommodation influence people's evaluations of their prospects in their relationships? In this stage, people encounter situations that are more *diagnostic* of their partners' responsiveness and the capacity of relationships to satisfy their needs. First, there is considerable opportunity for learning about partners because interests will more often diverge as people negotiate their terms of endearment. The situations that are confronted provide more optimal contexts for revealing people's attitudes. As patterns of choices make potential conflicts and risks more salient, there is more opportunity for distinctively expressing and attributing motives in relationships (Holmes, 1981; Kelley & Thibaut, 1978).

Second, the partner's willingness to respond to the person's preferences takes on a different hue, because accommodations are often required on core issues that are more deeply rooted in a sense of self (Altman & Taylor, 1973). When concerns about vulnerability and dependency are strongest, empathy and responsiveness by the partner are all the more meaningful and their impact on trust is magnified. In addition, the costs to the partner of compromises and personal adjustments in core domains facilitate confident attributions about the strength of attachment. The partner's adjustments convey caring by affirming the value of the person's separate identity as well as the value of the relationship itself. If the pair can successfully navigate this terrain by forging innovative arrangements tailored to their styles and needs, they are likely to develop a feeling that together they've created a special bond.

The process of self-disclosure also does much to strengthen this sense of connection. Berg and Clark (1985) suggested that at this stage, there is little urgency to reciprocate disclosures in kind, because expressions of understanding and support better convey a sense of caring. This kind of responsiveness is also affirming and eases anxieties about being oneself. However the process of communication usually involves mutual influence as well, and an actual convergence of preferences may start to occur (Borden & Levinger, in press). Sociologists have proposed that partners collude to construct a shared social reality, a "little world that crystallizes through the conversational process, with little apprehension by its authors" (Berger & Kellner, 1972, p. 63).

In summary, the accommodation process provides the opportunity to address latent concerns about dependency that come into focus as interdependence increases. Trust is strengthened if partners are responsive in ways that acknowledge individuals' particular needs and affirm their sense of worth. The responsiveness of partners is most clearly revealed in situations that require them to sacrifice their own interests. However, the sacrifices expected of each person cannot strain perceptions that interests in the relationship are ultimately convergent. On balance, confidence in the viability of the relationship results from a process that underlines shared interests and the unique ways in which each person's needs are furthered.

Control as a substitute for trust. Trust reflects a willingness to relinquish personal control, to put one's fate in the hands of another. In contrast, residual concerns about dependency foster efforts to exert influence to ensure that one's needs are met. Control serves as a security operation, as a *substitute* for trust. Experiences that are seminal to working through issues of trust often occur in a set of prototypical situations that highlight decisions to relinquish control in the face of risk (Holmes, in press). In these situations, individuals typically have safe choices available that do not leave them particularly dependent on the partner's actions and assure a degree of equality in outcomes. On the other hand, alternative courses of action may potentially be more satisfying and attuned to their needs. However these alternatives make them vulnerable to the partner's choice of responses, some of which could prove to be very hurtful or costly. Thus to satisfy their needs, people must permit increased dependency and leave themselves open to personal risk. The risk would be accepted with the hope that the partner would show concern for their needs and the joint welfare of the unit. It is important to note the paradoxical nature of this sequence: Individuals must first take the risk of trusting before the foundations of trust can be established (Strickland, 1958).

Concerns about relinquishing control will be most salient to people when responsiveness by partners would require behaviors seen as costly in terms of their outcomes. Despite this, it is often not the particular outcomes of an interaction that are of concern, but rather the implications of the interaction for deeper relationship issues. During this stage, people approach relationships tuned to detect evidence relevant to their concerns. They will value diagnostic information about their partners' attitudes more than the actual benefits received. Small acts of considerateness may feel more significant than displays of largesse that do not seem revealing. Thus people will raise their attributions for events to more general, abstract levels and the affect evoked will often derive from inferences about their partners' motivations (e.g., Kelley, 1984).

As risks are rewarded and trust grows, we suspect that the positive construals and good feelings generated in particular interactions lead people to entertain positive mental simulations of future episodes with similar features. This prospective affect or hope motivates individuals to take chances in a broader range of situations involving vulnerability and potential conflict of interest. As confidence increases, people will approach new circumstances less tentatively and exercise looser control in interactions where they are dependent on the partner's good intentions. However, if experiences fail to reduce uncertainty, individuals are likely to show a readiness to detect and avoid situations that mirror their concerns. Kelley (1984) described such failures in the adaptation process as causing a "lifestyle" for the relationship, one where the range of intimate situations in which partners will interact is narrowed and certain scenarios are deemed "off limits."

The issue of fairness in social exchange in the accommodation phase can also be viewed from the perspective of temporal control (Holmes, 1981). Initially, efforts are made to create a balance of exchange over the shorter term because it prevents exploitation or unfair advantage by a partner whose intentions are not yet clear to us. The accounting process will be tighter until sufficient trust develops to loosen the reins and extend the time frame within which fairness will eventually be served. People become increasingly able to set security concerns aside and respond more directly to each other's needs as they occur, less encumbered by the restraints of self-regulation. Concerns with control are also quieted to the extend that love comes to be seen in relational terms. After all, to give to the relationship is not to give anything *away* if people have come to see themselves as a natural unit (Lerner, Miller, & Holmes, 1976).

Mutual control and a sense of efficacy. The accommodation phase is a platform for confronting the issue of conflict over the conflict process itself, or metaconflict (Braiker & Kelley, 1979). To the extent that a couple learns that they can deal effectively with issues, and with cooperative efforts feel closer, they will experience the security that derives from a sense of control over the fate of the relationship. This type of control is the antithesis of the sort we discussed previously, because it involves the risk of *increasing* interdependence with a partner during times of stress rather than decreasing it. A sense of efficacy in dealing with problems and conflicts is predicated on people's assumption that their partners will be responsive if they take the risk of making their needs clear and that together, integrative solutions can be found. In contrast, if issues are avoided because of a clash of styles for resolving conflicts, confidence is liable to be eroded and areas of vulnerability will linger.

Perceptions of efficacy are most likely to develop in couples who engage issues in their relationships and who are willing to directly state their feelings. This orientation has been shown to result in better quality solutions in problem-solving sessions, more satisfaction with the outcomes, and increased mutual understanding (e.g., Miller, Lefcourt, Holmes, Ware, & Saleh, 1986). Individuals with an internal locus of control were found to engage issues most directly. Not surprisingly, locus of control correlates positively with trust (e.g., Sabatelli, Buck, & Dreyer, 1983). A shared sense of confidence in dealing with problems may become more central to trust as time passes. The solution of one problem is often followed by the discovery of another as the nature of interdependence continues to unfold (Levinger, 1983).

Attributions for responsiveness. Evidence that a partner is responsive to the person's needs is a necessary but not sufficient condition for the growth of trust. Behavior is coded not only for responsiveness, but also for the perceived *causes* of demonstrations of considerateness and altercentric concern. Rempel, Holmes, and Zanna (1985) distinguished three types of motivation that might be attributed to a partner. First, a partner's responsiveness might be perceived as an attempt to secure extrinsic resources facilitated by the relationship, such as money or status. Second, a partner's behavior might be seen as instrumental, designed to obtain the benefits that the person is capable of offering. The qualities that a partner values might have common currency, such as appearance, intellect, and social competence, or be targeted more directly, such as support, praise, and companionship. The common thread is that a partner may make sacrifices to maintain the relationship, precisely *because* it is expected to be rewarding.

Rempel et al. distinguished extrinsic and instrumental orientations from responsiveness that is seen as *intrinsically* motivated. Various theorists have stressed the notion that the pleasure derived from gratifying the needs of an intimate partner may become an end unto itself, through a process of empathic identification (e.g., Blau, 1964; Lerner et al., 1976; Levinger, 1979). The desire to be responsive to the partner is seemingly "without reason," in a way that suggests that the motive becomes functionally autonomous from its roots. Loving is its own reward. Earlier it was suggested that a sense of mutuality develops out of the dyadic process; people come to talk of "our love" rather than "my love" (Kelley, 1983). This experience of union, where the boundaries of people's own interests and their partners' interests become blurred, captures the meaning of intrinsic attachment.

The conviction that a partner is intrinsically motivated to be responsive and caring is hypothesized to be central to trust. The concept may seem ephemeral, but in one sense, it is the strongest evidence of attachment precisely because it goes *beyond* reasons (Brickman, 1987). The belief implies that the partner values the relationship over and above evaluations of the person's desirable features, features whose currency it is feared, are not written in stone for all time. In a less logical way, intrinsic attachment is appropriate to our cultural understanding about what "true love" really is. It seems inimical to people's thinking to conceive of their partners' love as rooted largely in the instrumental rewards they receive (Berg & Clark, 1985; Rempel et al., 1985; Seligman, Fazio & Zanna, 1980).

Rempel, Holmes, and Zanna (1985) attempted to test these notions by constructing scales to measure the three types of motives. They found that trust was strongly related to beliefs that a partner was intrinsically motivated to be in the relationship (r = .52), but not to beliefs that the other was motivated by instrumental (r = .17) or extrinsic (r = –.03) concerns. However, people's own instrumental motivation, their tendency to value what their partners provided, was associated with trusting them (r = .41). Qualities such as a partner's support and praise seem to be experienced as responsiveness and breed feelings of trust. Perceptions of intrinsic orientations in self and other were tightly linked (r = .77), as one might expect if the attachment process indeed promotes a sense of mutuality and shared feelings.

In contrast to the results for trust, love and satisfaction were both significantly associated with perceptions of instrumental motives in a partner (r = .52). It seems that being valued by a partner for what one has to offer, for one's qualities, is self-affirming and bolsters reciprocal good feeling. However, one's perceptions of being needed in this way seemed to do little to strengthen trust. Apparently, trust depends on the sense that a partner's caring transcends concerns about the direct benefits received. Caring should somehow reflect the special connection that has been created and should symbolize a lack of conditionality. The meaning of trust becomes truly relational in nature, with the metamorphosis reflecting seminal experiences that increasingly foster a shared sense of security.

THE IMPACT OF TRUST IN ESTABLISHED RELATIONSHIPS

Trust is not a static concept, an edifice that once erected simply continues to provide a warm place to house a relationship. One might get that impression however, given the dearth of research focusing on the impact of different levels of trust on experiences in established relationships. Studies have dealt almost exclusively with the development of feelings of security rather than its consequences. In this section we hope to take a step in the direction of remedying this imbalance by considering the dynamics of trust and its influence on the process of interpersonal evaluation in marriages.

In the early years of marriage, trust tends to be strong and its connection to love is restored as commitment to the relationship increases (Larzelere & Huston, 1980). Perhaps as people become pledged to a course of action, they need a sense of conviction to allow them to "avoid being forced to listen to the babble of competing inner voices" (Jones & Gerard, 1967, p. 181). However, psychological closure is seldom fully warranted by the evidence that is available. Trust is prospective in nature, and there will be times when the future does not mirror the past. Even if it did, the evaluation of a partner usually leaves a residue of ambivalence, as caregiving deficiencies are unmasked in the accommodation stage. In spite of or because of these forces, Rempel, Holmes, and Zanna (1985) speculated that at some point, most people need to act *as if* a sense of security were justified, and set their doubts aside. To do so requires a "leap of faith" in the face of evidence that can never be conclusive. Thus trust becomes a necessary construction, an emotionally charged sense of closure. It permits an illusion of control, an intimate life free from continual uncertainty, where one can plan ahead without anxiety.

The culmination of this process for high-trust individuals is an integrated attitude structure that reflects their convictions about their partners' motives. Attitudes of trust are comprised of people's abstract positive expectations that they can count on their partners to care for them and be responsive to their needs, now and in the future. Holmes and Rempel (1986) proposed that such attitudes will have a high degree of affective/cognitive consistency among elements seen as most relevant to trust. The structure will be organized in a hierarchical fashion, with core elements subsuming a variety of more specific beliefs and feelings about the partner. This attitude structure functions to regulate the interpersonal life space of trusting individuals, imparting *meaning* to the partner's behavior, in a top-down manner.

The Appraisal Process of High-Trust Individuals

The convictions of high-trust individuals are anchored both by positive conclusions about their partners' motives drawn from past evidence and by faith in what the future holds. Consequently, the impact of any given behavior is dampened as it is set against the broader context of attitudes about the relationship. A person in a trusting relationship is prepared to interpret a partner's actions in ways that are consistent with his or her abstract positive expectations. However, positive events merely confirm feelings of trust that already exist. This reasoning leads us to suggest that a wide range of behavior by a partner is liable to be assimilated to the benevolent expectations of a high-trust individual, and credited as further examples of the other's good intentions. Negative behavior by an intimate partner, on the other hand, will typically be inconsistent with a trusting person's general expectations. Nonetheless, confident beliefs about the partner's motives are not likely to be called into question if events are interpreted in the positive context of attitudes about the relationship. We suspect that negative behaviors are relegated to lower levels of concern by limiting their implications for core issues. Basically, trusting individuals do not treat their partners' central motives as an open question. Rather they attribute the offending behaviors to alternative, less threatening explanations.

These hypotheses were explored in a large-scale experiment that we conducted with established couples (Holmes & Rempel, 1986). Eighty-two couples participated in a laboratory session in which they were asked to discuss a difficult issue in their relationship. Trust in the relationship was measured using an 18-item trust scale (Rempel et al., 1985). The scale covers a range of trust-related experiences by measuring people's perceptions of their partner's predictability and dependability and their faith in the future of the relationship. Next, participants were asked to complete a short questionnaire comprised of semantic differential items designed to tap their expectations concerning the partner's behavior and motives in the forthcoming discussion. Couples then discussed the issue for fifteen minutes. The discussion was videotaped.

After a short break, participants were seated at tables facing a TV monitor. A computer-linked button-box with four keys labelled very negative, moderately negative, moderately positive, and very positive was placed on each table in front of them. The color videotape of the couple's discussion was played, and each person was asked to independently rate any of the partner's behaviors that "had some impact on you, resulting in either positive or negative feelings." Following the replay procedure, participants completed the same set of semantic differential scales that had been administered prior to the interaction. In this case, they were asked for their perceptions of the partner's actual behavior during the interaction, and then their inferences about the other's motives for acting that way. Couples were classified as high, medium, or low trust, based on a tertile split of their total Trust Scale scores.

High-trust couples entered their discussion with optimistic expectations and generously portrayed the partner's motives as even more positive than their own. When they punctuated their interaction using the button-box during the replay procedure, their reactions differentiated them from individuals at other levels of trust. They had more frequent reactions involving strong positive affect (19%) and far fewer involving strong negative affect (7%). Similarly, trusting individuals rated the partner's behavior and motives in the interaction as significantly more positive than did medium or low trust people. Finally, when the pre- and post-discussion ratings were compared, trusting individuals changed their opinions least of all and changes in evaluations were only weakly tied to their affective reactions during the replay procedure.

The impact of high trust on the interpretive process is more complex than these results indicate, however, as experimental manipulations included in our study demonstrated. We speculated that the confidence and clarity of the core attitudes held by trusting individuals lead them to react affectively to the partner's behavior in a relatively automatic, positive way and that little consideration of its meaning typically takes place (e.g., Fazio, in press). The potential cost of this process is that acts of caring may be taken for granted if the implications of events are not elaborated (Berscheid, 1983). Therefore, our manipulation was designed to promote a more active appraisal of trust-related issues in participants.

Our strategy was to remind people in a vivid way of either the darker or the brighter side of their formative experiences with trust. In a Positive Recall condition, we asked people to remember a specific problem in their relationship that, for the most part, was successfully resolved, a situation in which the partner was responsive to their needs and feelings. The wording in a Negative Recall condition was identical except for key phrases underlining people's sense of disappointment about the partner's lack of responsiveness when it counted. People were asked to describe a particular incident and their feelings associated with it. The procedure took only about five minutes and was tape recorded. The coding of the tapes indicated that the manipulation was very successful in priming emotionally charged memories and that level of trust was not related to the content of the memories or the ease with which they were recalled. For purposes of comparison, a Control group was included in the design. Participants in this condition were simply given several minutes to consider the issue they would be discussing.

The results depicted in Figure 8.1 indicate that trusting individuals in the Positive Recall condition changed their evaluations of the partner's behavior and motives more than their counterparts in the Control condition, even though trained observers could detect no behavioral differences in the interactions across conditions. Of course, this effect might be due to the impact of mood on judgment (e.g., Strack, Schwarz, & Gschneidinger, 1985), rather than to deeper elaboration of the attitude structure. However, the mood explanation cannot account for the failure of this same pattern to occur for couples at other levels of trust.

More critically, we found that recapitulating a negative relationship memory resulted in evaluations and attributions that were even more positive than those in the Positive Recall condition. This provocative result suggests that the challenge posed by the negative memory caused trusting individuals to more actively consider the wider issue of the partner's motives. We had expected that this elaboration process would

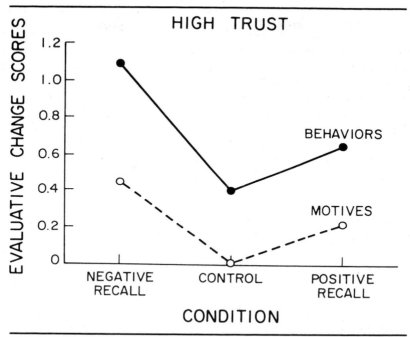

Figure 8.1 The impact of recall conditions on high-trust couples' evaluations of partners' behavior and motives.

simply dampen the impact of the memory by placing it into perspective. Instead, it appears that people defended against the threat by reaching back into their store of positive feelings. The result of activating considerations about their relationships was to further polarize their positive attitudes.

These results from the Negative Recall condition suggest that trusting individuals have developed a relatively unified representation of feelings about their partners and have avoided the separation of their hopes and fears into positive and negative compartments. We suspect that trust involves coming to terms with negative aspects of a partner and lingering doubts about his or her attachment by consolidating negative elements into a larger positive structure. This synthesis is achieved in part through a refutational network (e.g., Chaiken & Yates, 1985) that limits the adverse implications of negative elements for deeper relationship issues. In essence, recurring negative behaviors are encapsulated within the larger positive structure and relegated to less important relationship domains.

For example, an argument over the burden of household chores may cause very real frustration at the behavioral level. But the sting is largely removed for trusting individuals, because the conflict is not interpreted as a sign that the other doesn't care. A wife may see her husband as burdened by outside pressures, as lazy, or as pampered by his traditional mother. She may even accuse him of having been insensitive to her needs on this occasion. However, she is not likely to seriously contemplate the possibility that her husband is generally unconcerned about how she feels. Rather, she invokes dispositional or normative attributions at lower, less threatening levels in the attitude structure. Any anger coupled to these conclusions could be further drained by refutational thoughts of the "yes, but" kind: "He's lazy about cooking, but he's really considerate about helping with the children." His transgressions even serve to remind her of his virtues.

This charitable orientation reflects our premise that trusting individuals do not treat their partners' central motives as an open question. Behavioral transgressions can therefore be more easily endured because they have been largely discounted *in advance* of their occurrence. Of course events may sometimes conspire to challenge or threaten beliefs. When this happens, a more prolonged appraisal process may be triggered. The outcome of this process is liable to be largely over-determined, unless the partner's actions truly merit suspicion. This is because the *hypothesis* being tested is framed at the abstract level—does my partner really care? The evidence is at a specific, behavioral level, and the translation of it into diagnostic form is subject to considerable poetic license. Brickman (1987) has warned that constructions like these that serve to mask ambivalence are susceptible to "catastrophes" causing sudden swings in emotion if they become unraveled. However, the integrative solutions we are describing need not be fragile; they can be firmly rooted in people's history of dyadic experience and achieved without stretching perceptions or disavowing important issues in a premature search for closure.

In fact, a study by Rempel (1987) suggests that high-trust people do not seem to outrightly deny the negative elements in their relationships. In this study the discussions of 35 couples from the control condition of the experiment described earlier were transcribed, and attributional comments were identified on the transcripts. These attributions were then written on index cards, randomized, and coded on a variety of dimensions. The same rating dimensions were used to describe the type of events for which attributions were made. The results showed that high-trust people made more spontaneous attributions for positive events than people at lower levels of trust and their inferences were more stable and global than those of either medium- or low-trust people. Nonetheless, trusting individuals did not avoid communicating negative attributions when the type of event suggested such an attribution was warranted. What distinguished the negative attributions of trusting individuals was the manner in which these attributions were constrained. When explanations for very negative events were examined, trusting people made fewer very negative attributions, but a greater number of moderately negative attributions than would be expected by chance. Thus, high-trust people did not naively ignore negative events. Rather they tended to make attributions that placed some limits on the negative implications the event could have for the relationship.

Trust not only influences people's reactions in specific encounters, but it also shapes the *psychological perspective* they adopt in the overall evaluation process (Holmes, 1981). Trusting individuals tend to assess the flow of events in their relationships over a more extended period of time. Their broad time perspective has the effect of stabilizing their perceptions: Conclusions are moderated by aggregating the balance of rewards and costs over the longer term. This accounting practice *itself* has a leveling effect on impressions of momentary disturbances, smoothing out the ups and downs of everyday experience. Larger samples of behavior provide more stable inferences and give the *appearance* of less volatility in behavior. This is not to suggest that trusting individuals consciously calibrate the current ledger; rather, their sense of security tends to free them from concerns with monitoring contributions, permitting a looser, less deliberate accounting in their relationships.

In summary, our portrayal of a trusting relationship is one in which core issues of attachment are not a current concern. Thus there is little reason to monitor behavior for diagnostic signs of caring: In fact, trust can probably be recognized by the *absence* of an active appraisal process in the normal course of events (Holmes, 1981). This depiction of the *state* of trusting is compatible with the attachment theory notion that if one's partner has been available and responsive, the fear component becomes quiescent and a feeling of taken-for-granted security reigns (Hazan & Shaver, 1987). The subsequent dynamics we described also echo Sroufe's (1983) depiction of the "secure-base" metaphor in its more archaic form: The confident, benign expectations about attachment to adults in secure infants stretch the threshold for perceiving threats, cushion their impact, and hasten recovery after an experience of distress.

The Impact of Uncertainty on the Appraisal Process

For many people, a sense of trust in their partner may be an elusive goal. For some, experiences with a former partner or personal issues about dependency and closeness of the sort we described earlier make it difficult to forge a more permanent peace between their reasons to trust and their reasons to doubt. Others may feel that the fabric of their relationships simply does not merit a sense of conviction. Among them will be people who have retreated from the confidence they felt earlier in their relationship as the partner's inability to meet their expectations became difficult to comfortably explain away. Though the causes of people's ambivalence can vary considerably, the theme we will pursue is that feelings of uncertainty about a partner's motives have a pervasive influence on people's intimate lives. We believe that the goal of attaining a sense of security leads these individuals to *actively test the hypothesis* that their partner cares for them and is responsive to their needs. They will be relatively vigilant and monitor behavior for any diagnostic signs. We suggest that the ironic consequence of certain features of this appraisal process is often to accentuate the very concerns it aims to dispel.

The emotional tone of their relationships will reflect their latent approach/avoidance conflict, resulting in an unstable dialectic between polarities of feeling as they focus on one side of their attitudes or the other. On the one hand, the emotional investment of uncertain individuals leads them to be hopeful, primed to detect clear evidence of positive behavior and to code it for its relevance to larger issues. On the other hand, their hopes are constrained by feelings of vulnerability that lead them to consider the possibility that negative behavior is, in fact, the result of the partner's lack of concern for them. This elaboration process will amplify the reactions they have to events in their relationship, because they will be reacting not only to the behavior itself, but to the symbolic content it is perceived to convey (e.g., Kelley, 1984). Their reactivity will be further enhanced if their uncertainty evokes a more limited, shorter-term perspective: A particular experience can more easily take center stage, without being absorbed into the broader context of events.

There is evidence that distressed couples, broadly classified, have more polarized reactions to positive as well as negative behavior (Jacobson, Follette & McDonald, 1982). The results from the Holmes and Rempel (1986) experiment displayed in Figure 8.2 are also consistent with this view. They show that when the hopes of uncertain (medium-trust) individuals were primed in the Positive Recall condition, they evaluated the partner's

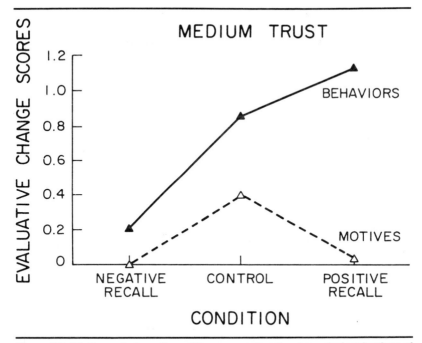

Figure 8.2 **The impact of recall conditions on medium-trust couples' evaluations of partners' behavior and motives.**

behavior in the subsequent interaction very positively, significantly more so than their counterparts in the Control condition. However, in a startling reversal in form, their attributions about the partner's motives were significantly *less* positive than in the control group. It is as if the prospect of a responsive partner leads ambivalent individuals to pull back, hardening their criteria for drawing positive inferences. Somehow, the specter of things going well is rather inextricably linked to an associated set of anxieties about the risk of feeling close but not truly having one's hopes realized.

We suspect that these individuals adopt what is essentially a *risk-aversive* strategy. For a variety of possible reasons they are constrained by feelings of vulnerability, by the risk of drawing positive conclusions that aren't justified, and being hurt, perhaps once again. These concerns translate into a conservative inference process for accepting positive behavior as truly diagnostic of corresponding motives of caring in their partner. This demand for relatively unequivocal evidence is like setting a high alpha level in statistical terms. It also appears that when people's hopes are raised and they approach a conclusion, the avoidance gradient

becomes even steeper, further sharpening the criteria for the attributional process. We speculate that to remove their final doubts,
uncertain individuals resort to a defensive style where positive behavior
is tagged to specific situational features and attributions are held in
abeyance until future evidence consolidates a generalization. Such
people may consider themselves to be "situationally skeptical" rather
than distrusting.

The reactions of uncertain individuals to negative experiences may
do little to redress this imbalance. Compared to trusting individuals,
they are likely to be more vigilant and ready to interpret a wide range of
actions in a negative way. The hurt will be greater because of their
willingness to consider the implications of a partner's negative behavior
for deeper issues about caring. The refutational structure of these
individuals is less capable of placing limits on the generalization process,
of containing the damage at lower levels of concern. In fact, Holmes and
Rempel (1986) found that their percentage of negative affect ratings and
frequency of very negative reactions as they watched the replay of their
discussion were almost identical to those of low-trust couples (see Table
8.1). In contrast, trained judges yoked by computer to rate behavior at
the same points in time viewed the partner as acting in a way that more
closely resembled high-trust spouses.

TABLE 8.1
Affective Reactions During the Replay Procedure

Percentage of Total Responses	Level of Trust		
	Low	Medium	High
Very positive reactions	12.5	15.5	19.0
Very negative reactions	16.8	16.8	7.2
Total negative reactions	54.9	54.4	43.3
Judges' negative reactions	53.2	42.6	37.5

Given their negative focus, it may come as a surprise to learn that
uncertain couples regarded their marriages as being relatively happy, far
more so than low-trust pairs. Thus one is left to speculate as to why they
do not draw on these accounts to stabilize their perceptions. We surmise
that on the whole, uncertain individuals' feelings about their partners
are less integrated and consistent than those of more trusting individuals.
Attitude structures that are sources of mixed messages are more
resistant to integration, and in uncertain individuals we may find that
hurts and fears are relatively compartmentalized and isolated from
areas of positive affect. If there is a weaker integration of component

attitudes in their associational networks, situations may prime a negative category without also priming the broader spectrum of positive feelings about a partner's attachment that could moderate their overall reactions. Thus people would be more susceptible to splitting their attitudes, to swings in emotion brought about when one side of their feelings is enhanced while the other is suppressed.

In the Holmes and Rempel (1986) experiment, the results in the Negative Recall condition are particularly relevant to this issue because feelings of vulnerability were made salient without also priming positive aspects of people's feelings. Uncertain individuals in this condition portrayed the partner's behavior in the discussion far more negatively than their counterparts in the control group and construed the partner's motives in an equally dark way. Unlike the trusting couples, there was no evidence of the negative relationship memory being buffered by positive aspects of their attitudes. This readiness to blame stands in contrast to their reactions in the Positive Recall condition, where they seemed extremely hesitant to grant any credit for behavior they viewed as very positive.

The same theme was apparent in the types of inferences uncertain individuals communicated to partners during their interactions. Rempel (1987) found that their discussions contained more negative and fewer very positive attributional statements than the discussions of either high- or low-trust couples. In addition, uncertain individuals made fewer specific and more frequent global attributions for very negative events than would be expected by chance. These various results lead us to believe that their threshold is lower for perceiving threats than it is for promises. They seem trapped in their ambivalence by a critical *asymmetry* in the types of conclusions they are willing to entertain. Ironically, it appears that uncertain individuals construct a social reality that mirrors their fears, but frustrates their hopes.

Reeder and Brewer (1979) suggested that inferences about moral dispositions such as honesty might follow such an asymmetrical pattern, where negative instances are treated as more diagnostic. If this is the case in the present context, it would be safer and more economical for these individuals to frame the hypothesis they are testing as, "Will my partner demonstrate that he or she *cannot* be counted on to respond to my needs" (e.g., Snyder, 1981). This bias may be particularly evident for people who believe their partners do not care as much as before, because the violation of standards would then be very salient. Alternatively, the risk-aversive bias may be less cognitive and reflect the accessibility of negative as opposed to positive categories of *affect*. Our emotional system is keyed to "trouble-shooting," to issuing warnings (Berscheid,

1983); one's fears may be easier to prime and have greater evocative power than one's hopes.

The Impact of a Breakdown in Trust

There has been little or no research focusing on factors that contribute to the erosion of trust, and we are left to conjecture as to the course it might take. Trust appears to be at its lowest in the group married from 6 to 20 years (Larzelere & Huston, 1980). One scenario for this decline involves an accumulation of violated expectations that exceeds the thresholds of tolerance and reminds people again of the risks of intimacy. The sources of strain may relate to facing novel problems of interdependence connected to careers, family, and lifestyle that surface old concerns thought to have been put to rest. These concerns are liable to be exposed in the process of resolving conflicts, which ultimately is the cradle for trust. Kelly, Huston, and Cate (1985) found that dissatisfaction several years into marriage was best predicted by the severity of conflict during the accommodation stage, even though conflict was not related to love at that time. The authors suggested that attributions for conflicts earlier in relationships tend to be charitable and people discount the import of the problem. But as time passes and similar patterns continue to be observed, blame is more likely to be attributed to a partner's chronic attitudes and dispositions (e.g., Fincham & Bradbury, 1987). People may further question their partners' feelings of love as emotional intensity fades in relationships, dampened by routines that tend to mask the areas of positive interdependence that remain intact (Berscheid, 1983).

As confidence declines, people develop a sense of defensive pessimism to protect themselves against further risk and vulnerability. In some ways, their attitudes are a mirror image of those of high-trust individuals. They are likely to have relatively closed minds and to react as if they have concluded that their partner is not truly concerned about them or the relationship. Positive behavior by the other will be viewed with suspicion. Low-trust couples may retain some residual hopes, but they understand all too well the risks of drawing positive conclusions about their partners' motives that later prove to be unwarranted. Their fears of being let down once again make them vigilant for signs of negative attitudes in their partners' behavior.

Holmes and Rempel (1986) found that low-trust individuals entered interactions expecting little of themselves and even less of their partners. Their affective responses on reviewing the replay of the discussion were predominantly negative, and trained observers had similar reactions to their partners' behavior (see Table 8. 1). Low-trust individuals' evaluations of the partners' behavior in the interaction were the least positive of any group and were not affected by the Recall manipulation. Their evaluations of the partners' motives seemed to be less firmly anchored by their expectations, however. In the Negative Recall condition, low-trust individuals were particularly inclined to distrust the partner's motives. Recalling the negative incident presumably primed a wider constellation of unhappy memories, cogently reminding them of the risks involved in depending on the partner's good intentions.

To our surprise, recalling positive memories induced low-trust couples to be somewhat more generous in their attributions. Unfortunately, any such vestiges of hope are often undercut by the self-fulfilling nature of a lack of trust. As people's fears grow, they are tempted to take out various forms of security insurance to protect themselves against the rising tide of risk. They essentially move to decrease interdependence in their relationships (Levinger, 1979) by forging an implicit social contract that puts their fate less in the hands of their partners (Holmes, 1981). Rules evolve to protect people's interests in contentious areas and more vulnerable domains are simply deemed off limits and avoided. The exchange process becomes less flexible and more measured as the issue of the partner's willingness to be responsive increases in salience. The theme is that more effort will be expended at controlling situations to ensure that one's needs are met, reducing dependency on the partner.

Consistent with this perspective, Holmes (1987, unpublished raw data) found that two effective markers of distrust in marriage were perceptions of neglect by a partner and perceptions that either person was trying to exert control in the relationship. These findings suggest that low-trust people withdraw psychologically from their relationships. As an aversion to taking risks grows, problems in relationships are often dealt with more superficially, in an arm's-length, avoidant way. Rempel (1987) found evidence of such behavior in his study of the attributional statements made by couples during their discussions. Compared to couples at other levels of trust, low-trust couples actually avoided focusing on contentious current issues and instead provided explanations for specific, less stable events from the past. This lack of commitment to solving problems removes the opportunity to restore trust by showing concern and caring. As people pull back, diminished evidence of concern by one person is likely to be reciprocated by the other. Trust draws its sustenance from the challenges of intimacy, and to restore a sense of confidence couples must find the strength to risk confronting the issues in their relationships.

CONCLUSIONS

This chapter departs from other portrayals of trust in its focus on the ways in which different states of trust influence people's emotions and perceptions in their relationships. In both developing and established relationships, people's current motivations to attain a sense of emotional security were postulated to have a significant impact on appraisals of their partners. In addition, there are reasons to believe that the foundations of trust change as relationships develop. In the early stages, feelings of love hold center stage and trust often does not become a salient issue unless signs of unequal attachment intrude. As relationships progress and people start to recognize the risks of increasing dependency, concerns about their prospects come into focus. The behavior of partners is increasingly coded for evidence of the quality of their feelings, and people's own level of involvement becomes regulated by their perceptions that their love is being reciprocated. The process of reducing uncertainty about partners' attitudes is facilitated by the demands of accommodation as interdependence grows. Couples face situations that are increasingly diagnostic of each person's motives, as differences in preferences and styles are gradually exposed. The partner's attachment is inferred from behavior that seems responsive to the needs of the person and the welfare of the unit. If adjustments are confronted successfully, people develop a shared sense of security that the relationship will endure and feelings of efficacy in controlling its future course.

Few people negotiate this terrain without discovering negative things about their partners. Despite this, high-trust individuals achieve a sense of closure by integrating such elements into the broader context of a coherent set of positive attitudes. Their optimistic expectations are maintained by interpreting partners' behavior in ways that confirm their attitudes. Negative experiences are tolerated by relegating them to lower levels of concern. In contrast, other people have difficulty resolving feelings of ambivalence by setting their doubts aside. Instead, they monitor their partners' behavior for diagnostic signs that might dispel uncertainty or provide substance to their fears.

The nature of the appraisal process triggered by their concerns may, in itself, structure their experiences in predictable ways. The results from several studies reported in the chapter suggest that the hypothesis-testing strategies of uncertain individuals are essentially risk-aversive. These individuals seemed to be very conservative in drawing positive inferences about partners' motives. They also showed a marked tendency to focus on negative behavior and a readiness to interpret it in line with their concerns that partners will ultimately fall short of their expectations. In an ironic way, uncertain individuals become directed toward the very fears they hope to surmount. If they are to avoid being trapped in a continuing cycle of doubt, they must find resources to deal with the issues in their relationships that reinforce their sense of caution.

REFERENCES

Ainsworth, M. D. S. (1979). Infant-mother attachment. *American Psychologist, 34*, 932-937.

Altman, I., & Taylor, D. A. (1973). *Social penetration: The development of interpersonal relationships.* New York: Holt, Rinehart & Winston.

Berg, J. H., & Clark, M. S. (1985). Differences in social exchange between intimate and other relationships: Gradually evolving or quickly apparent? In W. Ickes (Ed.), *Compatible and incompatible relationships* (pp. 101-128). New York: Springer-Verlag.

Berger, P., & Kellner, H. (1972). Marriage and the construction of reality: An exercise in the microsociology of knowledge. *Recent Sociology, 2,* 50-71.

Berscheid, E. (1983). Emotion. In H. H. Kelley, E. Berscheid, A. Christensen, J. H. Harvey, T. L. Huston, G. Levinger, E. McClintock, L.A. Peplau & D. R. Peterson (Eds.), *Close relationships* (pp. 110-168). New York: Freeman.

Berscheid, E., & Fei, J. (1977). Romantic love: Sexual jealousy. In G. Clanton & L. G. Smith (Eds.), *Jealousy* (pp. 101-109). Englewood Cliffs, NJ: Prentice-Hall.

Blau, P. M. (1964). *Exchange and power in social life.* New York: John Wiley.

Borden, V.M.H., & Levinger, G. (in press). Interpersonal transformations in intimate behavior. In W. H. Jones & D. Perlman (Eds.), *Advances in personal relationships* (Vol. 2). Greenwich, CT: JAI.

Braiker, H. G., & Kelley, H. H. (1979). Conflict in the development of close relationships. In R. L. Burgess & T. L. Huston (Eds.), *Social exchange in developing relationships* (pp. 135-168). New York: Academic Press.

Brehm, S. S. (1985). *Intimate relationships.* New York: Random House.

Brickman, P. (1987). *Commitment, conflict, and caring.* Englewood Cliffs, NJ: Prentice-Hall.

Chaiken, S., & Yates, S. (1985). Affective-cognitive consistency and thought-induced polarization. *Journal of Personality and Social Psychology, 49,* 1470-1481.

Clark, M.S., & Mills, J. (1979). Interpersonal attraction in exchange and communal relationships. *Journal of Personality and Social Psychology, 37,* 12-24.

Derlega, V. J., Wilson, M., & Chaiken, A. L. (1976). Friendship and disclosure reciprocity. *Journal of Personality and Social Psychology, 34,* 578-587.

Deutsch, M. (1973). *The resolution of conflict: Constructive and destructive processes.* New Haven, CT: Yale University Press.

Dion, K. L., & Dion, K. K. (1973). Correlates of romantic love. *Journal of Consulting and Clinical Psychology, 41,* 51-56.

Dion, K. L., & Dion, K. K. (1976). Love, liking and trust in heterosexual relationships. *Personality and Social Psychology Bulletin, 2,* 187-190.

Driscoll, R., Davis, K. E., & Lipetz, M. E. (1972). Parental interference and romantic love: The Romeo & Juliet effect. *Journal of Personality and Social Psychology, 24,* 1-10.

Eidelson, R. J. (1980). Interpersonal satisfaction and level of involvement: A curvilinear relationship. *Journal of Personality and Social Psychology, 39,* 460-470.

Erikson, E. H. (1963). *Childhood and society*. New York: Norton.

Fazio, R. (in press). On the power and functionality of attitudes: The role of attitude accessibility. In A. R. Pratkanis, S. J. Breckler & A. G. Greenwald (Eds.), *Attitude structure and function*. Hillsdale, NJ: Lawrence Erlbaum.

Fincham, F., & Bradbury, T. N. (1987). The impact of attributions in marriage: A longitudinal analysis. *Journal of Personality and Social Psychology, 53*, 510-517.

Hazan, C., & Shaver, P. (1987). Romantic love conceptualized as an attachment process. *Journal of Personality and Social Psychology, 52*, 511-524.

Hendrick, C., & Hendrick, S. (1986). A theory and method of love. *Journal of Personality and Social Psychology, 50*, 392-402.

Hill, C. T., Rubin, Z., & Peplau, L. A. (1976). Breakups before marriage: The end of 103 affairs. *Journal of Social Issues, 32* (1), 147-168.

Holmes, J. G. (1981). The exchange process in close relationships: Microbehavior and macromotives. In M. J. Lerner & S. C. Lerner (Eds.), *The justice motive in social behavior* (pp. 261-284). New York: Plenum.

Holmes, J. G. (in press). Trust and the appraisal process in close relationships. In W. H. Jones & D. Perlman (Eds.), *Advances in personal relationships* (Vol. 2). Greenwich, CT: JAI.

Holmes, J. G., & Rempel, J. K. (1986, August). *Trust and conflict in close relationships*. Invited address at the meeting of the American Psychological Association, Washington, DC.

Huesmann, L. R., & Levinger, G. (1976). Incremental exchange theory: A formal model for progression in dyadic social interaction. In L. Berkowitz & E. Walster (Eds.), *Advances in experimental social psychology* (Vol. 9, pp. 151-193). New York: Academic Press.

Jacobson, N. S., Follette, W. C., & McDonald, D. W. (1982). Reactivity to positive and negative behavior in distressed and nondistressed married couples. *Journal of Consulting and Clinical Psychology, 50*, 706-714.

Johnson-George, C., & Swap, W. (1982). Measurement of specific interpersonal trust: Construction and validation of a scale to assess trust in a specific order. *Journal of Personality and Social Psychology, 43*, 1306-1317.

Jones, E. E., & Gerard, H. B. (1967). *Foundations of social psychology*. New York: John Wiley.

Kelley, H. H. (1979). *Personal relationships: Their structures and process*. Hillsdale, NJ: Lawrence Erlbaum.

Kelley, H. H. (1983). Love and commitment. In H. H. Kelley, E. Berscheid, A. Christensen, J. H. Harvey, T. L. Huston, G. Levinger, E. McClintock, L. A. Peplau & D. R. Peterson (Eds.), *Close relationships* (pp. 265-314). New York: Freeman.

Kelley, H. H. (1984). Affect in interpersonal relations. In P. Shaver (Ed.), *Review of personality and social psychology* (Vol. 5, pp. 89-115). Beverly Hills, CA: Sage

Kelley, H. H., & Stahelski, A. J. (1970). The social interaction basis of cooperators' and competitors' beliefs about others. *Journal of Personality and Social Psychology, 16*, 66-91.

Kelley, H. H. & Thibaut, J. W. (1978). *Interpersonal relations: A theory of interdependence*. New York: John Wiley.

Kelly, C., Huston, T. L., & Cate, R. M. (1985). Premarital relationships correlates of the erosion of satisfaction in marriage. *Journal of Social and Personal Relationships, 2*, 167-178.

Larzelere, R. E., & Huston, T. L. (1980). The Dyadic Trust Scale: Toward understanding interpersonal trust in close relationships. *Journal of Marriage and the Family, 42,* 595-604.

Lerner, M. J., Miller, D. T., & Holmes, J. G. (1976). Deserving vs. justice: A contemporary dilemma. In L. Berkowitz & E. Walster (Eds.), *Advances in experimental social psychology* (Vol. 9, pp. 134-162). New York: Academic Press.

Levinger, G. (1979). A social exchange view of the dissolution of pair relationships. In R. L. Burgess & T. L. Huston (Eds.), *Social exchange in developing relationships* (pp. 169-193). New York: Academic Press.

Levinger, G. (1983). Development and change. In H. H. Kelley, E. Berscheid, A. Christensen, J. H. Harvey, T. L. Huston, G. Levinger, E. McClintock, L. A. Peplau & D. R. Peterson (Eds.), *Close relationships* (pp. 315-359). New York: Freeman.

Levitz-Jones, E. M., & Orlofsky, J. L. (1985). Separation-individuation and intimacy capacity in college women. *Journal of Personality and Social Psychology, 49,* 156-169.

Lloyd, S., Cate, R., & Benton, J. (1982). Equity and rewards as predictors of satisfaction in casual and intimate relationships. *Journal of Psychology, 110,* 43-48.

Miller, D. T., & Holmes, J. G. (1975). The role of situational restrictiveness on self-fulfilling prophecies: A theoretical and empirical extension of Kelley and Stahelski's triangle hypothesis. *Journal of Personality and Social Psychology, 31,* 661-673.

Miller, P. C., Lefcourt, H. M., Holmes, J. G., Ware, E. E., & Saleh, W. (1986). Marital locus of control and marital problem solving. *Journal of Personality and Social Psychology, 51,* 161-169.

Morton, T. U. (1978). Intimacy and reciprocity of exchange: A comparison of spouses and strangers. *Journal of Personality and Social Psychology, 36,* 72-81.

Newman, H. (1981). Communication within ongoing intimate relationships: An attributional perspective. *Personality and Social Psychology Bulletin, 7,* 59-70.

Pruitt, D. G. (1965). Definition of the situation as a determinant of international action. In H. C. Kelman (Ed.), *International behavior* (pp. 393-432). New York: Holt, Rinehart & Winston.

Reeder, G. D., & Brewer, M. B. (1979). A schematic model of dispositional attribution in interpersonal perception. *Psychological Review, 86,* 61-79.

Rempel, J. K. (1987). *Trust and attributions in close relationships.* Unpublished doctoral dissertation, University of Waterloo, Ontario.

Rempel, J. K., Holmes, J. G., & Zanna, M. P. (1985). Trust in close relationships. *Journal of Personality and Social Psychology, 49,* 95-112.

Rotter, J. B. (1967). A new scale for the measurement of interpersonal trust. *Journal of Personality, 35,* 651-655.

Rusbult, C. E. (1983). A longitudinal test of the investment model: The development (and deterioration) of satisfaction and commitment in heterosexual involvement. *Journal of Personality and Social Psychology, 45,* 101-117.

Sabatelli, R. M., Buck, R., & Dreyer, A. (1983). Locus of control, interpersonal trust, and nonverbal communication accuracy. *Journal of Personality and Social Psychology, 44,* 399-409.

Schmidt, G. W., Kelley, H. H., & Fujino, D. C. (1987). *Some new insights into interpersonal motives.* Paper presented at the 67th annual convention of the Western Psychological Association, Long Beach, CA.

Seligman, C., Fazio, R. H., & Zanna, M. P. (1980). Effects of salience of extrinsic rewards on liking and loving. *Journal of Personality & Social Psychology, 38,* 453-460.

Snyder, M. (1981). Seek, and ye shall find: Testing hypotheses about other people. In E. T. Higgins, C. P. Herman, & M. P. Zanna (Eds.), *Social cognition: The Ontario symposium on personality and social psychology* (Vol. 1, pp. 277-302). Hillsdale, NJ: Lawrence Erlbaum.

Sroufe, L. A. (1983). Infant-caregiver attachment and patterns of adaptation in preschool: The roots of maladaptation and competence. In M. Perlmutter (Ed.), *Minnesota symposium on child psychology* (Vol. 16, pp. 41-83). Hillsdale, NJ: Lawrence Erlbaum.

Sternberg, R. J. (1986). A triangular theory of love. *Psychological Review, 93,* 119-135.

Sternberg, R. J., & Barnes, M. (1985). Real and ideal others in romantic relationships: Is four a crowd? *Journal of Personality and Social Psychology, 49,* 1589-1596.

Strack, F., Schwarz, N., & Gschneidinger, E. (1985). Happiness and reminiscing: The role of time perspective, affect, and mode of thinking. *Journal of Personality and Social Psychology, 49,* 1460-1469.

Strickland, L. H. (1958). Surveillance and trust. *Journal of Personality, 28,* 200-215.

Swinth, R. L. (1967). The establishment of the trust relationship. *Journal of Conflict Resolution, 11,* 335-344.

Walster, E., Walster, G. W., & Traupmann, J. (1978). Equity and premarital sex. *Journal of Personality and Social Psychology, 36,* 82-92.

Wrightsman, L. S. (1972). *Social psychology in the seventies,.* Monterey, CA: Brooks/ Cole.

9

Envy and Jealousy in Close Relationships

PETER SALOVEY
JUDITH RODIN

Peter Salovey received his Ph.D. in clinical psychology from Yale University in 1986. He now serves as an Assistant Professor at Yale and contributes both to the social/personality and clinical psychology training programs. His primary area of research is the cognitive and behavioral consequences of moods and emotions, with special attention to complex affective states such as envy and jealousy. He is also interested in health beliefs and health behavior and in the role of emotion in shaping thoughts and beliefs about health and illness. In general, Salovey is concerned with the application of social psychological theory and research to problems in clinical psychology. He is the coauthor of *Peer Counseling* with Vincent J. D'Andrea and *Reasoning, Inference, and Judgment in Clinical Psychology* with Dennis C. Turk.

Judith Rodin is the Phillip R. Allen Professor of Psychology, and Professor of Medicine and Psychiatry at Yale University. Recipient of the Distinguished Scientific Award for an Early Career Contribution to Psychology and an award for outstanding contribution to Health Psychology, she has been elected to the Institute of Medicine of the National Academy of Sciences. She has served as President of the Eastern Psychological Association, the APA Division of Health Psychology, and the Yale Chapter of Sigma Xi. She is chair of the John D. and Catherine T. MacArthur Foundation Mental Health Research Network on the Determinants and Consequences of Health Promoting and Health Damaging Behavior. Rodin's research interests include obesity, bulimia and mechanisms of food intake and weight regulation, pregnancy, aging, the effects of psychosocial variables on neuroendocrine and immune system variables, and motivating emotional states such as envy and jealousy.

In the popular press, debate has often focused on whether negative states such as envy and jealousy are completely undesirable, even dangerous and pathological, or whether they are normal albeit unpleasant aspects of close personal relationships. Several sentences in a letter we received recently from a 35 year-old woman express this dilemma:

> Jealousy is one of those things that even though you know it's a destructive emotion and it won't accomplish anything, you can't help but

AUTHORS' NOTE: Preparation of this manuscript was supported in part by NIH Biomedical Research Support Grant S07 RR07015 and the Yale Social Science Faculty Research Fund. We would like to thank Clyde Hendrick and three anonymous reviewers for their very helpful comments on an earlier draft.

feel it. It grinds away at you like the horror of recognizing that all your worst fears are coming true. . . . It's an emotion so deeply imbedded in our genes that it's inescapable.

This writer advanced a view of jealousy that is quite different from the one to be taken in the present chapter. She believes that complex emotions such as jealousy or envy are biologically determined, invariant, and somehow sinister. In this chapter, however, we will describe the phenomenology of envy and jealousy, their situational antecedents, and some of their behavioral consequences. Research addressing the utility of differentiating jealousy and envy-provoking *situations* versus differentiating *feelings* of jealousy and envy will be presented. We will also discuss potential personality processes that drive envy and jealousy, especially attempts to maintain a high self-evaluation.

In the present chapter we will not attempt to review the entire psychological literature on jealousy and envy (see Bringle & Buunk, 1985, 1986, for thorough reviews of the jealousy literature). Rather, we will focus on situational and personological factors that they share and that differentiate them, with an eye toward understanding how threats to self-evaluation in important interpersonal domains often provoke these emotional states. We will also discuss how the behaviors that are motivated by envy and jealousy serve to protect individuals from such threats to self-worth. Our approach will be nomothetic; but Bringle and his colleagues have provided a full discussion of individual differences in proneness to jealousy (e.g., Bringle, 1981; Bringle & Evenbeck, 1979; Bringle, Roach, Andler, & Evenbeck, 1979).

SITUATIONALLY BASED CONCEPTUALIZATIONS
OF ENVY AND JEALOUSY

Traditionally, a distinction has been made between envy and jealousy. The word "jealous" is derived from the same Greek root as that for "zealous." Zealousness represents a fervent devotion to the promotion of some person or object; jealousy refers to the belief or suspicion that what has been promoted is in danger of being lost. Envy, on the other hand, is derived from *invidere*, a Latin word meaning to look upon with malice. Envy represents a discontent with and desire for the possessions or attributes of another person (Bryson, 1977).

The differences between envy and jealousy can be conceptualized using P-O-X triads, in which P is the individual experiencing the emotional state, O is another person, and X is a third person or a desired object. As seen in Figure 9.1 (based on Bryson's 1977 analysis), the crucial factor discriminating among definitions of jealousy, envy, and

GRAPH-THEORETIC DEFINITIONS
(P-Centric)

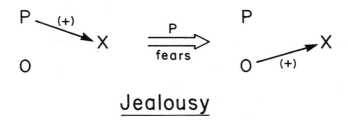

Jealousy

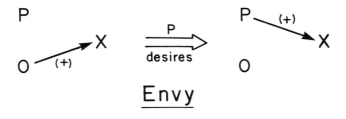

Envy

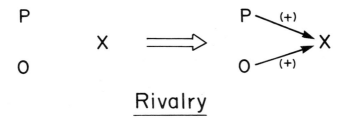

Rivalry

Figure 9.1 The differentiation of jealousy, envy, and rivalry (derived from Bryson, 1977).

rivalry is whether there is a previously established, emotionally invested relationship (traditionally termed a *unit* or *sentiment* relationship; see Heider, 1958) between two of the elements in the triad. Bryson (1977) defined jealousy as the consequence of P's belief that his or her previously established unique relationship with X is threatened by real or imagined attempts between O and X to form an equivalent relationship. We have referred to this situation as "social-relations jealousy," and, in its prototypical form in which the relationship between P and X is romantic, as "romantic jealousy" (Bers & Rodin, 1984; Salovey & Rodin, 1984).

When person O has a previously established relationship with X (X can be another person, object, personal attribute, or possession), attempts by P to supplant O in that relationship or to denigrate the O-X relationship can be considered envy. Individuals often use the term "jealousy" to describe this situation, and we have referred to it as "social-comparison jealousy" (Bers & Rodin, 1984; Salovey & Rodin, 1984). Rivalry (from the Latin *rivalis*, meaning your competitor for the water rights to a river or stream) can be depicted as the situation in which neither P nor O has a previous emotionally based relationship with X but both desire such a relationship (Bryson, 1977).

Our use of the phrases *social-relations jealousy* versus *social-comparison jealousy* as well as the P-O-X analysis implies that it may be especially useful to define jealousy and envy in terms of the situations that elicit these feelings rather than by focusing on the feelings themselves. These situationally based definitions, which we prefer, contrast with definitions that focus on emotional reactions, such as that of Buunk and Bringle (1987): "Jealousy is an aversive emotional reaction evoked by a relationship involving one's current or former partner and a third person. This relationship may be real, imagined, or expected, or may have occurred in the past" (p. 124). In their definition, the emotional component is "viewed . . . as necessary and sufficient for defining the jealous reaction" (p. 125). Although we do not deny that both jealousy and envy involve aversive emotional reactions, we believe that definitions with the greatest heuristic value will be those that attend especially to situational antecedents of these reactions (Bers & Rodin, 1984).

Situationally based definitions of envy and jealousy are evident in philosophical and fictional literature. For example, in commenting on Shakespeare's *Othello*, Neu (1980) noted, "Othello is jealous, Iago is envious. Jealousy is typically over what one possesses and fears to lose, while envy may be over something one has never possessed and may never hope to possess" (pp. 432-433). In terms provided by Tov-Ruach (1980): if Jack were envious, he would concentrate on Joan's gifts, comparing his gifts unfavorably to hers. If Jack were envious not only of Joan's gifts but of the attention she received from Henry, he would compare his situation unfavorably to hers and his envy would be transformed into jealousy if he considered Henry's attention to Joan as possibly depriving him of an important part of his personality or source of satisfaction.

PHENOMENOLOGICAL SIMILARITIES AND
DISTINCTIONS BETWEEN JEALOUSY AND ENVY

Although situational definitions of envy and jealousy may be especially useful, a central question in studies of jealousy and envy has been to identify the consequent feelings evoked by them. Are jealousy and envy characterized by differences in these subjective experiences? In a pilot study (Salovey & Rodin, 1986), we asked college students to list synonyms for the word "jealousy." The group described 74 distinct terms that we classified into five groups: (a) envy, coveting, wanting, (b) hate, anger, (c) hurt, deprivation, sadness, (d) rivalry, possessiveness, and (e) insecurity, low self-esteem, self-blame. These terms reveal the complexity of the subjective experience of jealousy. It is an affective experience with multiple emotional meanings, most centrally, anger, sadness, and perhaps fear or anxiety. The range of synonyms generated probably reflects the great variance in people's experience of jealousy. Bryson (1976) systematically studied the feelings and behaviors that individuals reported in jealousy-provoking situations. He described the phenomenology of jealousy in terms of eight factors: (a) emotional devastation (feelings of helplessness, insecurity, and depression), (b) reactive retribution (desire to "get back at" the betraying partner), (c) arousal (becoming more aware of the partner's sexuality and wanting to monopolize his or her time), (d) need for social support (seeking the support of others), (e) intrapunitiveness (blaming oneself for one's misery), (f) confrontation (desire to obtain an explanation from the partner or rival), (g) anger, and (h) impression management (engaging in "damage control" such as by acting as if nothing had happened or getting drunk). The experience of jealousy and envy was not especially consistent across individuals, and Bryson (1977) suggested that it is not usefully characterized as a simple type of emotional response with an obvious behavioral concomitant.

Many investigators have suggested that some of the variability in the subjective experience of jealousy might be explained by differentiating responses to envy- versus jealousy-provoking situations (e.g., Titleman, 1982). Spielman (1971) proposed that jealousy is a stronger feeling state than envy because "more hate is involved. . . . Envy bespeaks the desire to have what someone else has; jealousy is this as well as wanting the other person not to have it" (pp. 59-60). According to Spielman, when experiencing envy, one is unhappy that another person possesses something one would like to have for oneself and feels inferior because one does not have it. Jealousy, though, is an apprehension, anxiety, suspicion, and mistrust generated by the loss or potential loss of a highly valued possession or of affection and love. Similarly, in an article conceptualizing what he called "mixed emotions," Gellert (1976) viewed jealousy as the combination of anger plus fear of abandonment, while envy is the interaction of anger and sadness generated through self-pity.

In our own work on the phenomenology of envy and jealousy (Salovey & Rodin, 1986, Study 1), we found that subjects reliably distinguished these two states on the basis of their eliciting conditions (social-comparison failures versus threats to valued social relationships). However, both envy-provoking and jealousy-eliciting situations generated similar affective reactions, mostly involving anger, sadness, and some anxiety or embarrassment. The differences between the feelings evoked by envy versus jealousy were more noticeable in terms of their intensity rather than as categorically different emotional experiences. That is, subjects reported the same angry, sad, and anxious or embarrassed feelings in envy- and jealousy-provoking situations. They just reported more of them—especially sadness and anger—when jealous. In several follow-up studies in which subjects imagined themselves in situations expected to elicit envy (social-comparison failure) or jealousy (relationship threat), subjects reported more negative affect in the latter condition. But again, the experiences differed in emotional intensity rather than quality (Salovey & Rodin, 1986, Studies 2 & 3).

Parrott and Smith (1987), however, argued that the difference in intensity between jealousy and envy may serve to obscure real differences in the quality of these two feeling states. They conducted an experiment in which subjects rated an actual experience of envy or jealousy on a variety of feeling scales. Before attempting to differentiate envy and jealousy, Parrott and Smith equated subjects' responses for intensity by subtracting each subject's mean score from his or her individual scores. Using this approach, jealousy and envy *were* distinguishable in terms of their subjective experience. Jealousy was characterized by a sense of feeling lonely, betrayed, afraid, uncertain, and suspicious. Envy, however, elicited more shame, longing, guilt, denial, and a sense of inferiority.

Additionally, Smith, Kim, and Parrott (1988) noted that the self-involving scenarios used by Salovey and Rodin (1986) were difficult to equate for the robustness or intensity of feelings that they generated. When Smith et al. asked subjects to generate situations that produced *strong* envy or *strong* jealousy, envy was more often characterized by feelings of inferiority, longing, wishfulness, self-criticism, dissatisfaction, and self-awareness, while jealousy produced greater feelings of anger, hostility, hurt, fear of loss, suspiciousness, loss of control, rejection, being cheated, resentment, spite, malice, and a desire to get even. Smith et al. noted, however, that jealousy was consistently experienced as a more intense emotion than envy.

The results of these studies revealed that jealousy is experienced more intensely than envy. But it remains unclear whether the quality of what is actually experienced differs in the two situations. Using scenario and scaling methodologies and a dependent measure that often combined the terms jealousy and envy, Salovey and Rodin (1986) found support for intensity differences only. But Smith and his colleagues suggested that studies utilizing more precise definitions and measures of envy and jealousy might have better luck in qualitatively differentiating the two. They suggested that in the social-comparison context the two words might be considered synonymous, thus yielding ambiguous findings in attempts to distinguish envious from jealous feelings. But where linguistic confusion can be reduced, the differential phenomenology of envy and jealousy is likely to emerge.

Alternatively, the inconsistencies in results of studies attempting to define the feelings involved in envy and jealousy may reflect a more fundamental problem. As Hupka (1981, 1984) has argued, it simply may not be useful to conceptualize envy and jealousy as affects at all. Rather, he claims, words such as envy or jealousy are used to refer to situationally based *predicaments*, and these words better differentiate these predicaments than the associated feelings. It was in this spirit that we introduced the terms "social-comparison jealousy" and "social-relations jealousy" (Bers & Rodin, 1984; Salovey & Rodin, 1984). At least these terms clearly identify the situational antecedents of what might be rather complex and varying blends of emotions.

When focusing on situational antecedents, it seems that the typical jealousy-provoking situation is also laden with envy-producing characteristics. When one compares oneself to another and does not measure up, one experiences envy. When one's relationship is threatened by a rival, one experiences romantic jealousy as one imagines the loss of that relationship *and* envy when one reflects on the relatively superior attributes of the rival that have allowed him or her to seduce one's lover (Salovey & Rodin, 1986). As Sabini and Silver (1982) commented, "If my lover runs away with another man, I might be jealous of him. . . . I might be envious of him also if his *savoir faire* in seducing my lover highlights my lack of it" (p. 15). Jealousy is the whole; envy is a part. And jealousy's power lies in the simultaneous threat to a valued relationship and threat to self-evaluation via negative social-comparison. Perhaps this part-whole relationship between envy and jealousy is responsible for the use of the term "jealousy" to describe both jealousy and envy and the less generic use of the term "envy" in common parlance (see Silver & Sabini, 1978b; Smith, Kim, & Parrott, 1988).

The part-whole relationship between envy and jealousy is similar to the relationship between the two described by Spinoza:

> If I imagine that an object beloved by me is united to another person by the same or by a closer bond of friendship than that by which I myself alone held the object, I shall be affected with hatred toward the beloved object itself, and shall envy that other person. . . . This hatred toward a beloved object when joined with envy is called "jealousy," which is therefore nothing but a vacillation of the mind springing from the love and hatred both felt together, and attended with the idea of another person whom we envy. (1675/1949, *Ethics*, Part 3, Proposition XXXV, pp. 153-154)

SELF-EVALUATION IN ENVY AND JEALOUSY

Writers for both psychological and popular audiences quite commonly state that envy and jealousy must be a consequence, at least in part, of an individual's low self-esteem or perceived inadequacy (e.g., Mead, 1977; Rodgers & Bryson, 1978; White, 1981d). However, even when the relationship between jealousy or envy and a negative view of the self has been found, correlations are at best small to moderate (Aronson & Pines, 1980; Bringle, 1981; Hupka & Bachelor, 1979; Jaremko & Lindsey, 1979; Manges & Evenbeck, 1980), and at worst weak and inconsistent (Buunk, 1982a; Mathes & Severa, 1981; White, 1977, 1981c, 1981e). We believe that threat to global self-worth is not what drives envy and jealousy. Rather, envy and jealousy appear in close relationships when self-worth is threatened by another person in an area that is particularly *self*-defining for that individual. Envy and jealousy result when another person's performance or attributes "hit us where we live," both in the social-comparison sense, but also in threatening our important social and romantic relationships.

Some data supporting this view can be found in a reader survey on envy and jealousy conducted for *Psychology Today*, from which we received nearly 25,000 responses (Salovey & Rodin, 1985b). Although limited by its self-selected subject sample, this study did afford the opportunity to investigate relationships among self-regard, envy, and jealousy with a larger and more diverse population than is typically found with introductory psychology students. In constructing this survey, we hypothesized that jealousy and envy would be reported in situations particularly salient to one's self-definition. These situations should be especially likely to produce jealousy or envy when a large discrepancy exists between one's idealized view of oneself and one's actual view of oneself. Further, this discrepancy between real and ideal self-evaluations should lead to lowered self-esteem, particularly in contexts in which the self-definitional dimension is made salient. Lowered self-esteem should trigger attempts by the individual to raise it, and the behaviors engaged in to accomplish this goal should be easily identifiable as inspired by envy or jealousy.

Based on these ideas, we asked respondents what attributes were particularly important to them, how they would ideally like to perform on these attributes, and how they actually perceived themselves. We measured self-esteem using a standard scale (Rosenberg, 1965) and then obtained respondents' reports of their likelihood of engaging in a variety of jealous and envious behaviors. We also asked participants to indicate the situations in which they would experience the most jealousy or envy. Feelings of envy and jealousy, as well as a variety of specific envious and jealous behaviors, were predicted best by large discrepancies between actual and ideal self-descriptions on a highly valued, self-definitional attribute. These large real-ideal discrepancies were related to lowered self-esteem generally, and both the degree of discrepancy and low self-esteem were associated with greater experienced envy and jealousy. This association was strongest in the most self-defining areas. The single best predictor of envy or jealousy in an area was that area's importance to the self. For example, a subject with a large real-ideal discrepancy in personal wealth and who reported wealth as very important to her self-definition was likely to report great envy if her neighbor won the state lottery and great jealousy if her husband flirted with a wealthy woman at a party (more so than if her husband flirted with a woman with different attributes such as fame, attractiveness, or popularity). This pattern was strongest for subjects whose most self-defining area was physical attractiveness.

A Self-Evaluation Maintenance View of Envy and Jealousy

Tesser and his colleagues (Tesser & Campbell, 1982, 1983; Tesser, 1986) developed a model that views positive self-evaluation as a primary motive of most individuals. Positive self-evaluation is achieved through two, at times competing, processes: reflection and comparison. Reflection occurs when the successes of close others make us feel good about ourselves. We experience joy at our best friend's wedding; our parents experience *nachas* at our Bar (and Bat) Mitzvah or pride at our communions and confirmations. We delight in knowing that our next door neighbor once pitched for the Boston Red Sox. We even feel better about ourselves when our football team wins, an experience previously labeled "basking in reflected glory" (Cialdini, Borden, Thorne, Walker, Freeman, & Sloan, 1976). According to Tesser (1986), the reflection process can be initiated when the other person is emotionally close to us (a friend, relative, or significant other) and the performance of the other person is of high quality.

Under some conditions, however, high quality performances of close others can threaten our self-evaluations. At times, another's success makes us feel like a failure by comparison. Tesser labels such situations as ones that invoke the comparison process. One critical variable determines whether the successes of close others make us feel good about ourselves (reflection) or have the opposite effect (comparison): the *relevance* of the other's success or personal qualities to our self-definition. Reflection results when the other's performance is in a non-self-definitional domain. I am delighted when my close friend Dick notices his golf game gradually improving, even though mine seems to have plateaued. On the other hand, my self-evaluation is threatened when Dick tells me that his elegant theoretical masterpiece (on jealousy) will be next month's lead article in *Psychological Review*. What differentiates these two situations is the relevance of the other person's performance to my self-definition.

Because we are motivated to maintain high self-evaluation, we bask in the reflected glory of our friends' successes so long as they do not threaten our self-definitions. But when personal relevance is high, we maintain positive self-evaluation by engaging in other kinds of behavior such as: (a) changing our self-definition to reduce the relevance of the other's performance ("I'm not the kind of psychologist who publishes in *Psychological Review* anyway"), (b) reducing the closeness of the relationship with the other person ("Dick really isn't a friend of mine, I just put up with him because we needed a fourth for golf"), or (c) reevaluating the quality of the other person's performance or actually preventing it from happening (I write the editor of *Psychological Review* and point out several flaws in Dick's analysis; Tesser & Campbell, 1983).

These thoughts and behaviors seem to describe common reactions to various envy- and jealousy-provoking situations quite well (Salovey & Rodin, 1983). We tend to be attracted to others who perform well, so long as their superior performances are on dimensions not highly self-defining. We envy, however, those who perform highly in self-definitional domains because envy arises when our self-evaluation is threatened by the performance of others. Additionally, we jealously protect those aspects of ourselves that are particularly important to maintaining self-definition and self-evaluation (including attributes, possessions, but also close relationships). Finally, we perceive another person as envious or jealous when we see him or her inappropriately demean a third person in order to maintain his or her own self-worth (Silver & Sabini, 1978a).

A test of a self-evaluation maintenance view of envy and jealousy. Using the theoretical background provided by Tesser's work and by social comparison theory (Dakin & Arrowood, 1981), Salovey and Rodin (1984) proposed that envy or "social-comparison jealousy" would be reported under three eliciting conditions: (a) negatively valenced information about oneself relative to another person, (b) high self-relevance of this information, and (c) high similarity to or a close personal relationship with the comparison person. Under these conditions, individuals should experience a transient threat to positive self-evaluation, and engage in subsequent behaviors to bolster their threatened self-worth.

In Salovey and Rodin's (1984) experiment, subjects received false positive or negative feedback regarding aptitude that was either relevant to their self-definition or not relevant. We achieved this by recruiting subjects based on their expressed career commitments and then giving them feedback relevant to likely success, either in that domain or another one. Subjects then thought they would interact with a successful other person whose career interests were described as similar or dissimilar to theirs. Individuals reported the most envy when they received negative, self-relevant feedback and subsequently thought they would associate with a similar, successful other person. Anticipated meetings with this comparison other were greeted with feelings of depression and anxiety. Most interestingly, this situation had a profound impact on behavior. Subjects expressed diminished desire for the other person's friendship, and they disparaged him or her on a variety of trait scales. These consequent behaviors served to diminish the relative status of the comparison person and thus reduce the likelihood that he or she would be viewed as a relevant source of comparison feedback. These results regarding envy and derogation were consistent with those reported by Silver and Sabini (1978a), who presented subjects with video-taped scenarios and found that envy was especially likely to be attributed to an unsuccessful actor who behaved inappropriately, inconsiderately, or with insufficient restraint and respect toward a successful actor.

The development of self-definition. Bers and Rodin (1984) studied the developmental course of the expression of social-comparison jealousy. They hypothesized that older children, like adults, would report the most envy in the areas of their lives particularly important to them, but that young children would not show this effect because of their ill-defined sense of self. Rather, young children were expected to feel discomfort in all situations in which they did not measure up to someone else's performance.

Bers and Rodin read stories to children, ages 6 to 12, that described a child failing to excel or attain something in each of six different areas: possessions, sports, art, appearance, math, and reading. To manipulate social comparison, in some of the stories one child failed and another child excelled; in other stories only the failure was described, and there was no comparison other. The subjects were instructed to identify with the protagonist who failed in each story. As expected, children were much more likely to experience envy after hearing the comparison stories as opposed to the noncomparison stories as measured by spontaneous comparisons, affects like anger, entitlement, sadness, and desire, intentions to engage in competitive behaviors, and negative thoughts about the other child. For younger children, these feelings were high and occurred across all situations. For older children, these feelings were only elicited in the areas that they rated as particularly important to them. Thus, if sports ability was rated as especially self-defining, older children experienced envious thoughts and feelings after identifying with a child who failed in this domain as compared with another child. Young children, presumably with less well-defined areas of self-relevance, showed no differences in the experience of envy in different domains. Bers and Rodin (1984) thus demonstrated that the development of a sense of what is relevant or irrelevant to oneself is a necessary precursor to the powerful emotional experiences and anti-social behaviors that follow from negative or failed social comparison.

RELATIONSHIP FACTORS AND THE
EXPERIENCE OF JEALOUSY AND ENVY

Thus far we have focused on some of the more intrapsychic aspects of envy and jealousy, but several characteristics of close relationships themselves promote the experience of jealousy and envy. These relationship factors include physical characteristics and other attributes of the rival, the type of relationship involved, the perceived motives of the betraying partner, the type of threat to the relationship, and the degree of involvement or dependence on the relationship. We first consider romantic jealousy in terms of the characteristics of the relationship and in terms of the characteristics of the rival. We will then return to envy to consider the situational factors influencing social comparison when envy arises in close relationships.

Romantic Jealousy

Characteristics of relationships. Jealousy often involves a threat to an existing relationship, and the characteristics of that relationship often mediate the subsequent experience of jealousy. As part of a questionnaire study of 150 romantically involved couples, White (1980, 1981b, 1981d, 1981e) examined the effects of a variety of relationship variables on jealousy. Guided by the general hypothesis that people who are relatively more involved in their relationships than their partners are more likely to be jealous, White (1981e) studied the regression of jealousy scale scores on measures of relationship dependence, perceived dependence of partners, relationship exclusivity, and relationship stage (cohabitation versus less serious dating), among other variables.

White hypothesized that if a person feels that a relationship is relatively more rewarding than available alternatives, then a threat to a relationship may be viewed as particularly dangerous and anxiety producing. In fact, relationship dependence was strongly associated with jealousy, but only among women. White also expected that if an individual desires a sexually exclusive relationship, partner attraction to another would be particularly threatening and result in jealousy. Desire for exclusivity was, in fact, the strongest predictor of jealousy in both men and women. If the partner is perceived as dependent on the relationship (no other alternatives for the partner exist), then there should be little cause for jealousy since the likelihood of loss of that relationship would be low. However, White found that perceived dependence of the partner did not predict jealousy. Finally, because they have more emotional investment in their relationships, cohabiting couples were expected to be more jealous than casually dating couples. Married couples, having greater assurance of relationship stability, were expected to be less prone to jealousy. In actuality, none of these groups differed in reported jealousy, nor were significant correlations found linking length of relationship to jealousy.

In another analysis, White (1981d) examined several other relationship variables and their associations with jealousy. In this paper, relative involvement was again postulated as the underlying mediator of jealousy: more involved partners were expected to be more prone to jealousy. Several involvement variables were examined, including one's relative physical attractiveness as compared to the partner, relative availability of opposite-sex friends, belief that the partner is attracted to another person, perception of relative involvement, and partner's perceived dissatisfaction with the relationship. With few exceptions, these variables were associated with jealousy for both men and women, and White was able to devise an elegant causal model describing the relationships among these variables and jealousy.

Other relationship variables were examined by Buunk (1982a) in a Dutch sample. The first variable, emotional dependency, was defined as the relative importance of the relationship as compared with other aspects of the jealous person's life. Because individuals who are particularly dependent on their relationships for a variety of reinforcements have much to lose when the relationship is threatened, they were expected to report greater amounts of jealousy. Buunk also studied intended extramarital sexual involvement. He predicted that individuals engaged in or desiring extramarital affairs would be less likely to experience jealousy when their partners have such affairs (an hypothesis based on notions of exchange and reciprocity, e.g., see Ellis & Weinstein, 1986; Hansen, 1985).

Buunk (1982a) studied three populations: (a) a randomly selected sample, (b) individuals with considerable extramarital sexual experience, and (c) students at a Catholic university. In both the random and Catholic samples, emotional dependency was highly correlated with anticipated jealousy for both men and women. In the "sexually liberated" group, emotional dependence did not seem to be an important factor associated with jealousy. Interestingly, intended extramarital involvement was strongly related to jealousy in all three groups for both men and women. The greater one's intention to become involved in extramarital sexual behavior, the lower one's jealousy. Thus, jealousy seems related both to one's emotional dependence on a relationship and to one's own extramarital behavioral intentions.

Similar findings have also been reported by Bringle, Renner, Terry, and Davis (1983), who asked subjects to read scenarios describing jealousy-evoking events. Subjects then rated how upset they would feel if each event happened with their current, most recent, and next most recent romantic partner. The subjects also rated the balance of power in each of the three relationships. Congruent with the results of White and Buunk, Bringle et al.'s subjects who reported being more in love and more involved in their relationships felt greater threat and upset. Bringle et al. concluded that lack of interpersonal power (derived from how involved one is in a relationship) is an important predictor of jealous responses.

The results of the *Psychology Today* survey described earlier (Salovey & Rodin, 1985b) confirmed the importance of relationship involvement in provoking jealousy. Like White, Buunk, and Bringle et al., we found that respondents who placed great value on their current relationship and on the importance of exclusivity were more prone to feeling jealous. Although Buunk's subjects who intended to have affairs reported less jealousy, we did not find that individuals who actually had extramarital sexual experiences were less jealous. Quite the contrary; those individuals who admitted to extramarital affairs were even more suspicious of their current partners, a finding that supports Freud's (1934/1955) view that jealousy, in part, emanates from projected unacceptable sexual desires. Country singer Hank Williams warned his lover that her "cheating heart" would "tell on" her, perhaps by causing her undue anxiety and suspicion regarding his potential or imagined affairs.

Relative power may undergird differences in perceived relationship involvement. White (1980) discussed the relationship between power and jealousy, particularly with respect to the induction of jealousy in others. Clearly, the less-involved partner in a relationship has more power in that relationship. This partner can more easily threaten to leave the relationship, causing greater harm to the more-involved partner. White examined the phenomenon of the more involved or dependent partner (i.e., the least powerful partner) gaining greater control in the relationship by leading his or her partner to believe that an attractive alternative was available. To the extent that the inducement of jealousy is a strategy used to increase control, it is more likely to be used by those whose power is weakest, those more involved than their partners. White (1980) found that about 25% of the subjects in his study reported deliberate attempts to induce jealousy. Women were more likely to report attempted jealousy induction than men, probably reflecting the power imbalance in many traditional heterosexual relationships. Likewise, more involved (and therefore less powerful) women were more than twice as likely to attempt jealousy induction than less involved women. The most common motives reported for jealousy induction were to test the relationship and to increase rewards. Jealousy was most commonly induced in these situations by discussing or exaggerating attractions to others or by actually flirting, dating others, fabricating another attraction, or describing former lovers in vivid detail.

Characteristics of the rival. Two aspects of the rival (or interloper) have been examined with respect to jealousy: his or her physical attractiveness and the perceived motives of the partner's attraction to him or her. Shettel-Neuber, Bryson, and Young (1978) actually manipulated the attractiveness of a rival. Subjects in this study viewed a videotaped scene that depicted a party at which an individual's old boyfriend or girlfriend made an unexpected entrance and embraced and kissed his/her former partner. Shortly thereafter, the current partner entered and observed his/her lover and the former beau sitting together on a couch. Male and female interlopers were used in different versions of the tape, and the attractiveness of the interloper was manipulated with make-up and costume. Subjects were more likely to feel angry and embarrassed when the interloper was unattractive than when he or she was attractive, perhaps feeling distressed that this unappealing person was actually a rival.

Results from our survey (Salovey & Rodin, 1985b) suggested that for those individuals who place great importance on physical attractiveness, jealous reactions might be more likely when the rival is especially attractive. White (1981b) has studied the motives perceived by romantic partners for real or potential involvement with romantic rivals and how such motives are related to indicators of jealousy. Sexual attractiveness of the rival as a motive was associated with jealousy in both men and women, but the rival's nonsexual assets were associated with jealousy only among women.

Envy, Close Relationships, and Social Comparison

The contextual components of envy include a situation in which a person's possessions, attributes, and attainments have diminished the status of another (Silver & Sabini, 1978b). In such a situation, if the person whose status is diminished belittled the character of the successful person or undercut his or her success, envy is perceived. Silver and Sabini (1978a) tested these hypotheses by having subjects view videotapes depicting four actors describing their successes and failures regarding medical school applications. Several versions of the scenario were constructed in which one actor usually achieved this goal and another did not. After viewing a tape, subjects were asked to complete a questionnaire regarding how the characters felt toward each other. Most subjects stated that the unsuccessful character would feel "envious" or "jealous" toward the successful character in all conditions. For example, in a standard version of the scenario, 92% of the subjects thought the unsuccessful character would be envious or jealous. When the success was lower, 86% of the subjects still reported envy or jealousy. Envy was still expected by many subjects after viewing other scenarios: 86% reported envy when the two actors were depicted as friends, 59%

when one of the actors boasted, 55% when the unsuccessful actor wept, 54% when both actors obtained equal success, and 36% when the unsuccessful actor expressed admiration for the successful one. Silver and Sabini (1978a) saw these results as reflecting that the perception of envy is a recognition of two factors in close relationships: (a) that actor X has greater success than actor Y, and (b) that Y has acted inappropriately, inconsiderately, or disrespectfully toward X.

Dakin and Arrowood (1981) examined the situational conditions under which individuals will engage in one of three types of social comparison, competition (and resulting envy), cooperation, or conformity. Social comparison can be considered a process whereby an individual assigns values to self by using others as referents. Dakin and Arrowood predicted that competitive, envy-engendering comparisons should be made when two individuals are similar in ability and when one is clearly more successful than the other on a task. To test this hypothesis, subjects competed in pairs on a reaction-time task in which false feedback concerning the participant's success and failure was given after each trial. As predicted, competitive tendencies were related to interpersonal proximity. That is, competitive comparisons were more likely when subjects were close in ability. There was also a tendency for competitive comparisons to increase when subjects were comparing themselves to superior others. Thus "competition is greatest when P and O are similar and when P is losing" (Dakin & Arrowood, 1981, p. 105). We can expect, then, that such situations are particularly likely to foster envy, and, in fact, we found this result in our experiment described previously (Salovey & Rodin, 1984).

MANAGING ENVY AND JEALOUSY IN CLOSE RELATIONSHIPS

Although most people experience envy and jealousy, they are usually not moved to the violent extremes we will describe later. Strategies are somehow learned in order to cope with these emotional states. One aspect of coping with negative experiences that has been investigated fairly systematically is the appraisal of stressors and stressful situations. Once individuals appraise a situation, in this view, they will adopt some cognitive or behavioral coping strategy in an attempt to adjust to it. Defining a situation as envy- or jealousy-provoking requires not only an appraisal of the stressful elements in the immediate situation, but also self-reflection, that is, determining what it is about the situation that is particularly threatening to one's self-worth. As a result, the coping strategies that might then be invoked are often self-focused and involve changing one's view of oneself, thinking about non-threatened aspects of the self, or deciding that a relationship or personal attribute is simply not that important (but see White, 1981a, for an alternative view).

Three studies have been reported that investigated ways in which envy and jealousy are managed. Jaremko and Lindsey (1979) predicted that jealousy-prone individuals might lack the skills to cope with social stress more generally. However, using laboratory self-disclosure as their stress inducer, nonjealous and jealous individuals (as differentiated using the Self-Report Jealousy Scale, Bringle et al., 1979) did not differ in psychophysiological reactivity or in their effective use of a coping technique called "reversal of affect," involving viewing the positive aspects of the stressor.

Buunk (1982b) investigated coping with romantic jealousy aroused in nonexclusive relationships. Three primary coping strategies were used to deal with extramarital involvements of one's spouse: (a) avoidance, (b) reappraisal, and (c) communication, although evidence of the efficacy of these activities was not available.

Salovey and Rodin (in press) assessed the amount of jealousy and envy (and other negative emotions) experienced in several different life domains. We then determined the coping strategies used to deal with these jealousy-provoking situations and assessed their association with relief from jealousy and other affective distress. In this study, and consistent with our theoretical framework, we were especially interested in strategies that involved changing the way one viewed oneself or the importance of the other person or event for one's self-definition. Three strategies were identified by factor analysis: (a) self-reliance (avoiding emotional outbursts, maintaining activities, not asking others for help), (b) self-bolstering (thinking about one's good qualities, doing nice things for oneself, thinking positively about oneself), and (c) selective ignoring (reevaluating the importance of the desired goal). Self-reliance was most strongly associated with reports of less intense jealousy. Selective ignoring appeared related to a further small, but significant, reduction in jealousy. Self-bolstering was not associated with lower jealousy, but it was related to reduced depression and anger among subjects already experiencing jealousy. Self-reliance also was associated with lower anger in some subjects.

Contrary to our original expectations, self-bolstering may be a particularly poor strategy for dealing with the initial flash of jealousy, because the immediate responses to jealousy include such powerful, negative self-relevant imagery. When individuals are confronted with negative social comparison, it is at first difficult to evoke thoughts about one's good qualities (i.e., engage in self-bolstering). Rather, the attributes on which one does not measure up are precisely those that are most salient (Salovey & Rodin, 1985b; Silver & Sabini, 1978a). Self-reliance and selective ignoring, rather than involving thoughts about oneself, are stimulus-focused coping strategies. One either becomes even more committed to attaining one's goals, trying harder and avoiding emotional outbursts, or one simply decides that reaching the goal is not important. Rather than being forced to confront and change one's self-concept, as with self-bolstering, self-reliance and selective ignoring are reassessments of the desired object or relationship. As jealousy-provoking experiences in a relevant life domain begin to accumulate, more generalized affective distress, probably in the form of anger and depression, becomes associated with that domain. At this point, self-bolstering might be an effective coping strategy.

Problems with envy and especially jealousy are commonly brought to psychotherapists (Constantine, 1977; Ellis, 1977; Margolin, 1981; Teismann, 1979), and there is some evidence that the kinds of cognitive coping strategies described above are helpful. For example, Teismann (1979) asked clients to reframe negative attributes of jealousy (e.g., possessiveness, dependence) as positive qualities (e.g., romance, passion). Similarly, Margolin (1981) used cognitive reframing to help jealous couples, asking them to think of their jealousy as a sign of caring and devotion, and their staying together, despite suspected extramarital affairs, as a sign of the relationship's strength rather than the individual's weakness.

ENVY, JEALOUSY, AND CRIMES OF PASSION

Although most individuals learn to cope with the experiences of envy or jealousy, there is a belief by those working in the legal arena that unbridled envy and jealousy are at the root of much criminal activity. Unfortunately, this question has received little systematic attention by social scientists. Consideration of crimes of passion is fraught with political overtones. Many commentators (e.g., Jordan, 1985) have noted that the classic crime of passion, the murder of a lover and rival upon discovering them in the midst of a sexual indiscretion, is a myth. Rather, such so-called crimes of passion are preceded by years of psychological abuse and physical battering, and, in fact, very little passion at all.

Still, homicide committed in the alleged heat of passion is considered manslaughter rather than murder in 49 states (Dressler, 1982). Although this conceptualization may have originally served to prevent the death penalty from being inflicted on an unfortunate soul who killed someone in a barroom brawl, the American Law Institute's Model Penal Code still lists manslaughter as any intentional killing committed under the influence of extreme mental or emotional disturbance for which there is a reasonable explanation or excuse. Yet confusion reigns in the courts' interpretation of the law in what are called "sight of adultery" cases. For example, a married person who kills upon "sight of adultery" can be convicted of manslaughter, but an unmarried person who kills under similar circumstances has committed murder (Dressler, 1982). There is no real evidence that "sight of adultery" by a married person arouses any more intense and cognitively disrupting "passion" than that in the unmarried. As Dressler noted, "this rule is really a judgment by courts that adultery is a form of injustice perpetrated upon the killer which merits a violent response, whereas 'mere' sexual unfaithfulness out of wedlock does not" (p. 438).

Despite the legal confusion over the proper use and disposition of a "heat of passion" defense, the psychiatric literature is the source of a variety of studies of murderers, with the typical finding that many experienced intense jealousy immediately preceding the killing. Several in-depth case studies were described by Lehrman (1939) and Cuthbert (1970), and in an analysis of reported homicides, Psarska (1970) found that in nearly one-fourth, nondelusional jealousy was a causal factor. In these 38 cases, 16 involved actual unfaithfulness, and the remaining 22 cases comprised situations where long-standing marital conflicts developed into jealousy. Further, morbid (i.e., delusional) jealousy has been reported to be one of the leading motives of murderers judged insane (Mowat, 1966).

Only a few social scientists have addressed these disturbing trends. Most place the blame on several interrelated factors: (a) societal sanctioning of aggression and battering (mostly by men) in the context of marital relationships, (b) an emphasis on exclusivity rather than permanence in what couples value in their marital relationships, (c) a lack of resolution of how couples should deal rationally with the availability of extramarital sexuality, and (d) unrealistic visions of what can be expected in a normal marital relationship (Whitehurst, 1971).

SOCIOCULTURAL ASPECTS OF ENVY AND JEALOUSY

We will conclude with some thoughts regarding the sociocultural basis for envy and jealousy in close relationships. Although many theorists see envy and jealousy as fundamental to all human existence, describing these feelings as "instinctual" (see, for example, Darwin, 1888; James, 1890) and even observing infrahuman evidence for them (Mathes & Deuger, 1982), there is no doubt that the experience and expression of envy and jealousy can be viewed profitably from a sociological perspective.

Sociocultural Origins of Jealousy

Kingsly Davis (1936) was among the first social scientists to claim that jealousy is rooted in social structure. Davis described jealousy in terms of the violation of sexual property norms. Such norms (and therefore jealousy) served to protect relationships valued by the community. According to this view, a given culture defines which relationships are particularly valued and guides an individual's interpretation of events threatening this valued relationship. Further, cultures also prescribe behaviors that protect these relationships.

Hupka (1981) identified several characteristics that differentiate jealous from nonjealous cultures. Cultures low in jealousy discourage individual property rights and view sexual gratification and companionship as easily available, but do not engender in their members a desire for sex as a pleasurable pastime. Such cultures place little value on personal descendants or the need to know whether the children in the family are one's own progeny. Marriage is not required for economic survival, companionship, or recognition of the individual as a competent member of the society.

Whitehurst (1977) proposed that jealousy thrives in cultures with rigidly prescribed sex-roles. In these cultures, sex-role sanctioned divisions of labor lead to a sense of inadequacy in which one spouse (usually the wife) may feel uneasy about her role relative to the other, and this anxiety is expressed as jealousy. Similarly Clanton and Smith (1977) noted that in rigid sex-role prescribed relationships, jealousy is used to gain power and control, to generate self-righteousness, to excuse one for vicious or physically abusive behavior, or to justify withdrawal from a relationship.

Sociocultural Origins of Envy

Most advanced societies use envy to encourage the talents, abilities, and productivity of their members (Rorty, 1971). In a competitive culture, individualistic concerns for material possessions, status, and affection are often manifested as envy. Envy can easily become jealousy when competition for the sole affections of a lover produces suspiciousness and self-doubt (Whitehurst, 1977). But the promotion of envy is not part of the ideology of all cultures. Schoeck (1966) observed that societal development is premised on gaining social control over envy.

For example, in some less-developed societies, when one member of a group deviates from social norms by achieving something the other group members lack, envy is aroused. Members of these cultures fear arousing envy in others (and then becoming the focus of their rage), and this fear inhibits such deviant behavior in the society. There is widespread belief in many cultures that experiencing envy of another person will result in personal calamities (Foster, 1972). Schoeck (1966) thus advanced the provocative thesis that envy functions as a positive mechanism of social development in industrial societies and a negative one in less-developed societies.

CONCLUSION

The experiences of envy and jealousy are characteristic of close relationships in a wide variety of cultures (e.g., Hupka, Buunk, Falus, Fulgosi, Ortega, Swain, & Tarabrina, 1985). However, there is considerable variance in the phenomenology of the experience of these affective states, in the situations that elicit them, in the behaviors motivated by them, and in the way individuals try to manage them. We propose that one ubiquitous aspect of envy and jealousy is that they are experienced most intensely when an especially self-relevant or self-definitional attribute, accomplishment, or relationship is threatened or desired. There is a seemingly close tie between emotional intensity and the self, and the self may be the link between affective experiences and motivated social behaviors (see Salovey & Rodin, 1985a). Such is probably the case for jealousy and envy. We do not experience jealousy when the exclusivity of unimportant relationships is threatened; envy cannot be expected when others accomplish goals about which we simply do not care. Because of their close ties to self-definition, envy and jealousy are states with some utility for the individual. Their existence helps us to identify those relationships and attainments that are truly important to us. Without envy and jealousy, close relationships might be more pleasant, but would they be as meaningful? As psychoanalyst Robert Seidenberg (1967) reflected, "Who would want to live a life in which one cared so little about another ... that nothing he [or she] did ... mattered?" (pp. 586-587).

REFERENCES

Aronson, E., & Pines, A. (1980, April). *Exploring sexual jealousy*. Paper presented at the annual meeting of the Western Psychological Association, Honolulu.

Bers, S., & Rodin, J. (1984). Social-comparison jealousy: A developmental and motivational study. *Journal of Personality and Social Psychology, 47*, 766-779.

Bringle, R. G. (1981). Conceptualizing jealousy as a disposition. *Alternative Lifestyles, 4*, 274-290.

Bringle, R. G., & Buunk, B. (1985). Jealousy and social behavior: A review of person, relationship, and situational determinants. In P. Shaver (Ed.), *Review of Personality and Social Psychology* (Vol. 6, pp. 241-264). Beverly Hills, CA: Sage.

Bringle, R. G., & Buunk, B. (1986). Examining the causes and consequences of jealousy: Some recent findings and issues. In R. Gilmour & S. Duck (Eds.), *The emerging field of personal relationships* (pp. 225-239). Hillsdale, NJ: Lawrence Erlbaum.

Bringle, R. G., & Evenbeck, S. E. (1979). The study of jealousy as a dispositional characteristic. In M. Cook & G. Wilson (Eds.), *Love and attraction: An international conference* (pp. 201-204). Oxford: Pergamon.

Bringle, R. G., Renner, P., Terry, R., & Davis, S. (1983). An analysis of situational and person components of jealousy. *Journal of Research in Personality, 17*, 354-368.

Bringle, R. G., Roach, S., Andler, C., & Evenbeck, S. (1979). Measuring the intensity of jealous reactions. *Catalog of Selected Documents in Psychology, 9* (2), 23-24.

Bryson, J. B. (1976, September). *The nature of sexual jealousy: An exploratory study.* Paper presented at the annual meeting of the American Psychological Association, Washington, DC.

Bryson, J. B. (1977, September). *Situational determinants of the expression of jealousy.* Paper presented at the annual meeting of the American Psychological Association, San Francisco.

Buunk, B. (1982a). Anticipated sexual jealousy: Its relationship to self-esteem, dependency, and reciprocity. *Personality and Social Psychology Bulletin, 8*, 310-316.

Buunk, B. (1982b). Strategies of jealousy: Styles of coping with extramarital involvement of the spouse. *Family Relations, 31*, 13-18.

Buunk, B., & Bringle, R. G. (1987). Jealousy in love relationships. In D. Perlman & S. Duck (Eds.), *Intimate relationships: development, dynamics, and deterioration* (pp. 123-147). Newbury Park, CA: Sage.

Cialdini, R. B., Borden, R. J., Thorne, A., Walker, M. R., Freeman, S., & Sloan, L. R. (1976). Basking in reflected glory: Three (football) field studies. *Journal of Personality and Social Psychology, 34*, 366-375.

Clanton, G., & Smith, L. G. (Eds.). (1977). *Jealousy.* Englewood Cliffs, NJ: Prentice-Hall.

Constantine, L. L. (1977). Jealousy: Techniques for intervention. In G. Clanton & L. G. Smith (Eds.), *Jealousy* (pp. 190-198). Englewood Cliffs, NJ: Prentice-Hall.

Cuthbert, T. M. (1970). A portfolio of murders. *British Journal of Psychiatry, 116*, 1-10.

Dakin, S., & Arrowood, A. J. (1981). The social comparison of ability. *Human Relations, 34*, 80-109.

Darwin, C. (1888). *Descent of man* (Vol. 2). Chicago: University of Chicago Press.

Davis, K. (1936). Jealousy and sexual property. *Social Forces, 14*, 395-405.

Dressler, J. (1982). Rethinking the heat of passion: A defense in search of a rationale. *The Journal of Criminal Law and Criminology, 73*, 421-470.

Ellis, A. (1977). Rational and irrational jealousy. In G. Clanton & L. G. Smith (Eds.), *Jealousy* (pp. 170-179). Englewood Cliffs, NJ: Prentice-Hall.

Ellis, C., & Weinstein, E. (1986). Jealousy and the social psychology of emotional experience. *Journal of Social and Personal Relationships, 3*, 337-357.

Foster, G. (1972). The anatomy of envy: A study in symbolic behavior. *Current Anthropology, 13*, 165-202.

Freud, S. (1955). Some neurotic mechanisms in jealousy, paranoia, and homosexuality. In J. Strachey (Ed. and Trans.), *The standard edition of the complete psychological works of Sigmund Freud* (Vol. 18). London: Hogarth. (Original work published 1934)

Gellert, S. (1976). Mixed emotions. *Transactional Analysis Journal, 6*, 129-130.

Hansen, G. L. (1985). Perceived threats and marital jealousy. *Social Psychology Quarterly, 48*, 262-268.

Heider, F. (1958). *The psychology of interpersonal relations.* Hillsdale, NJ: Lawrence Erlbaum.

Hupka, R. B. (1981). Cultural determinants of jealousy. *Alternative Lifestyles, 4*, 310-356.

Hupka, R. B. (1984). Jealousy: Compound emotion or label for a particular situation? *Motivation and Emotion, 8*, 141-155.

Hupka, R. B., & Bachelor, B. (1979, April). *Validation of a scale to measure romantic jealousy.* Paper presented at the annual meeting of the Western Psychological Association, San Diego, CA.

Hupka, R. B., Buunk, B., Falus, G., Fulgosi, A., Ortega, E., Swain, R., & Tarabrina, N. V. (1985). Romantic jealousy and romantic envy: A seven-nation study. *Journal of Cross-Cultural Psychology, 16*, 423-446.

James, W. (1890/1983). *The principles of psychology.* Cambridge, MA: Harvard University Press.

Jaremko, M. E., & Lindsey, R. (1979). Stress coping abilities of individuals high and low in jealousy. *Psychological Reports, 44*, 547-553.

Jordan, N. (1985). Till murder do us part. *Psychology Today, 19*(7), 7.

Lehrman, P. R. (1939). Some unconscious determinants in homicide. *Psychiatric Quarterly, 13*, 605-621.

Manges, K., & Evenbeck, S. (1980, April). *Social power, jealousy, and dependency in the intimate dyad.* Paper presented at the annual meeting of the Midwestern Psychological Association, St. Louis.

Margolin, G. (1981). A behavioral-systems approach to the treatment of marital jealousy. *Clinical Psychology Review, 1*, 469-487.

Mathes, E. W., & Deuger, D. J. (1982). Jealousy, a creation of human culture? *Psychological Reports, 51*, 351-354.

Mathes, E. W., & Severa, N. (1981). Jealousy, romantic love, and liking: Theoretical considerations and preliminary scale development. *Psychological Reports, 44*, 23-31.

Mead, M. (1977). Jealousy: Primitive and civilized. In G. Clanton & L. G. Smith (Eds.), *Jealousy* (pp. 115-127). Englewood Cliffs, NJ: Prentice-Hall.

Mowat, R. R. (1966). *Morbid jealousy and murder: A psychiatric study of morbidly jealous murderers at Broadmoor.* London: Tavistock.

Neu, J. (1980). Jealous thoughts. In A. O. Rorty (Ed.), *Explaining emotions* (pp. 425-464). Los Angeles: University of California Press.

Parrott, W. G., & Smith, R. H. (1987, August). *Differentiating the experiences of envy and jealousy.* Paper presented at the annual meeting of the American Psychological Association, New York.

Psarska, A. D. (1970). Jealousy factor in homicide in forensic psychiatric material. *Polish Medical Journal, 6*, 1504-1510.

Rodgers, M. A., & Bryson, J. B. (1978, April). *Self-esteem and relationship maintenance as responses of jealousy.* Paper presented at the annual meeting of the Western Psychological Association, San Francisco, CA.

Rorty, A. O. (1971). Some social uses of the forbidden. *Psychoanalytic Review, 58*, 497-510.

Rosenberg, M. (1965). *Society and the adolescent self-image.* Princeton, NJ: Princeton University Press.

Sabini, J., & Silver, M. (1982). *Moralities of everyday life.* Oxford: Oxford University Press.

Salovey, P., & Rodin, J. (1983, April). *A self-esteem maintenance model of envy.* Paper presented at the annual meeting of the Eastern Psychological Association, Philadelphia.

Salovey, P., & Rodin, J. (1984). Some antecedents and consequences of social-comparison jealousy. *Journal of Personality and Social Psychology, 47,* 780-792.

Salovey, P., & Rodin, J. (1985a). Cognitions about the self: Connecting feeling states and social behavior. In P. Shaver (Ed.), *Review of Personality and Social Psychology* (Vol. 6, pp. 143-166). Beverly Hills, CA: Sage.

Salovey, P., & Rodin, J. (1985b). The heart of jealousy. *Psychology Today, 19*(9), 22-25, 28-29.

Salovey, P., & Rodin, J. (1986). Differentiation of social-comparison jealousy and romantic jealousy. *Journal of Personality and Social Psychology, 50,* 1100-1112.

Salovey, P., & Rodin, J. (in press). Coping with envy and jealousy. *Journal of Social and Clinical Psychology.*

Shettel-Neuber, J., Bryson, J. B., & Young, L. E. (1978). Physical attractiveness of the "other person" and jealousy. *Personality and Social Psychology Bulletin, 4,* 612-615.

Schoeck, H. (1966). *Envy: A theory of social behavior.* New York: Harcourt Brace & World.

Seidenberg, R. (1967). Fidelity and jealousy: Socio-cultural considerations. *Psychoanalytic Review, 54,* 583-608.

Silver, M., & Sabini, J. (1978a). The perception of envy. *Social Psychology, 41,* 105-117.

Silver, M., & Sabini, J. (1978b). The social construction of envy. *Journal for the Theory of Social Behavior, 8,* 313-331.

Smith, R. H., Kim, S. H., & Parrott, W. G. (1988). Envy and jealousy: Semantic problems and experiential distinctions. *Personality and Social Psychology Bulletin, 14,* 401-409.

Spielman, P. M. (1971). Envy and jealousy: An attempt at clarification. *Psychoanalytic Quarterly, 40,* 59-82.

Spinoza, B. (1675/1949). *Ethics.* (J. Gutmann, trans. and ed.). New York: Hafner.

Tesser, A. (1986). Some effects of self-evaluation maintenance on cognition and action. In R. M. Sorrentino & E. T. Higgins (Eds.), *Handbook of motivation and cognition* (pp. 435-464). New York: Guilford.

Tesser, A. & Campbell, J. (1982). Self-evaluation maintenance and the perception of friends and strangers. *Journal of Personality, 50,* 261-279.

Tesser, A. & Campbell, J. (1983). Self-definition and self-evaluation maintenance. In J. Suls & A. Greenwald (Eds.), *Social psychological perspectives on the self* (Vol. 2, pp. 1-31). Hillsdale, NJ: Lawrence Erlbaum.

Teismann, M. W. (1979). Jealousy: Systematic problem-solving therapy with couples. *Family Process, 18,* 151-160.

Titleman, P. (1982). A phenomenological comparison between envy and jealousy. *Journal of Phenomenological Psychology, 12,* 184-204.

Tov-Ruach, L. (1980). Jealousy, attention, and loss. In A. O. Rorty (Ed.), *Explaining emotions* (pp. 465-488). Los Angeles: University of California Press.

White, G. L. (1977, September). *Inequity of emotional involvement and jealousy in romantic couples.* Paper presented at the annual meeting of the American Psychological Association, San Francisco, CA.

White, G. L. (1980). Inducing jealousy: A power perspective. *Personality and Social Psychology Bulletin, 6*, 222-227.

White, G. L. (1981a, August). *Coping with romantic jealousy: Comparison to rival, perceived motives, and alternative assessment.* Paper presented at the annual meeting of the American Psychological Association, Los Angeles.

White, G. L. (1981b). Jealousy and partner's perceived motives for attraction to a rival. *Social Psychology Quarterly, 44*, 24-30.

White, G. L. (1981c). A model of romantic jealousy. *Motivation and Emotion, 5*, 295-310.

White, G. L. (1981d). Relative involvement, inadequacy, and jealousy: A test of a causal model. *Alternative lifestyles, 4*, 291-309.

White, G. L. (1981e). Some correlates of romantic jealousy. *Journal of Personality, 49*, 129-147.

Whitehurst, R. N. (1971). Violence potential in extramarital sexual responses. *Journal of Marriage and the Family, 33*, 683-691.

Whitehurst, R. N. (1977). Jealousy and American values. In G. Clanton & L. G. Smith (Eds.), *Jealousy* (pp. 136-140). Englewood Cliffs, NJ: Prentice- Hall.

10

A Model of the Causes of Date Rape
in Developing and Close Relationships

R. LANCE SHOTLAND

R. Lance Shotland is a Professor of Psychology at Pennsylvania State University. His research interests include bystander behavior, crime, methodological issues, the use of social science in the creation of public policy, perceptions and misperceptions between men and women, and date rape. He is the author of *University Communication Networks: The Small World Method*, coauthor (with Stanley Milgram) of *Television and Antisocial Behavior: Field Experiments*, and a coeditor (with Melvin M. Mark) of two books, *Social Science and Social Policy* and *Multiple Methods in Program Evaluation*.

Rape, whether the aggressor is a stranger, a nonromantic acquaintance, or a date, is a major problem on American college campuses. Kanin and his colleagues, in a series of surveys over a 20-year period, found that between 20% and 25% of college women surveyed reported forceful attempts at sexual intercourse by their dates in which the women reacted by screaming, fighting, crying, and pleading (Kanin, 1957, 1967, 1971; Kanin & Parcell, 1977; Kirkpatrick & Kanin, 1957). More recently Wilson and Durrenberger (1982) found that 18% of their sample of women indicated that they were the victims of attempted rape, and a additional 15% indicated that they had been raped. Likewise, Korman and Leslie (1982) reported that 20% of their sample were offended by attempts at intercourse, while Skelton (1982) found that 25% had experienced at least one incident of coerced intercourse. Another study (Muehlenhard & Linton, 1987) found that approximately 15% of their sample of college women had been involved in unwanted sexual intercourse.

Koss and her colleagues have performed the only two probability sample surveys on college campuses. The first survey was conducted on one campus (Koss & Oros, 1982), while the second was conducted at 32 institutions (Koss, Gidycz, & Wisniewski, 1987). These researchers found that 13% and 15.4% (respectively) of the women had experienced incidents of sexual aggression that met the legal definition of rape. The

AUTHOR'S NOTE: I would like to thank Barry Burkhart, Lynne Goodstein, and Clyde Hendrick for their careful reading, helpful comments, and editorial suggestions on previous drafts of this chapter.

survey of 32 campuses showed that 11% of the victimized women were raped by strangers, 25% by nonromantic acquaintances (friends, co-workers or neighbors), 21% by casual dates, 30% by steady dates, and 9% by husbands or other family members (Koss, Dinero, Seibel & Cox, in press). Two probability sample surveys have been conducted in cities using different methodologies. The results from these studies are quite disparate, indicating that 24% of San Francisco women had been raped (Russell, 1984), while 5% of Charleston, South Carolina women had been raped (Kilpatrick et al., 1985).

Many epidemiological surveys that used college students were not based on probability samples and tended to come from similar sources (for example, introductory psychology classes) subject to the same potential biasing factors. Nevertheless, the consistency of the results from nonprobability college samples with those of probability based college samples suggests that the contemporary rate of rape victimizations on college campuses is approximately 15%; one-half of these occur during a date. The observed rate, however, appears partially to depend on the age of the population, the method of data collection, and the criteria on which the estimate is based.

PRELIMINARY CONSIDERATIONS

The purpose of this chapter is to review the relevant literature on date rape and to present a preliminary model of the causes of date rape (see Shotland, 1985a, 1985b, for earlier versions). The model focuses on different processes that may lead to rape that are likely to occur at different points in a relationship's development. This typology, to my knowledge, has not been previously proposed or researched. Therefore the literature cited does not differentiate among the types of date rape that I will develop. Accordingly, the association of a research finding with a particular variety of date rape reflects my own theorizing and not that of the authors cited.

A caveat concerning legal responsibility, morality, and social science research is in order. The purpose of this chapter is to describe different types of date rape from a social science perspective, without assignment of moral blame or discussion of legal culpability. Part of the analysis involves the identification of characteristics of women and men that relate to the likelihood of their becoming victims or perpetrators of date rape. One should not infer, however, that possessing higher risk factors implies blameworthiness for women or mitigates responsibility or culpability for men. The fact that some of the victim's attributes may make her vulnerable does not make her responsible for her victimization.

Nor does the fact that sexual aggression can be predicted by certain perpetrator characteristics reduce the rapist's culpability.

Let me provide an analogy. Because Milgram (1974) discovered the power of obedience and suggested that it played a role in the Holocaust does not mean that the Nazis were any less morally responsible for the acts they committed. Similarly, one can identify victims of the Holocaust by their political, religious, and sexual beliefs and practices. This knowledge does not mean that the victims were responsible for their extermination. Correspondingly, no research or theory that I will present should be perceived as either diminishing the responsibility of the rapist or increasing the responsibility of the victim in either a moral or legal sense.

Inconsistencies exist in explanations of the causes of date rape. On one hand, some investigators have characterized date rape as a deviation in degree but not in kind from normative sexual behavior (Kanin, 1969; Weis & Borges, 1973). These researchers suggest that sexual aggression is primarily the result of cross-sex communication failure and male attitudes supportive of rape myths. Indeed, the fact that epidemiological evidence indicates that date rape is a widespread phenomenon may suggest that some fraction of date rape results from "normal" sociological processes of courtship. Normal or traditional processes of courtship include the male's initiation of both dates and sex, with females limited to the more passive response of either declining or consenting to these advances. These role expectations may lead to misunderstandings by both men and women, at times resulting in males initiating and proceeding with sex when it is not wanted (Weis & Borges, 1973).

Other researchers have relied upon psychopathological explanations to account for sexual aggression (see Groth, 1979). These authors look for characteristics in the personalities of aggressors and victims that create either aggression-prone or victim-prone behavior.

One reason for these different perspectives may be that date rape is not a unidimensional phenomenon. There may be different types of date rape, with each type caused by somewhat different factors. It seems reasonable that elements from both the normal process of courtship as well as psychopathological models may be needed to account for these different kinds of date rape. Furthermore, different types of rape may occur at different stages of a relationship.

The results of research allow the inference that date rapes do indeed occur at different stages of relationships. Skelton (1982) reported that 36% of women's most upsetting coercive sexual experiences occur on a first date or by an acquaintance, 26% by an occasional date (not a regular suitor), and 31% by a steady or regular date. Similar findings with somewhat different percentages have been reported by other researchers (e.g., Kanin, 1969; Koss et al., in press).

It would seem that a rape that occurs on a first date, before the male "knows" his partner well or could reasonably expect to have a sexual relationship with her, has a cause quite different from a rape that occurs after the couple has had a number of dates. After a couple has been dating, but before each person has a full understanding of the other's position concerning sex, the male's misperception of his date's sexual intent can set the stage for rape. After a couple has a full understanding about each other's relative position concerning sex, misperception becomes an unlikely cause of date rape, and another explanation becomes necessary.

There are other reasons to expect that there are several varieties of date rape, with different causal patterns. First, 39% of rape victims and 12% of attempted rape victims date their attacker subsequent to the assault (Wilson & Durrenberger, 1982). One might assume that the experience of the rape would be different for a woman who continues to see her attacker compared to a woman who does not. For example, while a woman who is attacked on a first date would be unlikely to see her rapist again, this might not be the case for a woman who feels that she had miscommunicated her intentions or for a victim with an investment in a long-term relationship with her rapist (there may be other explanations as well). The causal factors leading to these different responses to sexual victimization may also be causal factors of rape. Second, victimized women appear to have dated or had sex with more men than their nonvictimized counterparts and hence have a higher probability of dating a rapist (Koss, 1985; Koss & Dinero, 1987; Skelton, 1982). Similarly, sexually aggressive males have more sexual experience and consistently seek new sexual involvements (Kanin, 1967). Such males and females are unlikely to be involved in steady relationships. However, 30% of college rape victims have been raped by a steady date (Koss et al., in press). This suggests that several groups of date rapists and victims with different characteristics and motivations may exist.

Thus it seems reasonable that there may be several different types of date rape, with each variety having somewhat different causes. Furthermore, each type of date rape is likely to occur at different times in the life of a relationship.

A major tenet of the model that I will propose is that date rape can be separated along three different but not independent causal pathways. I believe that each causal sequence is *likely* to occur at different temporal points in the relationship. However, these causal processes can also overlap in time, and in such instances may combine to cause an incident of date rape. Nevertheless, I will label the hypothesized causal paths with the name of the time period of the dating relationship in which they are most likely to occur.

I discuss psychological and lifestyle characteristics of victims and aggressors as a unit because I believe that the best unit of analysis is neither victim nor aggressor, but the couple. Previous investigators have taken either the aggressor or the victim as the unit of analysis. However, in date rape the victim knows the identity of the aggressor, so it may be possible to study date rape with the couple as the unit. Researchers frequently judge the advance of knowledge by the amount of variance in the phenomenon that can be predicted. If the research focus is on only a fraction of the equation (i.e., either the victim or aggressor), the predictive fit is unlikely to be good, resulting in slow progress in knowledge. If couples are not the unit of analysis, potentially important interactions between aggressor and victim characteristics will be ignored.

For instance, it is unlikely that many date rapists attempt to rape every woman that they date. (Unfortunately, no data exist that provide a ratio of dates to rapes for these men.) Similarly, a woman might be more at risk with one date rapist than another. For example, let's assume that some aggressive male is willing to rape if necessary to obtain the coitus he expects by the fifth date (see Knox & Wilson, 1981). One woman might find this male boring, so that she stops seeing him after their third date; therefore, she is not raped. A second woman finds him interesting but not sexually appealing, so that she dates him five times and is raped. A third woman may find him very sexually attractive and is willing to sleep with him on the fourth date, so that the man does not feel the need to resort to rape. Therefore, the second woman is raped, while the first and the third women are not. Similarly, an aggressive male may stop dating a woman because she does not share his interests. He may continue to date a woman for companionship but not be sexually interested in her, or he may date a woman that he finds sexually interesting and whom he eventually rapes. This example underlines the potential importance of interactions between victim and aggressor variables in the prediction of date rape.

A MODEL FOR THREE TYPES OF DATE RAPE

The three types of date rape that I will discuss are *beginning date rape* which, as the name indicates, occurs during the first few dates at the beginning of a relationship. The second type of date rape occurs early in the relationship, after several dates, as the couple is getting to know one another and are still establishing the rules of their relationship. I will call this variety *early date rape*. The third type occurs after the couple has been dating for some time and believe that they know what to expect from each other. This variety is called *relational date rape*.[1]

The major focus of the chapter is on early date rape. I emphasize this type of rape because (1) like relational date rape, it can be explained more completely in terms of "normal" courtship processes that affect men and women of college age and (2) I believe there is more empirical evidence relevant to early date rape than to the other two types. I will start my analysis with early date rape rather than beginning date rape. While starting with early date rape disregards the chronology of the three types of date rape, it provides the best perspective from which to understand both the need and explanations for beginning and relational date rape.

Much of the empirical evidence relevant to early date rape relates to gender differences in perceptions of sexual intent, a process which may play an important role in setting the stage for early date rape. Gender differences in the perception of sexual intent are considered below, as well as the mechanisms for the prediction of early date rape from such gender differences. After these considerations, a model for early date rape is defined, followed by preliminary models for beginning date rape and relational date rape.

EARLY DATE RAPE

Gender Differences in the Perception of Sexual Intent

That men are more preoccupied with sex than women is a common observation in contemporary America. Perhaps because of the pervasiveness of this observation, relevant research testing the existence of this gender difference and its consequences is quite sparse. Surprisingly, no theory comes to mind, and little research has been performed that illuminates how such a difference may affect relationships between men and women.

One area in which research demonstrates a difference between men and women is in the perception that a person is "sexually interested." Men tend to perceive people as having more sexual interest than do women. The understanding of this phenomenon may be important to an analysis of early date rape.

Gross (1978) theorized that the socialization experience causes men to perceive sex more favorably than women perceive sex. Several investigations of nonverbal cues support the presence of such a gender difference in perception. In one study, males who imagined a hypothetical touch "of their sexual area" delivered by an opposite sex *stranger* judged it to be more pleasant than females did. However, the ratings of males and females were similarly high for such contact with a *close* opposite sex person (Heslin, Nguyen, & Nguyen, 1983). These authors also found that single men were more likely than single women to associate a hypothetical sexual touch with love and pleasantness (Nguyen, Heslin, & Nguyen, 1976).

A survey of ethnically diverse males and females between fourteen and seventeen years of age found that males "view[ed] the world" in a more sexualized manner than females in response to hypothetical situations. For example, males judged some female apparel as a sign that the wearer "wanted sex," while females did not make such an inference (Zellman, Johnson, Giarrusso, & Goodchilds, 1979). Another investigator asked mixed-sex couples to sustain eye contact for a period of time. Afterward, many more males than females indicated that they were sexually attracted to their partner (Rytting, 1976). In addition, males in their twenties are much more likely than females to engage in sexually flirtatious behavior (Montgomery, 1987). Males are more likely than females to rate both male and female actors as higher on sexual desire (Abbey, 1982; Abbey, Cozzarelli, McLaughlin, & Harnish, 1987; Abbey & Melby, 1986; Hendrick, 1976; Major & Heslin, 1982; Shotland & Craig, in press).

In conclusion, the available evidence strongly supports the proposition that males view females in more sexual terms than females view males. Several studies also suggest that males are more likely to judge male desires and intentions in sexual terms as well (e.g., Abbey, 1982; Hendrick, 1976; Shotland & Craig, in press). Do these effects suggest that (1) men and women see the relationships among friendship, sexual interest, and love differently, and that (2) men cannot tell the difference between friendly and sexually interested behavior?

The available evidence suggests that males and females do perceive the relationships among friendship, sexual interest, and love differently. Rubin (1970) reported that liking and loving a dating partner were more strongly related for males than for females. These results were confirmed by Frevert and Kahn (1976).

Can men tell the difference between platonic and sexually interested behavior? Abbey (1982) suggested that men frequently misjudge a woman's friendly intent as an indication of sexual interest. Abbey hypothesized that men cannot tell the difference between a woman's seductive and friendly behaviors, and reported an experiment in which pairs of male and female strangers interacted while being observed by two other subjects. Abbey found that males, whether actors or observers, rated the female actor as being both more "seductive" and "promiscuous," than did females. Male actors also found their female partners to be more sexually attractive and were more eager to date them. Female actors felt less strongly about their male partners. Similar results were found for the observers' ratings of the male and female actors. It is also important to note that all of the differences between males and females were found only on the most sexually explicit items.

However, in order to determine whether people can tell the difference between platonic and sexually interested behavior, their responses must be compared across conditions of friendship and sexual interest. Two studies have made this comparison, and both used similar methodologies (Muehlenhard, Miller, & Burdick, 1983; Shotland & Craig, in press). Both studies had actors interact in either a sexually interested or a merely friendly manner. Videotapes were made of these interactions, and other subjects made judgments of the actors after watching the videotape. Both studies found that males could distinguish between sexually interested and friendly behavior exhibited by women. In addition, Shotland and Craig found that (1) women can distinguish between sexually interested and friendly behavior exhibited by women, (2) both men and women can make this distinction for male actors as well, and (3) consistent with previous work, male and female observers differed in amount of sexual interest attributed to both male and female actors.

If both men and women can discriminate between "friendly" and "interested" behavior, what accounts for the gender difference in the perception of sexual intent? Whether men or women are more frequently correct cannot be experimentally determined. What is needed is a "true" criterion on which a perceptual bias may be judged. As long as a gender-based perceptual difference persists, sexually interested behavior will probably be misjudged as friendly behavior by a group with a high threshold for labeling sexually interested behavior, that is, women. Likewise, friendly behavior is likely to be misjudged as sexually interested behavior by a group with a low threshold for labeling such behavior, that is, men. Obviously, a mild expression of interested behavior and an exuberant expression of friendly behavior are most likely to be misjudged. A person may feel that he or she is only indicating friendly intent when others might interpret this behavior as a sign of sexual interest. In such a situation the communication that is sent is unclear. However, neither the sender nor the receiver is objectively correct in some absolute sense as to what was sent, or what was received. All that can be said about men and women *generally* is that men have lower thresholds for labeling sexually interested behavior than do women. This perceptual mismatch is important because it is structured so that if a miscommunication around sexual intent occurs within a couple, a likely outcome is for the man to perceive sexual intent when the woman felt she communicated none.

Gender Differences as a Predictor of Early Date Rape

There are two possible way that this perceptual gender difference may lead to early date rape. First, one might expect that early date rapists and their victims are near the extremes of their respective gender distributions on the perception of sexual intent. For example, victims may be less likely than the average woman to monitor their communication and to perceive the sexual intent of their dates. The early date rapist may be more likely than the average man to perceive sexual intent when none was intended. Therefore, such a couple has a greater chance of sexual miscommunication than an average couple. However, it is not necessary for the members of an early date rape couple to be at the extremes of their respective gender distributions. All that is necessary to set the context for an episode of early date rape is a simple misinterpretation of the woman's sexual intent by her date.

If, however, sexually coercive males and victimized females *are* at the extremes of their distributions, one might expect support for the following proposition: If perceptual thresholds are permanent individual characteristics of both victims and aggressors, then victims and aggressors should be involved in multiple incidents of sexual aggression over an extended time period. Several studies have found that a large percentage of college-age women reported being offended by *some type of erotic behavior* by a male escort during the previous year. The estimates of offended women vary between 38% and 56%, with the mean numbers of aggressive episodes varying between 5.1 and 8.7 (see Kanin & Parcell, 1977; Kirkpatrick & Kanin, 1957; Korman & Leslie, 1982).

While these data may be seen to support my hypothesis, they are certainly not conclusive, because these findings may result from several other causes. First, women who report being offended may not experience a greater number of potentially offensive behaviors but may simply be more easily offended, and thus be more likely to remember and report experiences as offensive. Another possibility is that victimized women date more frequently (Koss, 1985; Skelton, 1982) and hence are more frequently exposed to sexual aggression. Whether or not victimized women perceive less sexual intent than do nonvictimized women must wait a direct empirical test.

Two studies directly bear on the repetitive behavior of sexually aggressive men. One study found that 17 of 1,152 male introductory psychology students admitted that they: "had sexual intercourse with a woman when she didn't want to" by using "some degree of physical force." Of these 17 men, 8 (47.1%) reported only a single incident, 3 (17.6%) reported between two and five incidents, 2 reported six to twenty incidents, and 4 reported more than twenty incidents (Muehlenhard & Falcon, 1987). One might expect that *some* of the males who committed a *few* sexually coercive (physical) incidents were at first confused by miscommunication. However, males who use physical coercion to gain sex many times probably belong in the beginning date rape category because of an assumption that communication mistakes are usually self-correcting. Other researchers have found that 13% of their male subjects (n = 190) acknowledged having engaged in forced sexual intercourse on one or two occasions, while 2% stated that they engaged in this behavior "several times," with no subject admitting that they carried out this behavior "often" (Rapaport & Burkhart, 1984).

One possible explanation for the different perceptions of sexual intent between males and females is that males have greater sexual desire than do females (see Kinsey, Pomeroy, & Martin, 1948; Kinsey, Pomeroy, Martin & Gebhard 1952), and that males thus attribute greater sexual desire to their partners. If sexually aggressive males are at the high end of the male sexual desire distribution, then one might expect the date rape literature to support the proposition that these males do desire more sex and are dissatisfied with the level of sexual contact that is available to them. There are at least some data supporting this proposition.

Kanin (1967, 1969, 1983) found that sexually aggressive males had more sexual experiences and were more dissatisfied with their sexual activity than nonaggressive males, and that although these males had more sexual experience, they report needing a much higher level of sexual activity in order to be satisfied (also see Koss, Leonard, Beezley & Oros, 1985). Another researcher discovered that sexually aggressive males (acquaintance rapists and sexually coercive men) responded with more sexual arousal to rape presentations as well as presentations of consenting intercourse than did a control group (Rapaport, 1984, as reported by Burkhart & Stanton, in press). However, similar results were not found with incarcerated rapists (Abel, Barlow, Blanchard, & Guild, 1977).

A Model of Early Date Rape

The model I propose for early date rape, the type that occurs after the couple has had several dates but before the couple has established a relationship, is a relatively simple one. It combines the elements of differential life style, misperceptions of sexual intent between males and females, personality characteristics, and social attitudes.

Males tend to view the world in a more sexualized fashion than do females. Sexually aggressive males are assumed to be more extreme than nonsexually aggressive males on this dimension. Such males want more sexual contact, and they assume that their dates have similar desires but disguise them and feign disinterest.

Such males may be particularly likely to misperceive a woman with a high threshold for sexual intent. She may be eager to engage in mild forms of foreplay without the realization that her behavior leads her date to believe that coitus is forthcoming. As a result, when told to stop, the man feels "led on." Approximately half of high school males (and 30% of females) believe that it is acceptable for males to force sex on females if the female exhibits "suggestive" behavior (Giarrusso, Johnson, Goodchilds, & Zellman, 1979). Feeling led on, the male may ignore the female's pleas and force her to engage in sexual intercourse.

These males expect their dates to "play the feminine role" and to deny her own interest in sex. Muehlenhard and Hollabaugh (1987) indicate that 40% of 610 undergraduate women had engaged in token resistance to sex, that is, saying "no" when they really "had every intention to and were willing to engage in sexual intercourse" (Muehlenhard & Hollabaugh, 1987, p. 5). Furthermore, about 20% of these women had engaged in token resistance between 6 and more than 20 times. If only sexually experienced women were considered, the percentage using token resistance increased to approximately 60%. The reasons for engaging in this behavior consisted of (1) *practical reasons,* including the "fear of appearing promiscuous," a fear of expressing "how much I liked him," and fear of sexually transmitted diseases; (2) *inhibition-related reasons* such as emotional, religious, and moral worries; and (3) *manipulative reasons,* including a desire for more physical aggression, getting him more aroused, wanting "him to beg for sex," being "in control," and because of anger with her partner. Obviously, this situation can create confusion and miscommunication so that women who are serious when they say "no" are not taken seriously and are sometimes forced to have sexual intercourse. Such miscommunication can work to prevent desired sexual intercourse as well. Approximately 12% of sexually *inexperienced* women used token resistance. These women, because of their partners' reaction to their misleading behavior, did not engage in sexual intercourse even though they desired it (Muehlenhard & Hollabaugh, 1987).

Because women may have a greater tendency than men to signal their sexual responsiveness indirectly (Craig, in preparation), sexually aggressive males may watch for nonverbal cues and ignore their partners' "misleading" verbal protests. Due to the greater ambiguity associated with nonverbal cues and due to the male's own level of sexual interest, he is likely to find sexual interest where it does not exist.

Adding to this confusion, men and women are more likely to have different expectations concerning the appropriate time in the couples' dating history when sex is acceptable. For example, approximately half of male undergraduates believe that intercourse is acceptable by the fifth date, but only about one-quarter of females hold a similar view. Furthermore, "less than 15% of both sexes said that their dates always shared their understanding of how long people should wait before engaging in kissing, petting, and intercourse" (Knox & Wilson, 1981, p. 257).

There is also evidence that misperception and poor communication are directly related to sexual aggression. Muehlenhard and Linton (1987) asked men and women college students to describe "their worst" sexually aggressive date and their most recent date. Both women (40.9%) and men (50.8%) indicated that the man believed that he was "led on" during sexually aggressive dates in comparison to recent dates (10.8% and 13.7%, respectively). Women nearly always said that it had been unintentional and that their date had misinterpreted their actions, while men were evenly divided about the intentionality of their date's behavior.

In conclusion, misunderstandings about sex are likely to arise between dating couples because (1) many men and women do not discuss their sexual intentions openly and frankly; (2) differences exist in perceptions of sexual intent; (3) the use of token resistance by some women may create a belief in some males that the protest encountered is of a token nature; and (4) there are differing expectations concerning the stage of the relationship when sexual intercourse is appropriate. Until the couple honestly discuss their sexual wants and desires, or until a sufficient history is in place by which future behavior is predictable from past behavior, miscommunication and misperception are likely to occur.

However, the fact that males hold different beliefs than females is not per se a sufficient condition for date rape. *If misperceptions were all that were involved, and the woman made it clear that she was misunderstood, most males would probably cease and desist.*

Males who engage in date rape have different characteristics than ordinary males. Because such males place a higher value on sexuality and feel greater sexual deprivation (Kanin, 1967), they *may* be poorer at coping with sexual frustration and impulse control. The level of sexual excitation and/or anger experienced by these aggressive men may be inadvertently heightened by their victims' refusals and protest through the cognitive process known as *excitation-transfer* (Zillmann, 1984). If one assumes that early date rape couples engaged in foreplay before the rape, it is logical to infer that the aggressive male was sexually aroused. The female's refusal of more advanced forms of sexual intimacy may result in surprise and embarrassment for the male, leading to sexual frustration and anger. If the couple goes back to milder forms of foreplay, the male's feelings of sexual arousal may return, only now they may be heightened by the residual arousal from the previous episode in which he experienced surprise, embarrassment, and anger. As a result, the male may try to advance sexual foreplay once again and may again be frustrated, thereby raising further his level of sexual arousal. Furthermore, if at some point the predominant emotion becomes anger, the residual sexual arousal may enhance the male's state of anger. Thus sexual arousal and anger may enhance each other, each raising the level of the other.

In summary, if periods of sexual excitation are interrupted by brief episodes of anger-aggression, or if the two excitatory states occur concurrently, there is a probability that residual arousal from anger-aggression in the male may be misinterpreted by him as sexual excitation. Similarly, a state of anger-aggression may be heightened by residual sexual arousal that is misinterpreted as anger-aggression. Under these circumstances, the sexually aggressive male may have reduced impulse control.

The belief systems of date rapists further contribute to their sexually aggressive behavior. Such males hold rape supportive beliefs (Koss, Leonard, Beezley, & Oros, 1985; Muehlenhard & Linton, 1987; Rapaport & Burkhart, 1984), including "adversarial sexual beliefs," the "acceptance of interpersonal violence," and "coercive sexuality." After reaching high levels of sexual frustration, they are motivated by their belief system to take what they want. Therefore they rape.

Focusing upon potential victims, some women may be more vulnerable to early date rape than are others. Women who have a tendency to be socially anxious may be hesitant to signal their displeasure sufficiently early and in a form that will inhibit rapists, that is, with disgust, abhorrence, shock, and terror (see Malamuth & Check, 1980). They may only exhibit pleading and pain, which may simply facilitate the males' sexual arousal (see Malamuth, 1981). These women may not be taken seriously by their dates and consequently are raped.

There is some indication that socially anxious women may be victimized more frequently. Rogers (1984) found anxiety and poor social adjustment to be positively associated with experiences of higher levels of sexual victimization. While Rogers assumed that this condition was the consequence of sexual aggression, it could conceivably be a cause. Rogers found that these factors were not related to the recency of the victimization of the women. If these factors are the consequence of coercive sex, one might expect the consequences to become less acute with time.[2] Further support for the role of these personality factors was found by Skelton (1982), who discovered the women's self-esteem and assertion levels were negatively correlated with the number of victimizations that a woman experienced.

BEGINNING DATE RAPE

Most college students do not expect to have sexual intercourse during their first few dates (Knox & Wilson, 1981). Furthermore, it is likely that most males understand that their sexual values are likely to be more liberal than their dates' sexual values. Therefore, when rape occurs on one of the first few dates, it seems unlikely that poor communication per se could play a significant role. In beginning date rape, a male may date a woman with the intent to rape her, realizing that such an action is less likely to be labeled as rape than would the action of raping a stranger on the street. Such a male may simply date the woman in order to isolate his victim. In fact, in this regard, beginning date rape may be similar to nonromantic acquaintance rape. A beginning date rapist is likely to be simply antisocial.

Rapaport (1984), as described by Burkhart and Stanton (in press), found that sexually aggressive males were much more likely to hold misogynist views and to have histories of a variety of antisocial acts in addition to coercive sexual practices. In further support, Rapaport and Burkhart (1984) found that sexually aggressive males scored lower than normal males on the "socialization" and the "responsibility" subscales of the California Personality Inventory. Indeed, beginning date rapists may tend toward sociopathy (although Koss et al., 1985, contrary to their expectations, found no evidence for psychopathy among sexually aggressive males). Such an individual is insensitive to the plight of others but hypersensitive about his own welfare (see Penner, Escarraz, & Ellis, 1983). Such a person may feel that he has been treated unjustly. Unfortunately, common mores of courtship may provide reasons why such an individual may feel that he has been treated unfairly and therefore has a "right" to have sex with a woman that he is dating. For example, as I mentioned in the early date rape section, a male may feel that he has been treated unfairly by believing that he has been sexually "led on" by a woman and then been told to stop (Giarrusso et al., 1979).

Beginning date rapists may also have a greater need for more, and more varied, sexual experiences. "The sexually aggressive male, in contrast to his non-aggressive peers, has not only had considerably more sexual experience but is persistently seeking new sexual involvements and utilizing more surreptitious techniques with greater frequency to obtain sexual activity" (Kanin, 1967, p. 429; also see Koss et al., 1985). This type of date rapist will have sexually coerced a larger number of women than will early and relational date rapists. This characterization is more consistent for the beginning date rapist formulation than for the early or relational rapists, because the early and relational rapists, by definition, have a greater probability of being involved with one woman.[3]

Women who date or have had sex with a large number of different males increase their chances of exposure to a sexually aggressive male (Koss, 1985; Koss & Dinero, 1987; Skelton, 1982). In addition, research evidence indicating that date rape victims report less conservative sexual values also supports this interpretation (e.g., Koss & Dinero, 1987).

This increased risk *may be even further compounded* by being labeled "sexually accessible." Such a woman has had many dating partners and may be rumored to "sleep around."[4] This label may artificially increase the male's expectations that sexual intimacy will be forthcoming. This aggressor, upon receiving the woman's sexual refusal, may feel that he has provided the services furnished by other males who obtained her sexual favors. He has spent money, provided transportation, and so on, and therefore may feel that a refusal of his sexual advances is particularly unwarranted and *inequitable*. Thus he may be motivated to sexual aggressiveness by anger and frustration. Excitation transfer may increase both his sexual arousal and anger. His antisocial personality and rape supportive beliefs then may lead him to rape. The labeling of the victim as sexually accessible is an enhancing but not a necessary precondition for beginning date rape.

RELATIONAL DATE RAPE

The average male does not expect sexual intercourse until roughly the fifth date (Knox & Wilson, 1981) and therefore is *unlikely* to engage in date rape on the first date because of miscommunication about sex.

Similarly, miscommunication is *not likely* to be the cause of a rape that occurs after the couple has been dating regularly. Couples at this stage of a relationship understand their partner's position regarding sex. Although they may not be in perfect agreement with each other concerning sex, they nevertheless have an understanding (Peplau, Rubin & Hill, 1977). Likewise, the male involved in relational date rape, unlike the male involved in beginning date rape, probably did not date his victim with the sole intention of having sexual intercourse with her. If that were the case, one would expect him to force sexual intercourse sooner. Rather, exchange and social comparison processes are likely causal factors of relational date rape.

Investigators have hypothesized that if a man pays for the date he may feel justified in forcing sex on his partner (McCormick & Jesser, 1983; Weis & Borges, 1973). Research provides some support for this contention. Approximately 40% of high school males (and 12% of females) believed that it is acceptable for a male to force sex on his date if he has spent a lot of money on her. Similar results have been found with college students (see Muehlenhard, in press; Muehlenhard, Friedman, & Thomas, 1985). However, the utility of sharing the expense of a date or not, as either a predictor of victimized women (Korman & Leslie, 1982) or of sexually aggressive dates, is ambiguous (Muehlenhard & Linton, 1987). Nevertheless, these studies do not specify or measure the length of time that the couple has been dating. In addition, the researchers use a limited range of the goods and services that a couple, particularly a couple involved in a long range relationship, usually supplies to each other. One might expect that some males who have been exclusively dating and showing affection toward a woman for a period of time, paying for the dates, and so on, may begin to feel shortchanged if intercourse is not obtained. However, other reasons may cause a relational rapist to feel that his relationship is an inequitable one.

First, the usual power relationship between a couple in a long-term dating relationship is either one of equality or one in which the man has more control. This does not appear to be the case in couples that are refraining from sexual intercourse. In these couples the women were "twice as likely to describe themselves as having greater overall power and less likely to report male power" (Peplau, 1984, p. 103).

Not surprisingly, it is the man who expresses a greater desire than the woman to engage in coitus. Furthermore, the woman's attitude is "the major restraining influence," with both partners being aware of each others' views (Peplau et al., 1977). Moreover, when there is unequal power, one of the factors that is related to it is unequal involvement, in this case on the part of the woman (Peplau, 1984).

Most people who have been dating for a long period of time expect their relationship to develop toward marriage. The worth of a dating relationship is judged in part by its movement toward this permanent state (Surra & Huston, 1987). Certainly one sign of movement and involvement, at least for the male, may be sexual intercourse. Men may understand that coitus may be a sign of love for some women. Research shows that 72% of those women who were involved in long-term relationships and who engaged in sexual intercourse, in comparison to 51% of abstaining women, reported feeling love for their partner. In addition, relationships in which sex did not occur were judged to be less serious relationships (Peplau et al., 1977).

Therefore the occurrence of sexual intercourse may be a sign of "movement" within a relationship that some women are willing to take only when they are in love. The need for such a sign may be so important that a sexually conservative male might abandon his own conservative values so that if he is given the opportunity to engage in coitus with his girlfriend he does so. Research demonstrates that women's values, but not men's, are predictors of couples engaging in sexual intercourse (Peplau et al., 1977).

It seems reasonable that after some interval men may view their relationships as stationary or deteriorating if they do not engage in sexual intercourse with their dating partner. With time they may become more dissatisfied with their relationship and may feel that the situation is inequitable, but may be unwilling to end the relationship because they have a sizable investment of time, emotion, material resources, have no alternative partner, and so on.

These feelings may be exacerbated through social comparison processes. Two types of comparisons can create or further exacerbate these feelings of inequity. First, these men may compare their relationships to those of other males in long-term relationships. They may know or assume that other males with similar relationships are involved sexually with their partners and thus have a relationship that is "going somewhere," while theirs is not. Second, if their partners have had, or are assumed to have had, previous sexual experience, the males may compare themselves to the women's prior partners and conclude that they come off second best. Therefore, because of anger and the belief that with sexual intercourse the relationship will gain momentum, sometime during the couple's usual "petting," this type of male extends his usual sexual practice by forcing intercourse.

The women victimized by relational date rape, like their partners, are likely to have conservative sexual values. Such conservatism seems to be a characteristic of those couples in long-term relationships who are sexual abstainers (Peplau et al., 1977). Furthermore, although conservative, these women may tend to waver and express uncertainty about whether they want to engage in premarital sex. Therefore, like the early date rape victim, the woman may feel partly to blame and hence may continue to date her assailant because of self-blame and her own investment in the relationship.

The man involved in relational date rape certainly does not have liberal sexual values. If he did, it is likely that he would have ended the relationship at an earlier stage because of the couple's incompatibility on sexual issues (Peplau et al., 1977). Rather, he too has traditional values, but his values are not as conservative as those of his partner. In addition, sexual intercourse may have such great symbolic importance to him that he is willing to overlook his values.

For example, the woman may be against premarital sex, may express the wish that she did not feel this way, and may even question whether she should have sex at this stage of their relationship. The man may believe that sexual intercourse is not appropriate between people who are not in love but believes that it is proper for a loving couple at "their" stage of relationship. However, such males also have traditional masculine sex-role beliefs (as previously described in the early date rape section) that allow him to force sexual intercourse on his partner. Given that men tend to have romantic beliefs about love (Rubin, Peplau, & Hill, 1981), these males may believe and be sexually excited by the idea that their partners will resist their advances at first and then will be overcome with passion (Malamuth, Heim, & Feshbach, 1980) and will willingly and even enthusiastically take part in intercourse.

If the woman decides to resist, she may produce anger-aggression in the man, which may through excitation-transfer cause a heightened sense of sexual excitation and/or anger. In addition, because of the man's traditional sex role beliefs, he may feel that he has been treated unfairly through the withholding of coitus. Therefore he continues his aggressive behavior and rapes his partner.

HYPOTHESES AND CONCLUSIONS

I have proposed three types of date rape and probable causes for each variety. The model that I proposed treats the couple rather than the rapist or victim as the unit of analysis because I believe that a model based on this assumption has greater explanatory power and will yield stronger relationships.

As a useful means of summarizing the model, I will provide a *partial* list of hypotheses that can be used to test some of the model's components. I will state the hypotheses in terms of comparisons between the three types of couples involved in date rape and a control group of males and females who have never been involved in sexual aggression and have dated for an equivalent length of time. In order to give the list of hypotheses greater continuity and meaning I have, for the most part, grouped the hypotheses into sets based on the type of date rape to which the hypotheses refer. A partial list of the hypotheses that can be generated from this model follows.

(1) Early date rapists will be more likely to have a lower threshold for judging the sexual intent of both males and females than are other date rapists or control males and females. In the context of sexually aggressive dates, early date rapists will be more likely to overestimate the sexual intent of their partners than are other date rapists or control males (with the exception of beginning rapists who believe they are dating promiscuous women).

In a complementary fashion, early date rape victims will generally have a higher threshold for judging the sexual intent of both males and females than other date rape victims or control males and females. In the context of sexually aggressive dates, early date rape victims will be more likely to underestimate the sexual intent of their partners than are other date rape victims or control females and males.

Early date rapists may have poorer impulse control than do other rapists and controls. In addition, these males will have a greater history of other antisocial acts and may score higher on sociopathy measures than do relational rapists and controls but lower than beginning rapists. Early date rapists are likely to have fewer sexual partners and aggressive incidents than are beginning date rapists but more partners and incidents than are relational rapists and controls.

Communications by the victim indicating a lack of consent may be delivered later in foreplay and with less force, so her date is less likely to listen than would be the case for other date rape victims or the control group. If the message is delivered late and less forcefully, it may occur because of lower assertiveness and self esteem, and higher levels of social anxiety than are found in other date rape victims and control women.

(2) Beginning date rapists are more likely to state they have large appetites for sexual encounters and different partners and to claim a higher number of sexual partners and admit to a greater number of aggressive incidents than are either early or relational rapists or controls. Beginning date rapists will have a greater history of antisocial acts and may have the highest sociopathy and antisocial personalities scores in comparison to other groups of date rapists and controls. On the other hand, beginning date rape victims are more likely to have

dated more men and have had more sexual partners then are other categories of victims or female controls.

A beginning date rapist may also follow a different path. Such a beginning date rapist may be more likely to assume that his date is promiscuous. He may request a date expecting to have consensual sex. When his date refuses his sexual advances he feels that he has been treated inequitably in comparison to early date rapists and controls. Therefore he rapes his date.

(3) Relational date rapists and victims are likely to have more conservative sexual values and fewer prior sexual partners than other rapists, victims, or controls. Furthermore, unlike most other couples involved in long-term relationships, the woman is perceived by both partners to have more control and to be less committed to the relationship than the man. The rapist is more likely than beginning and early rapists and controls (and other people involved in long-term relationships) to feel that this relationship is inequitable and not moving toward marriage. This type of rapist, in comparison to other rapists, believes that the rape would follow a romantic script in which the woman would protest at first but then willingly comply. When protest does not turn to compliance, he rapes.

(4) All types of rapists are more likely to hold rape-supportive attitudes than a control group of nonsexually aggressive males.

The study of date rape is a recent research topic that is beginning to receive the attention it deserves, both because of its social relevance and because of its importance in understanding relationships between men and women. I hope that in the future, information concerning date rape will continue to amass at an accelerated rate, and I look forward to the changes that new knowledge may demand of this model.

NOTES

1. These three types of date rape only address the situation in which the first incident of coitus between a dating couple occurs through rape, and the rapist's purpose is not degradation or sadism (with the possible exception of beginning date rape). Rape that occurs after a number of previous consensual sexual encounters and/or is performed for degradation or sadistic purposes (see Groth, 1979) is probably a different phenomenon with very different causes, and therefore is not considered in this chapter.

2. I should point out that all individual difference measures are taken after the aggressive incident. As a result, one cannot determine whether differences in the variable of interest are "causes," "consequences," or are spuriously related to the aggressive act. I should also point out that some of the personality studies that I report correlate the personality measures with a more general measure of sexual aggression rather than restricting it to the more circumscribed measure of coerced sexual intercourse.

3. These men may be sexually different in other ways as well. They may be physiologically sexually aroused while not experiencing psychological sexual arousal, as is found with samples of incarcerated rapists (e.g., Kercher & Walker, 1973; Abel, Barlow, Blanchard & Guild, 1977). Hence they may need the added arousal produced by aggression either directly as aggressive arousal or misinterpreted as sexual arousal through the excitation transfer mechanism.

4. In fact, as R. Ashmore indicates (personal communication, October 5, 1987), she may be described by her fellow women students as "trying too hard" and by the men as an "easy lay."

REFERENCES

Abbey, A. (1982). Sex differences in attributions for friendly behavior: Do males misperceive females' friendliness? *Journal of Personality and Social Psychology, 42*, 830-838.

Abbey, A., Cozzarelli, C., McLaughlin, K., & Harnish, R. (1987). The effects of clothing and dyad sex composition on perceptions of sexual intent: Do women and men evaluate these cues differently. *Journal of Applied Social Psychology, 17*, 108-126.

Abbey, A., & Melby, C. (1986). The effects of nonverbal cues on gender differences in perceptions of sexual intent. *Sex Roles, 15*, 283-298.

Abel, G. G., Barlow, D. H., Blanchard, E. B., & Guild, D. (1977). The components of rapists' sexual arousal. *Archives of General Psychiatry, 34*, 467-475.

Burkhart, B. R., & Stanton, A. L. (in press). Sexual aggression in acquaintance relationships. In G. Russell (Ed.), *Violence in intimate relationships.* Englewood Cliffs, NJ: Spectrum.

Craig, J. M. (in preparation). *Perception and analysis of cues for sexual intent.* Unpublished doctoral dissertation, Pennsylvania State University, University Park.

Frevert, R. L., & Kahn, A. (1976). *Observers' perceptions of affection in heterosexual pairs: Does like = love = sex?* Unpublished manuscript, Iowa State University.

Giarrusso, R., Johnson, P., Goodchilds, J., & Zellman, G. (1979, April). *Adolescents' cues and signals: sex and assault.* Paper presented at the meeting of the Western Psychological Association, San Diego, CA.

Gross, A. E. (1978). The male role and heterosexual behavior. *Journal of Social Issues, 34*(4), 87-107.

Groth, A. N. (1979). *Men who rape: The psychology of the offender.* New York: Plenum.

Hendrick, C. (1976). *Person perception and rape: An experimental approach.* Unpublished grant proposal, Kent State University, OH.

Heslin, R., Nguyen, T. D., & Nguyen, M. L. (1983). Meaning of touch: The case of touch from a stranger or same sex person. *Journal of Nonverbal Behavior, 7*, 147-157.

Kanin, E. (1957). Male aggression in dating-courtship relations. *American Journal of Sociology, 63*, 197-204.

Kanin, E. (1967). An examination of sexual aggression as a response to school frustration. *Journal of Marriage and the Family, 29*, 428-433.

Kanin, E. (1969). Selected dyadic aspects of male sex aggression. *The Journal of Sex Research, 5*, 12-28.

Kanin, E. (1971). Sexually aggressive college males. *Journal of College Student Personnel, 112*, 107-110.

Kanin, E. (1983). Rape as a function of relative sexual frustration. *Psychological Reports, 52*, 133-134.

Kanin, E., & Parcell, S. R. (1977). Sexual aggression: A second look at the offended female. *Archives of Sexual Behavior, 6*, 67-76.

Kercher, G. A., & Walker, C. E. (1973). Reactions of convicted rapists to sexually explicit stimuli. *Journal of Abnormal Psychology, 81*, 46-50.

Kilpatrick, D. G., Best, C. L., Veronen, L. J., Amick, A. E., Villeponteaux, L. A., & Ruff, G. A. (1985). Mental health correlates of criminal victimization: A random community survey. *Journal of Consulting and Clinical Psychology, 53*, 866-873.

Kinsey, A. C., Pomeroy, W. B., & Martin, C. E. (1948). *Sexual behavior in the human male.* Philadelphia: Saunders

Kinsey, A. C., Pomeroy, W. B., Martin, C. E., & Gebhard, P. H. (1952). *Sexual behavior in the human female.* Philadelphia: Saunders.

Kirkpatrick, C., & Kanin, E. (1957). Male sex aggression on a university campus. *American Sociological Review, 22*, 52-58.

Knox, D., & Wilson, K. (1981). Dating behaviors of university students. *Family Relations, 30*, 255-258.

Korman, S. K., & Leslie, G. R. (1982). The relationship of feminist ideology and date expense sharing to perception of sexual aggression in dating. *Journal of Sex Research, 18*, 114-120.

Koss, M. P. (1985). The hidden rape victim: Personality, attitudinal, and situational characteristics. *Psychology of Women Quarterly, 9*, 193-285.

Koss, M. P., & Dinero, T. E. (1987). *Discriminant analysis of risk factors for sexual victimization among a national sample of college women.* Unpublished manuscript, Kent State University, OH.

Koss, M. P., & Oros, C. J. (1982). Sexual experiences survey: A research instrument investigating sexual aggression and victimization. *Journal of Consulting and Clinical Psychology, 80*, 455-457.

Koss, M. P., Dinero, T. E., Seibel, C. A., & Cox, S. L. (in press). Stranger and acquaintance rape: Are there differences in the victim's experience? *Psychology of Women Quarterly.*

Koss, M. P., Gidycz, C. A., & Wisniewski, N. (1987). The scope of rape: Incidence and prevalence of sexual aggression and victimization in a national sample of higher education students. *Journal of Consulting and Clinical Psychology, 55*, 162-170.

Koss, M. P., Leonard, K. E., Beezley, D. A., & Oros, C. J. (1985). Nonstranger sexual aggression: A discriminant analysis of the psychological characteristics of undetected offenders. *Sex Roles, 12*, 981-992.

Major, B., & Heslin, R. (1982). Perceptions of cross-sex and same-sex nonreciprocal touch: It is better to give than to receive. *Journal of Nonverbal Behavior, 6*, 148-162.

Malamuth, N. M. (1981). Rape proclivity among males. *Journal of Social Issues, 37*(4), 138-157.

Malamuth, N. M., & Check, J. (1980). Sexual arousal to rape and consenting depictions: The importance of the woman's arousal. *Journal of Abnormal Psychology, 89*, 763-766.

Malamuth, N. M., Heim, M., & Feshbach, S. (1980). Sexual responsiveness of college students to rape depictions: Inhibitory and disinhibitory effects. *Journal of Personality and Social Psychology, 38*, 399-408.

McCormick, N. B., & Jesser, C. J. (1983). The courtship game: Power in the sexual encounter. In E. R. Allgeier, & N. B. McCormick (Eds.), *Changing boundaries: Gender roles and sexual behavior* (pp. 64-86). Palo Alto, CA: Mayfield.

Milgram, S. (1974). *Obedience to authority.* New York: Harper & Row.

Montgomery, B. M. (1987). *Sociable vs. sensual flirting: The influence of gender.* Unpublished manuscript, Department of Communication Sciences, University of Connecticut, Storrs.

Muehlenhard, C. L. (in press). Misinterpreted dating behaviors and the risk of date rape. *Journal of Social and Clinical Psychology.*

Muehlenhard, C. L., & Falcon, P. L. (1987). *Social skills and attitudes of nonincarcerated forceful rapists.* Unpublished manuscript, Department of Psychology, Texas A&M University, College Station.

Muehlenhard, C. L., Friedman, D. E., & Thomas, C. M. (1985). Is date rape justifiable? *Psychology of Women Quarterly, 9,* 297-309.

Muehlenhard, C. L., & Hollabaugh, L. C. (1987). *Why a woman would say no when she meant yes: The incidence and correlates of women's token resistance to sex.* Unpublished manuscript, Department of Psychology, Texas A&M University, College Station.

Muehlenhard, C. L., & Linton, M. A. (1987). Date rape and sexual aggression in dating situations: Incidence and risk factors. *Journal of Counseling Psychology, 34,* 186-196.

Muehlenhard, C. L., Miller, C. L., & Burdick, C. A. (1983). Are high-frequency daters better cue readers? Men's interpretations of women's cues as a function of dating frequency and SHI scores. *Behavior Therapy, 14,* 626-636.

Nguyen, M. L., Heslin, R., & Nguyen, T. D. (1976). The meaning of touch: Sex and marital status differences. *Representative Research in Social Psychology, 1,* 13-18.

Penner, L. A., Escarraz, J., & Ellis, B. (1983). Sociopathy and helping: Looking out for number one. *Academic Psychology Bulletin, 5,* 209-220.

Peplau, L. A. (1984). Power in dating relationships. In J. Freeman (Ed.), *Women: A feminist perspective* (3rd ed., pp. 100-112). Palo Alto, CA: Mayfield.

Peplau, L. A., Rubin, Z., & Hill, C. T. (1977). Sexual intimacy in dating relationships. *Journal of Social Issues, 33* (2), 86-109.

Rapaport, K. (1984). *Sexually aggressive males: Characterological features and sexual responsiveness to rape depictions.* Unpublished doctoral dissertation, Auburn University, AL.

Rapaport, K., & Burkhart, B. R. (1984). Personality and attitudinal characteristics of sexually coercive college males. *Journal of Abnormal Psychology, 93,* 216-221.

Rogers, L. C. (1984). *Sexual victimization: Social and psychological effects in college women.* Unpublished doctoral dissertation, Auburn University, AL.

Rubin, Z. (1970). Measurement of romantic love. *Journal of Personality and Social Psychology, 16,* 265-273.

Rubin, Z., Peplau, L. A., & Hill, C. T. (1981) Loving and leaving: Sex differences in romantic attachments. *Sex Roles, 7,* 821-835.

Russell, D. E. H. (1984). *Sexual exploitation: rape, child sexual abuse, and workplace harassment.* Beverly Hills, CA: Sage.

Rytting, M. B. (1976, May). *Sex or intimacy: Male and female versions of heterosexual relationships.* Paper presented at the annual meeting of the Midwestern Psychological Association, Chicago.

Shotland, R. L. (1985a). A preliminary model of some causes of date rape. *Academic Psychology Bulletin, 7,* 187-200.

Shotland, R. L. (1985b, November). *A preliminary model of the causes of date rape.* Paper presented at the meeting of the American Society for Criminology, San Diego, CA.

Shotland, R. L., & Craig, J. (in press). Can men and women differentiate between friendly and sexually interested behavior? *Social Psychology Quarterly.*

Skelton, C. A. (1982). *Situational and personological correlates of sexual victimization in college women.* Unpublished doctoral dissertation, Auburn University, AL.

Surra, C. A., & Huston, T. L. (1987). Mate selection as a social transition. In D. Perlman & S. Duck (Eds.), *Intimate relationships: Development, dynamics and deterioration* (pp. 88-212). Newbury Park, CA: Sage.

Weis, K., & Borges, S. S. (1973). Victimization and rape: The case of the legitimate victim. *Issues in Criminology, 8,* 71-115.

Wilson, W., & Durrenberger, R. (1982). Comparison of rape and attempted rape victims. *Psychological Reports, 50,* 198.

Zellman, G. L., Johnson, P. B., Giarrusso, R., & Goodchilds, J. D. (1979, August). *Adolescent expectations for dating relationships: Consensus and conflict between the sexes.* Paper presented at the meeting of the American Psychological Association, New York.

Zillmann, D. (1984). *Connections between sex and aggression.* Hillsdale, NJ: Lawrence Erlbaum.

NOTES

NOTES